THINKING LIKE
EINSTEIN

THINKING LIKE
EINSTEIN

RETURNING TO OUR VISUAL ROOTS WITH THE EMERGING REVOLUTION IN COMPUTER INFORMATION VISUALIZATION

Thomas G. West

Prometheus Books

59 John Glenn Drive
Amherst, New York 14228-2197

Published 2004 by Prometheus Books

Inquiries should be addressed to
Prometheus Books
59 John Glenn Drive
Amherst, New York 14228–2197
VOICE: 716–691–0133, ext. 207
FAX: 716–564–2711
WWW.PROMETHEUSBOOKS.COM

08 07 06 05 04   5 4 3 2 1

Library of Congress Cataloging-in-Publication Data

West, Thomas G., 1943–
    Thinking like Einstein : returning to our visual roots with the emerging revolution in computer information visualization / Thomas G. West.
        p. cm.
    Includes bibliographical references (p.   ) and index.
    ISBN 1–59102–251–7 (hardcover : alk. paper)
    1. Thought and thinking. 2. Visualization. 3. Information visualization—Psychological aspects. I. Title.

BF441.W455 2004
153.3'2—dc22
                                                                    2004014556

Printed in the United States of America on acid-free paper

Contents

PART 3. VISUAL BRAINS

PART 4. VISUAL PEOPLE

In memory of

William J. Dreyer, 1928–2004

Molecular biologist, strong visual thinker

Prescient inventor, instrument maker

Who loved to fly high to see

What others could not see

Frequently alone

Albert Einstein, twenty-six years old, published in the Annalen der Physik *in 1905 five papers on entirely different subjects. Three of them were among the greatest in the history of physics. One, very simple, gave the quantum explanation of the photoelectric effect—it was the work for which, sixteen years later, he was awarded the Nobel Prize. Another dealt with the phenomenon of Brownian motion, the apparently erratic movement of tiny particles suspended in a liquid. . . . The third paper was the special theory of relativity, which quietly amalgamated space, time, and matter into one fundamental unity. This last paper contains no references and quotes no authority. All of them are written in a style unlike any other theoretical physicist's. They contain very little mathematics. There is a good deal of verbal commentary. The conclusions, the bizarre conclusions, emerge as though with the greatest of ease; the reasoning is unbreakable. It looks as though he had reached the conclusions by pure thought unaided, without listening to the opinions of others. To a surprisingly large extent, that is precisely what he had done.*

—C. P. Snow

I sometimes ask myself . . . how did it come that I was the one to develop the theory of relativity. The reason, I think, is that a normal adult never stops to think about problems of space and time. These are things he has thought of as a child. But my intellectual development was retarded, as a result of which I began to wonder about space and time only when I had already grown up. Naturally, I could go deeper into the problem than a child with normal abilities.

—Albert Einstein

The words or the language, as they are written or spoken, do not seem to play any role in my mechanism of thought. The psychical entities which seem to serve as elements in thought are certain signs and more or less clear images which can be "voluntarily" reproduced and combined.

There is, of course, a certain connection between those elements and relevant logical concepts. It is also clear that the desire to arrive finally at logically connected concepts is the emotional basis of this rather vague play with the above mentioned elements. But taken from a psychological viewpoint, this combinatory play seems to be the essential feature in productive thought—before there is any connection with logical construction in words or other kinds of signs which can be communicated to others.

The above mentioned elements are, in my case, of visual and some of muscular type. Conventional words or other signs have to be sought for laboriously only in a secondary stage, when the mentioned associative play is sufficiently established and can be reproduced at will.

—Albert Einstein

FOREWORD

In the late nineties, I was fortunate to have the opportunity to take over as editor of *Computer Graphics*. At this time, the prevailing technology environment was one of high optimism, and nowhere was this more widely felt than in the community of artists and technologists that made up the membership of ACM SIGGRAPH. There was a palpable sense that what was happening in the world of computer graphics could impact society in innumerable ways—witness the creative optimism of the many efforts to merge the Internet and three-dimensional interactive techniques, for example.

To try to reflect this excitement, in addition to producing targeted focused issues, my intention was to build a "stable" of regular columnists for the magazine and provide a degree of consistency and depth that would intrigue readers from both technical and artistic backgrounds. I also wanted to help promote cross-fertilization in ideas between the two fields, as well as attract into the fray those who perhaps had only a passing knowledge of or interest in the fields of computer graphics and interactive techniques.

It was clear to me that Tom West's writing spanned all these bases in a unique fashion—helping those in the industry think in a more expansive way about their own work, while helping those outside the industry form an understanding of where the emerging technology might lead in terms of visual communication. I was delighted when Tom agreed to become one of the regular writers for the magazine. Over the years, he has continued to create thoughtful essays that have engaged a generation of readers, helping them to imagine how things could be if only we set our minds to realizing the full potential of visual thinking linked to these new visual technologies.

THE EARLY DAYS OF SUPERCOMPUTING

My first exposure to SIGGRAPH the organization came from reading *Computer Graphics* in the library of the university where I worked for a while in Scotland. I particularly remember one of the most intriguing issues being a special edition focusing on the burgeoning field of scientific visualization. This was in the early nineties, very much the glory days of the supercomputer, with various centers cropping up around the globe to service the needs of scientists with a thirst for computational power.

I worked briefly at one of these supercomputer centers, where "big science" was using parallel computers such as Thinking Machine Corporation's "Connection Machine," which had many thousands of processors, to compute, calculate, process, and produce vast amounts of data. It was clear that to understand such data required new, visual methods in addition to the traditional analytical techniques. At the time, scientific visualization as a research field was enormously rich and ambitious, full of new ideas. Scientists working in the areas of fluid simulation, weather modeling and predication, molecular biology, genetics, traffic simulation, medical analysis, and many, many others had a new set of tools for trying to determine patterns, extract meaning, and understand the relationships in the tremendously complex data sets that had been created.

INCLUSIVE SYNERGY

There was an intriguing symbiosis between the scientists creating the science, the technologists creating the tools and techniques (and, in doing so, borrowing liberally from prior and current research in pure computer graphics, artificial intelligence, and computer vision) and, indeed, the artists who were very often involved in helping craft the visualizations. In short, there was a wonderfully creative and inclusive synergy between various groups, one that remains a typical and unique characteristic of the SIGGRAPH organization itself.

At the same time, revolutionary general-purpose visualization tools (such as aPE, AVS, and Iris Explorer) running on graphical workstations were allowing researchers to experiment with data in a truly fluid fashion. These developments offered hope for collaborative communication of visual ideas. It really seemed that visualization was gaining momentum as a potential enabling technology, as Tom West observes, heralding "a return to our visual roots." With these new technologies, interactive visual tools became available to encourage the exploration of information (of which there is, of course, no shortage nowadays, thanks to the growing popularity of the Internet) and provided a basis for new visual curricula being taught to a new wave of students.

Fast-forward to the present day, where the graphical power in even the cheapest of current personal computers challenges that of the highest-end workstation from the nineties. Indeed, the capabilities of the machine I use to help develop software for animated films (or one that a graphics researcher would employ to develop new visualization techniques) differ very little from the power of an average home computer.

Because today's personal computers are so powerful, one would imagine that computer visualization as an enabling tool for visual thinking would be ubiquitous at this stage. However, in terms of general public awareness and adoption, one would be wrong. Visualization's place in the arsenal of tools employed by researchers in the sciences and other areas such as financial modeling is now well established. In other areas, as in education, students are commonly using software tools such as Steve Wolfram's Mathematica to reason visually. However, there remains a certain resistance and significant untapped potential for the more widespread adoption of interaction and visualization techniques—both in our schools and our places of work. Nonetheless, there is a slowly growing awareness that there is more to computer graphics than film effects and games.

WITHIN A BIGGER PICTURE

Tom's new book, *Thinking Like Einstein*, shows us just where the technology may lead us, while providing a historical context that expertly helps us understand why we may wish to go there and what a wonderful and naturally empowering place it may end up being.

Tom understands graphical technology and how it is currently being employed both in the consumer and scientific space. But he is also able to step back and see the bigger picture, showing how the techniques being developed can fit into a larger, more holistic context. He brings a focus and a rare thirst for knowledge to his writing that compels the reader to think outside the ordinary.

As he delivered to me each of his columns for *Computer Graphics* over the years, I felt some of the excitement I had encountered on picking up my first issue of the magazine years before. With the collection of his essays in this book, I believe readers will feel that same excitement, enthusiasm, and thirst for further understanding.

In reading the manuscript for *Thinking Like Einstein*, I have also found myself reflecting on the field in which I was lucky to toil for a while, and I discovered a newfound respect for the pioneer visualization researchers. I believe they have developed—and are continuing to develop—new ways of helping us to see the world around us. Their efforts may indeed ultimately lead us to benefit from a set of technologies that will encourage us to feel less afraid to experiment, learn, communicate, and think visually—"like Einstein."

Gordon Cameron
Former editor, ACM SIGGRAPH *Computer Graphics*
Software Engineer, Pixar Animation Studios, Emeryville, California
Florence, Italy
June 2004

INTRODUCTION

*No one could hope to convey so much true knowledge without an
immense, tedious and confused length of writing and time, except through
this very short way of drawing from different aspects.*
                    —Leonardo da Vinci, *Anatomical Notebooks*

MEDIEVAL CLERK TO RENAISSANCE VISUAL THINKER

For some four or five hundred years we have had our schools teaching
skills that are basically those of a medieval clerk—reading, writing,
counting, memorizing texts, learning foreign languages. But now it seems
that we might be on the verge of a truly new era, when we will wish to and
will be required to value a very different set of skills—the skills of a Renaissance visual thinker such as Leonardo da Vinci. With such a change, traits
that are considered desirable may change gradually but dramatically.

If we continue to turn out people who have primarily the skills (and
outlook) of the clerk, however accomplished, we may increasingly be
turning out people who will (like the unskilled laborer of the last century)
have less and less to sell in the global marketplace. It seems clear that sometime in the not-too-distant future, machines will be the best clerks. Given
this situation, we must learn to maximize what is most valued among
human capabilities and what machines cannot do. It seems clear that many
of these most valued skills will increasingly involve the insightful and integrative capacities associated with visual modes of thought.

I believe we are now at the early stages of a major transition—moving from an old world of education and work largely based on words and numbers to a new world largely based on images that are rich in content and information. (What I am talking about is quite different from the images of television—poor in information content and providing no interaction.)

If a picture is worth a thousand words, a moving diagram based on highly complex computer data is worth a million words. This transition promises to be true revolution—not about how we will use technology, but about how we will learn (or relearn) to use our brains.

Going Forward by Going Backward

For most of us—contrary to what might be expected—these newest technologies will seem more like the natural world than the word- and number-linked technologies that have dominated education and work for hundreds of years. Strangely, the further ahead we move, the more we will learn to feel at home, once again, relearning how to use our familiar and ancient visual talents and capabilities. After two decades of development in supercomputer centers and in various scientific disciplines along with continuing reductions in cost and increases in power, computer information visualization technologies and techniques are becoming more widely available.

The process of broad adoption is much slower than I would have ever thought possible. However, as these technologies demonstrate their effectiveness (i.e., their comparative advantage) to skeptics in business after business, discipline after discipline, it seems all but inevitable that in time a great many of us will come to rely more and more on very different ways of working with and understanding information—seeing patterns and trends in information in ways that were never possible before (or were limited to extraordinarily gifted visual thinkers alone). With these changes, a whole new set of visual talents will come to be highly valued—just as many capabilities that are now highly valued will come to be seen as associated with obsolescent technologies and will be valued less and less over time.

Computer Graphics Radiating Outward

This book is largely based on a series of columns written at the invitation of the editors of *Computer Graphics*, a quarterly publication of the international professional association for computer graphic artists and technologists known as ACM SIGGRAPH—the Association on Computing Machinery's Special Interest Group on Graphics. I came to write these columns not as an expert with deep technical knowledge in the field but as an outside seeker and observer long interested in visual thinkers and visual technologies, watching with great interest the unfolding story and trying to figure out what it all meant in the larger context.

Some twenty-five or thirty years ago, SIGGRAPH was the smallest of the many special interest groups of the ACM, with only two or three dozen individuals attending the earliest conferences. With rapid increases in the capabilities of the technologies and broad applicability, annual SIGGRAPH conferences grew to attract attendees of fifty to sixty thousand in the late 1990s—making SIGGRAPH the largest by far of all the ACM interest groups. It was the one place in the world each summer where the leaders from industry and academia could meet to show each other their best work.

I had originally attended my first SIGGRAPH conference in 1989 in Boston in an attempt to better understand the rapid development of computer graphic technologies as they related to research for my earlier book *In the Mind's Eye: Visual Thinkers, Gifted People with Dyslexia and Other Learning Difficulties, Computer Images, and the Ironies of Creativity* (Prometheus Books, 1991, updated edition 1997).

TIME MACHINE

Once I had attended the first conference, I continued to attend nearly every year thereafter. I realized that all the most innovative work was shown there first. Consequently, for me the conference became a kind of time machine, allowing me to see first what would be seen at other conferences and industries twelve, eighteen, or even twenty-four months later. It became a way for me to gain a deeper understanding of powerful developments—as they unfolded before my eyes, year after year.

In addition, I had discovered that many SIGGRAPH members seemed to fit the profile that I was originally most interested in—highly creative visual thinkers with varied language and academic difficulties who nonetheless showed an extremely high degree of talent and ability when working with visual materials and with the newest computer graphics technologies.

Indeed, as I often noted in the public talks associated with *In the Mind's Eye*, it was at the SIGGRAPH conferences that I came to realize that those who had often been at the bottom of the class in an old educational system (based on words and numbers) were now already at the top of the class in an emerging new system based on visual technologies—leading the way into a new era where the most advanced work in science, art, or business will be done using modern information visualization technologies and techniques. This visually talented group is leading the way for all of us into the sophisticated use of the newest and most powerful technologies—yet most people are totally unaware of this most important trend, even now.

It seems clear to me that these new technologies will necessarily be adapted broadly first by imaginative businesses, because they will be seen to work—to confer an advantage over the competition. In contrast, conventional education may be expected to be the last to embrace these new ideas and techniques, since these ideas are so much in opposition to traditional "word-bound" thinking—long defined as reading, writing, counting, and memorizing texts. One group sees the technology as an instrument, whereas the other group sees the technology as an absolute, as an end in itself. In time, however, it seems clear that the power of these new technologies and techniques will spread to every discipline and every economic pursuit. The inherent power of these technologies makes it seem inevitable—although, again, I must admit that the process is taking much, much longer than I would have originally expected.

BROAD MUTUAL RESPECT

At SIGGRAPH I also observed a truly remarkable thing—broad mutual respect and appreciation among many very different individuals and occupational groups. In most fields of knowledge, there seems to be a natural and irreversible tendency toward specialties, subspecialties, and sub-subspecialties. With SIGGRAPH I observed the opposite tendency. The levels of excitement and energy were always high, especially during the golden years of the 1990s, when everything was new and each year seemed to bring such giant leaps forward. But it was also truly remarkable how artists and engineers, filmmakers and technologists, surgeons and astronomers, game designers and mathematicians seemed to speak the same language and pursue similar interests.

I recall especially when one mathematician who had developed a computer graphic video on geometry gave a detailed talk on how it had been put together. She gave high praise to those who helped her, the animator who formed the moving objects, the artist who provided the color and lighting, the writer who helped with humor, and even the choreographer who had shown how to treat the moving geometrical figure and its analysis like a complex dance routine.

THE UNFOLDING STORY

This collection of essays, written in the years since 1995, will serve to indicate, from a broader perspective, the unfolding story of the growing power of these new computer graphic and visualization technologies—how they relate to the human brain and how they relate to a group of people who seem exceptionally well suited to their sophisticated use. Because I deal with both technology and the brain, there has been some exchange between these columns and my book *In the Mind's Eye*: parts of several relevant columns found their way into the epilogue of the updated version in 1997. Similarly, parts of the book seemed to quite naturally form the basis for several columns. Remarkably, most of the columns seem to have aged rather well, partly because I was usually focusing on the longer-term significance of certain technological events and trends (such as links between creativity and visualization or the continuing tension between words and images through history). Occasionally, the columns have dealt with particular SIGGRAPH conferences or particular trends and events (the brief animation boom or the early boom in technology stocks). Some of these have been preserved for historical interest, with endnotes where appropriate to provide timely comment.

Most columns were written to a fairly strict two-thousand-word limit to fit the given space. I had intended to expand several columns for this book, but then I found that the expansion tended to destroy a certain crispness and simplicity that I thought should be preserved. In addition, I am fully aware that many of my image-loving readers would much prefer a brief and evocative treatment rather than the painful, extended elaboration that one sometimes sees. Nonetheless, I hope I have illuminated some of the core elements, perhaps providing some small flash of insight or, as Robert Frost said, a "momentary stay against confusion," expecting that readers will move on to other more substantial resources as they are inclined.

FORWARD INTO THE PAST

The first chapter, "Forward into the Past," is based on an article that was specifically requested by *Computer Graphics* issue editor Karen Sullivan and other SIGGRAPH members. They wanted, they said, an article that they could hand to university deans, provosts, and professors who seemed to be so deeply committed to the world of words that they could not see that computer graphics and information visualization were not just another form of vocational training—that, instead, they were the beginning of a new technology that promised to be at least as powerful, in time, as the old technology of writing and printed books.

In this requested article, I tried to argue that much of the knowledge that universities most treasure, whether in science, mathematics, or literature, in fact often comes from strong visual thinkers such as Albert Einstein, Henri Poincaré, or William Butler Yeats. Such visual thinkers should be recognized as such and treated with high respect, in spite of their language problems, eccentricities, and academic difficulties. I was afterward told that some SIG-GRAPH members had in fact handed this article to their own deans and provosts. They were delighted to report some measure of success in making their case—noting that the extensive references and footnotes did seem to help the conventional academic mind to take the matter more seriously.

I had based the article on an invited talk I had just given to some fifty Max Planck Institutes in Germany—a group highly interested in how computer information visualization was likely to affect the future of their scientific research in various fields. It seemed to be clear that one had to be bold (in some fields) to try to break down the centuries-old belief that words and mathematical symbols were for serious professionals—whereas pictures and diagrams were only for the lay public and children.

After this initial article, the editorship of *Computer Graphics* was taken over by Gordon Cameron. Originally from Scotland, Gordon had been working with supercomputers in Edinburgh, animation and image capture with Softimage in Montreal, and most recently (and currently) developing software animation tools with Pixar in Emeryville, California. Gordon recruited several regular columnists, myself included—thus beginning my series of columns called "Images and Reversals." With his patient prodding of his columnists as well as artists and production staff, Gordon reshaped and vastly improved the publication. He has been kind enough to read (and reread) the manuscript and provide a brief foreword.

ON THE *HOKULE'A*

The title of this book, *Thinking Like Einstein,* is the result of weeks of e-mail in an extended discussion with my publisher. I had originally wanted to call the book *Insight* (loving the gentle wordplay as well as the conventional definition provided by *Webster's Ninth New Collegiate Dictionary*: "the power or act of seeing into a situation, penetration; the act or result of apprehending the inner nature of things or of seeing intuitively, see discernment").

Being persuaded finally that *Insight* was not sufficiently evocative, I suggested several alternatives, including the title of one of the original columns: "Thinking Like Einstein on the *Hokule'a.*" They loved the first part but thought the reference to the famous traditional Polynesian canoe to be too obscure. I argued that even this obscurity might pique the interest and curiosity of some—and, as I thought, it did nicely underscore the connections between the very new and the very old as well.

Finally consenting to what seemed to me a slightly pretentious title, I consoled myself with the belief that any possible misunderstanding would be clarified by the long subtitle. And then, thinking again, I realized that I agreed with them that the coming anniversary of the publication of Einstein's famous papers in 1905 was not a bad time for an extended song of praise for visual thinking and visual thinkers.

REFORMING THE REFORMERS

Now, in the thin leading edge of the twenty-first century, computer graphics and visual technologies are in use around us everywhere, yet most of us have no idea of the real power of these technologies. Our children live in a visual world of television and video games (unfortunately with too little visual observation of the natural world), yet most schools continue to be increasingly obsessed with the narrow skills linked to the ancient technologies of writing, reading, and the book. These are important, of course, but these alone are not enough to prepare our children and grandchildren for really high-value work in a global marketplace.

Education experts and politicians talk of school reform, yet none seem to be aware that, in a sense, our reforms are moving us backward, not forward. No one is yet beginning to focus on the new technologies and undeveloped talents that will likely be most important over time for the children of today and tomorrow—learning to use the new visual technologies and the old visual talents that will be needed to do the highest-level work in a world of increasingly intense global competition.

We talk of basic skills and literacy, yet there is almost never any talk about visual literacy. All the studio art courses were scrapped long ago. We teach the sciences as a series of facts to be memorized with machine-like accuracy and recall. (Why do we think we should be competing with machines—just because it gives impressive test results?) Facts are easy to test and allow us to avoid having to teach critical thinking or having to understand deep patterns in nature. We focus on the facts, yet no one acknowledges that the essence of science is not a list of facts but a process that, for many of the best scientists, is largely visual—making discoveries about patterns in nature through seeing patterns in complex visual information.

PART

1   VISUAL THINKING

CHAPTER

1

FORWARD INTO THE PAST
*A REVIVAL OF OLD VISUAL TALENTS
WITH COMPUTER VISUALIZATION*

AN ANCIENT STANDARD

As we move forward into the future, we may expect a revival of visual talents and skills once highly valued but long considered of lesser value in word-dominated modern culture. Indeed, it may be significant that our culture is so word-bound that we find it difficult to even talk about visual proficiencies without referring to word-oriented terminology. It is apparent but not often noted that "visual literacy" really has nothing to do with words or with literature.

Each technology has its limits. Long ago, Socrates described some second thoughts he had about the new and questionable technology called a "book." He thought it had several weaknesses. A book could not adjust what it was saying, as a living person would, to what would be appropriate for certain listeners or specific times or places. In addition, a book could not be interactive, as in a conversation or dialogue between persons. And, finally, according to Socrates, in a book the written words "seem to talk to you as if they were intelligent, but if you ask them anything about what they say, from a desire to be instructed, they go on telling you just the same thing forever."[1] After more than two millennia, it now seems that a new kind of technology, with interactive multimedia capabilities, may be beginning to address some of Socrates' concerns. As we move forward, we might measure our relative success by his ancient standard.

Just as print technologies added to and superseded the oldest oral traditions, so, too, in the new visual era we might expect that a whole new generation of powerful, interactive visualization technologies and techniques could soon turn many long-held beliefs upside down, including conventional evaluations about what is worth learning, what is worth doing, and about who is intelligent.

For a very long time, serious academic work has been word-based. It seems evident that this is about to change. We should expect to move in fits and starts from a world based on words to a world based on images. And, as these changes occur, it would seem likely that the wonderfully diverse and innovative membership of the SIGGRAPH computer graphics association, along with strong visual thinkers everywhere, could have a special role in pressing ahead and guiding these developments—bringing together the arts and the sciences in powerful combinations impossible in other spheres.

More and more of those working at the edge of these new technologies, in the sciences as well as business or the professions, are coming to recognize the emerging power of these developments. For example, Dr. Larry Smarr, a physicist, astronomer, and former director of the National Center for Supercomputing Applications (NCSA), has commented, "I have often argued in my public talks that the graduate education process that produces physicists is totally skewed to selecting those with analytic skills and rejecting those with visual or holistic skills. I have claimed that with the rise of scientific visualization as a new mode of scientific discovery, a new class of minds will arise as scientists."[2]

Consequently, the further ahead we advance with the newer computer technologies, surprisingly, the more we seem likely to see a revival of visual approaches and perspectives largely abandoned in many fields long ago. In some areas, disdain for visual, graphical, or diagrammatic approaches has been strikingly strident. For example, for many decades, most mathematicians and some scientists have tried to turn away from visual approaches as much as possible. Now in many disciplines these visual approaches are seen as having great value once again.[3]

Data Visualization

As many computer professionals are aware, visual modes of thought and learning are increasingly being given serious attention—partly because of growing capabilities of new computers but also partly because of the great difficulty of dealing effectively with the enormous masses of data that now have to be assessed. Increasingly, computer-generated, multidimensional graphic displays are helping scientists detect relationships in data that could never have been detected by conventional methods.

For example, some years ago scientists using computer graphics at Stanford University were beginning to see "patterns in data that never would have been picked up with standard statistical techniques." In cases such as these, the purpose of data analysis is to "discover patterns, to find nonrandom clusters of data points." In the past this was usually done with mathematical formulas. However, with the use of animated computer graphics, "it has become possible to look at three-dimensional projections of the data" and to employ "the uniquely human ability to recognize the meaningful patterns in the data."[4]

Developments such as these are encouraging in themselves, as new ways are found to recognize meaningful patterns and slowly peel away, in a most unexpected and surprising manner, whole other layers of reality. But these developments are of special interest because of the way they shift emphasis to primarily visual modes of analysis and thought.

Such trends are especially important in the newly developing fields of chaos theory and fractals. Some see these fields as now excessively fashionable; others see them as genuinely new tools that will permit, in time, genuinely new approaches to understanding patterns in nature. In any case, these new approaches are clearly providing additional cause to consider a return to visual thinking. Developments associated with chaos research suggest the beginning of a major new trend away from traditional mathematical analysis and, instead, toward the analysis of visual images.

As James Gleick, an observer of the early development of chaos theory, has noted, "Chaos has become not just theory but also method, not just a canon of beliefs but also a way of doing science. . . . To chaos researchers, mathematics has become an experimental science, with the computer replacing laboratories full of test tubes and microscopes. Graphic images are the key. 'It's masochism for a mathematician to do without pictures,' one chaos specialist would say. 'How can they see the relationship between that motion and this? How can they develop intuition? Some carry out their work explicitly denying that it is a revolution; others deliberately use the language of paradigm shifts to describe the changes they witness."[5]

In other areas, some observers suggest that in general data visualization in business applications is about ten years behind visualization in the sciences.[6] Few are using these techniques, and those few that are apparently do not like to talk much about it. However, there is evidence that mainstream business users are gradually beginning to take visualization techniques seriously. For example, years ago *The Economist* magazine carried a story about visualization of trading and financial data, featuring the products of a small Canadian company that provides an "entire portfolio encapsulated as a three-dimensional moving picture." Using language familiar to visualizers of scientific data, the article speaks of the increased capacity of the New York Stock Exchange to handle complex information visually: "We're drowning in lots of data and we need ways of making sense of it." Indeed, the article suggests that the use of these techniques might have saved Barings, the British bank that collapsed in February 1995 through the hidden manuverings of a Barings trader in Singapore. Spotting such a rogue trader "is often a matter of luck rather than judgment." However, "with a 3-D view of what traders are doing, strange strategies or dangerous positions jump right out of the picture."[7]

Thus a new pattern may be emerging. New tools will increasingly require new skills and talents. With the further development of smaller and cheaper but more powerful computers having sophisticated visual-projection capabilities, we expect a new trend to be emerging in which visual proficiencies will play an increasingly important role in areas that have been almost exclusively dominated in the past by those most proficient in verbal-logical-mathematical modes of thought. However, although the application of these techniques may now be expanding to new segments of the population, they have long been used by a gifted and dedicated few.

VISUALIZATION AND STATISTICS

In the words of psychologist Howard Gardner, those who naturally gravitate toward a visual approach have "often seemed to be in the minority—although they seemed to be part of an especially creative and productive minority."[8] For example, late nineteenth-century English statistician Karl Pearson and his son E. S. Pearson both relied heavily on visual modes of images in their innovative statistical work. They were surprised that their professional colleagues and students used visualization rarely, if at all. These associates believed that visualization was useful only for presentation to ordinary laypersons—whereas the Pearsons saw visualization as the essential grounding for their most creative work.

In his lecture notes, Karl Pearson observed, "Contest of geometry and arithmetic as scientific tools in dealing with physical and social phenomena. Erroneous opinion that geometry is only a means of popular representation; rather it is a fundamental method of investigating and analyzing statistical material."[9] Writing in the 1950s, younger Pearson lamented that "the prestige of mathematical procedures based on algebra formulae is deeply entrenched in our lecture courses and our text-books, so that few mathematical statisticians will use to the full their visual faculties unless they are trained to do so."[10]

VISUALIZATION AND MATHEMATICS

In the past, visualization was rare in many fields. This is changing. In the past few years, the world of the professional mathematician has been undergoing fundamental change—reversing, in many respects, more than a hundred years of development in the opposite direction. In recent years, professional mathematicians have been rethinking the way they view their whole discipline, as well as the ways they think their discipline should be taught. In the old days (not very long ago), logic and rigorous proof were seen as the most important aspects of serious mathematics. In recent years, however, this has changed. Currently, "many leading professional mathematicians now see that visualization, experimentation, and original discovery are of prime importance—a position unthinkable by most respectable mathematicians only a short time ago."[11]

An emerging consensus point of view was described some years ago by Lynn Arthur Steen, a mathematics professor familiar with years of debate within the profession:

> Mathematics is often defined as the science of space and number, as the discipline rooted in geometry and arithmetic. Although the diversity of modern mathematics has always exceeded this definition, it was not until the recent resonance of computers and mathematics that a more apt definition became fully evident. Mathematics is the science of patterns. The mathematician seeks patterns in number, in space, in science, in computers, and in imagination. . . . To the extent that mathematics is the science of patterns, computers change not so much the nature of the discipline as its scale: computers are to mathematics what telescopes and microscopes are to science. . . . Because of computers, we see that mathematical discovery is like scientific discovery. . . . Theories emerge as patterns of patterns, and significance is measured by the degree to which patterns in one area link to patterns in other areas.[12]

The far-reaching consequences of this change in perspective can be partly seen in the concurrent major reevaluation of certain university-level mathematics courses in recent years. Although this reevaluation has been widespread—with many alternative proposals for improvements and extensive debate among professional mathematicians—in most instances real change has been slow to take place. And in many cases those changes actually implemented have been relatively modest in scope.

In some cases, on the other hand, the changes have been quite extensive, with dramatic results. In one case, for example, three professors have developed innovative courseware for teaching calculus as an interactive laboratory course using a graphics computer together with a high-level mathematics program—one designed to do mathematics in all to its three major forms: numerical, symbolic, and graphical.

Unlike many other course innovations, such changes are not just additions to the regular class lectures, but rather they have had enormous impact in transforming all aspects of the teaching and learning process. Instead of spending valuable time learning by hand routines that can be quickly done by the computer, students are pressed to move rapidly to high-level conceptual matters and a variety of practical problems, focusing mainly on examples from medicine, biology, and the life sciences. This is in marked contrast to the traditional calculus problem sets, which are now seen by professional mathematicians in Europe as well as in America as being highly contrived and artificial, with little relevance to real mathematics in either research or application.

An unpublished evaluation summarizes some of the radical curricular innovations and the increased effectiveness of this new type of laboratory calculus course:

> The new course changed the delivery of calculus from lectures and texts to a laboratory course through an electronic interactive text. . . . One of the most remarkable characteristics was the student's exploration through calculus and plottings. In the traditional calculus courses, the instructor announces the mathematical theory and then reinforces it with examples and exercises, and students recite the theory and solve the problems illustrating the theory. In the new course, however, the learning pattern of students. . . . was dramatically different. The experimentation by redoing, reformatting, rethinking, adapting and making changes led students to discover the basic concepts and principles for themselves. . . . The students . . . indicated that they had a feel for "doing" mathematics instead of "watching" mathematics.[13]

As we try to identify the causes of success in this approach, it may be no small matter that the students are encouraged to think and learn visually first—before traditional lectures and verbal description. A major shift in learning technique (along with a delightful informality and irreverence) is apparent in the authors' explanation to their students: "One of the beauties of learning the CALCULUS & *Mathematica* way is your opportunity to learn through graphics you can interact with. In this course, your eyes will send ideas directly to your brain. And this will happen without the distraction of translating what your eyes see into words. Take advantage of this opportunity to learn visually with pure thought uncorrupted by strange words. The words go onto an idea only after the idea has already settled in your mind. This aspect of CALCULUS & *Mathematica* distinguishes it from other math courses."[14]

It perhaps also is of no small importance that students who learn in this new way have shown that, in comparison with the traditional course, they understand the basic concepts better, can remember the information longer, and can apply the concepts to practical uses more effectively. It is increasingly apparent that many of the consequences seen in this new teaching approach—using interactive graphical computer systems with advanced software and courseware—may indicate possibilities for effective innovation in many other disciplines. Thus these new teaching approaches may be merely the manifestation of a much larger trend, as many disciplines find distinctive ways to return to visual thinking and learning.

VISUAL TALENTS AND VERBAL DIFFICULTIES

There is increasing evidence that many highly original and productive thinkers have clearly preferred visual over verbal modes of thought for many tasks. Some psychologists and neurologists argue that visual-spatial abilities should in fact be seen as a special form of intelligence, on a par with verbal or logical-mathematical forms of intelligence. Historically, it is apparent that some of the most original and gifted thinkers in the physical sciences, engineering, mathematics, and other areas relied heavily on visual modes of thought, employing images instead of words or numbers. However, it is notable that some of these same gifted thinkers have shown evidence of a striking range of learning problems, including difficulties with reading, spelling, writing, calculation, speaking, and memory. What is of greatest interest here is not the difficulties themselves but their frequent and varied association with a high degree of visual and spatial talent.

Several neurologists believe that sometimes such talents are closely associated with various kinds of learning difficulties because of certain early patterns of neurological development. Research suggests that in some forms of early brain growth the development of the verbal left hemisphere is suppressed while the development of the visual right hemisphere is increased—producing an unusual symmetry of brain form and function.[15] In ordinary people, the left hemisphere tends to be larger than the right; in visual thinkers with verbal difficulties, the left and right hemispheres tend to be approximately the same size. Varied visual talents mixed with verbal difficulties are evident in a diverse group of highly gifted historical figures, such as Michael Faraday, James Clerk Maxwell, Albert Einstein, Henri Poincaré, Thomas Edison, Leonardo da Vinci, Winston Churchill, Gen. George S. Patton, and William Butler Yeats.[16]

MICHAEL FARADAY

It is instructive to look at the example of Michael Faraday (1791–1867), an English scientist of the early and mid-nineteenth century. The son of an unemployed blacksmith, Faraday was for years a welfare recipient and had virtually no formal education. However, after eight years as an apprentice bookbinder—with a Frenchman who had fled to London to escape the French Revolution—he started work as a bottle washer and junior laboratory assistant. Through years of self-education and intensive laboratory work, he eventually became director of the laboratory, the Royal Institution, and earned a reputation for being the greatest experimental scientist of his time—formulating, among many accomplishments in chemistry and physics, the basic ideas of electricity and magnetism.

Faraday started with chemistry and moved on to physics and the study of electricity, light, and magnetism. He thought of himself as a philosopher and hated being called a chemist or a physicist—because he hated the limited worldview of the specialist approach. He liked to look at wholes, not pieces.

Among many original discoveries, he developed the first electric motor. But most importantly, he developed utterly original ideas about the fundamental nature of energy and matter—the electromagnetic "field" and "lines of force." These ideas were later translated into proper mathematical form by James Clerk Maxwell and later still became a powerful influence on the young Albert Einstein. Remarkably, these ideas have proved to be valid and useful since the time they were first developed in the middle of the nineteenth century. With each new scientific revolution since, many of the old theories and concepts have become rapidly outdated. But on the whole, those of Faraday and Maxwell just keep looking better and better.[17]

As a youth, Faraday explained, he was not precocious or a deep thinker. But he said that he was a "lively imaginative person" and could believe in the *Arabian Nights* as easily as the encyclopedia. However, he found a refuge from this too lively imagination in experimentation. Known especially as a great experimenter, he found that he could trust an experiment to check the truth of his ideas as well as to educate and inform his intuition, his mental models. In experimentation, he said, he "had got hold of an anchor" and he "clung fast to it."[18] Finally, Faraday is seen by later scientists as being like Einstein in that he had a remarkable ability to get to the heart of the matter and not be distracted by details or blind alleys. Historians of science said that Faraday "smells the truth." They thought he had an "unfailing intuition." They wondered at his "inconceivable instinct."[19]

JAMES CLERK MAXWELL

Maxwell was the sort of scientist who was able to deal in an extraordinary way with two entirely different worlds—the world of conventional mathematics and analysis, on one hand, and the visual world of images and models and diagrams on the other—which he, along with Faraday, favored. Indeed, he understood and admired Faraday's visualizations as did no other scientist of their time. Eventually he converted Faraday's ideas into mathematics for what are now known as "Maxwell's equations," although he always maintained that these were originally Faraday's ideas.[20]

A native of Scotland, Maxwell received his education in science and mathematics at the University of Cambridge in England. He showed himself to be a brilliant student; however, Maxwell's troubles with words manifested itself in severe, lifelong speech problems. He was a stutterer and had continuous career difficulties as a result—although he is thought to be the most brilliant physicist of the nineteenth century. In fact, Richard Feynman, a Nobel Prize–winning American physicist, said in 1963 that "from the long view of the history of mankind—seen from, say, ten thousand years from now—there can be little doubt that the most significant event of the nineteenth century will be judged as Maxwell's discovery of the laws of electrodynamics. The American Civil War," Feyman said, "will pale into provincial insignificance in comparison with this important scientific event of the same decade."[21]

Like Faraday, Maxwell was a strong visual thinker. There are many references in the biographies and letters as well as the commentaries of historians of science. He could understand Faraday's highly visual ideas much better than others, presumably because his visualization abilities were as exceptional as Faraday's. But in addition, he was familiar with the relevant mathematics—Faraday was not—and was able to translate the conceptual clarity of Faraday's theories into the language of mathematics. He much preferred Faraday's conceptions to those of the other professional mathematicians of his day. Indeed, he felt that following Faraday's way of looking at things produced a conceptual clarity and simplicity impossible through the other, more acceptable scientific approaches of their time.[22]

Maxwell's visual orientation was evident in many aspects of his work. In mathematics and physical science, his starting point was often geometry. He used mechanical analogies and resorted to diagrams and pictures whenever possible. Much of his work involved the interaction of force and substance in a largely visual-spatial arena. And, finally, one historian of science, writing of Maxwell, puzzled at the appearance of artists in his family, generation after generation, although the family seemed to be otherwise a uniformly practical group.[23]

ALBERT EINSTEIN

In the life of Albert Einstein, the importance of visual learning and visual talents in conjunction with verbal difficulties has long been recognized. His poor memory for words and texts made him hate the rote learning methods of his early school years. However, he tended to thrive later at the progressive school in Switzerland where he prepared to take his university examinations—no doubt partly because the unconventional school was based largely on visually oriented educational principles.[24]

There is a debate among biographers as to whether the young Einstein was a brilliant student or whether he was a dullard. After some time looking at these conflicting points of view, one realizes that to some extent he was both—a pattern typical of highly gifted visual thinkers with verbal difficulties. Einstein's sister Maja recorded a number of details about his early life, commenting about his late development of speech, his slow answers but deep understanding in mathematics, and his frequent calculation errors despite a clear understanding of the main mathematical concepts involved.[25]

Einstein dropped out of secondary school in Germany (contrary to plan) to follow his parents after they moved to Italy. His reason was that because of his "poor memory," he preferred to endure all kinds of punishments rather than to have to learn to "gabble by rote."[26] After he failed his first set of university entrance examinations, Einstein went to a new and unconventional school—one that was based on the highly visually oriented ideas of Johann Heinrich Pestalozzi. It was at this school that Einstein's abilities began to blossom, and the great theories that would be published in 1905 began to take their initial shape.[27]

The fact that Einstein possessed both visual talents and verbal difficulties has been noted by several observers. Physicist and historian of science Gerald Holton has remarked: "An apparent defect in a particular person may merely indicate an imbalance of our normal expectations. A noted deficiency should alert us to look for a proficiency of a different kind in the exceptional person. The late use of language in childhood, the difficulty in learning foreign languages may indicate a polarization or displacement in some of the skill from the verbal to another area. That other, enhanced area is without a doubt, in Einstein's case an extraordinary kind of visual imagery that penetrates his very thought processes."[28]

Later, in his own writing, Einstein made clear references to what he saw as two very different modes of thought, especially with regard to his own most creative and productive work. He pointed out that when he did really productive thinking, he always used "more or less clear images" and what he called "combinatory play" as the "essential feature" in his "productive thought," as well as of some "visual and some muscular type."[29] But he explains that if he wanted to communicate these thoughts to others, he had to go through a difficult and laborious translation process, proceeding from images to words and numbers that could be understood by others.

It is anticipated that modern visualization technologies and techniques may eventually permit many more ordinary people to do what Einstein did with mental models in his mind's eye—and permit the communication of sophisticated visual ideas without having to resort to poorly suited verbal and mathematical substitutes.

The power of the visual approach is found in one rather surprising account of Albert Einstein's development as a professional scientist. In his later career, Einstein did become increasingly sophisticated in higher mathematics. However, some have argued that this increased sophistication may have been more of a hindrance than a help in his later creative work. Mathematician David Hilbert made clear, with some exaggeration, that Einstein's creative scientific accomplishments were not a result of his mathematical skill: "Every boy in the streets of Göttingen understands more about four-dimensional geometry than Einstein. Yet, in spite of that, Einstein did the work and not the mathematicians."[30]

Hilbert was not alone in his assessment. Indeed, Abraham Pais, the author of a scientific biography of Einstein, observes that Einstein's increasing reliance on mathematics over time also involved a reduced dependency on the visual methods that he used so heavily and so productively in his earlier work. Pais suggested that this change in approach may have contributed to Einstein's comparatively reduced productivity in his later years. Pais observes, "It is true that the theoretical physicist who has no sense of mathematical elegance, beauty and simplicity is lost in some essential way. At the same time it is dangerous and can be fatal to rely exclusively on formal arguments. It is a danger from which Einstein himself did not escape in his later years. The emphasis on mathematics is so different from the way the young Einstein used to proceed."[31]

CONCLUSION

These examples should help to provide weight to the argument that we can be seen to be moving forward into the past—that we might very well expect a revival of old-fashioned visual talents and skills as greater use is made of computer visualization. Thus we might expect a revival of the kinds of visual learning and visual thinking that have been relatively unfashionable in many disciplines for as much as a century. These examples should also provide some sense of how visual thinking has been a major source of creative thought in several extraordinarily gifted individuals.

However, as these changes take place, we should also expect significant reassessment of the kinds of skills and talents that are considered valuable. In the past, there has been general high regard for strong verbal, mathematical, and memorization skills—"academic skills."

In the future, however, we might expect to see a higher regard for visualization skills and talent—for detecting subtle patterns in moving computer images representing complex systems, whether they be the immune system of the body or the weather systems of the globe or fluctuations in international financial markets.

The extent of these changes might be very great. It is useful to remind ourselves of a remarkable continuity: that for centuries our schools and universities have been essentially working with the skills of the clerk—reading, writing, counting, symbol manipulation, and memorizing texts. In spite of obvious value, the technology of the book has always been somewhat one-dimensional, using the shorthand of a sequence of symbols representing sounds. No matter how evocative, rich with information, or precise, there have always been limits—as Socrates observed long ago.

Today, however, we may be on the verge of a really new era, when we will be required to go much further and develop a very different set of visually based talents and skills—like those of a hands-on visual thinker such as Leonardo da Vinci rather than those of the clerk or scholar or schoolman of the Middle Ages. (Seeing the caps and gowns in an academic procession, we should be reminded of the largely medieval—and word-based—indicators of prestige and status that still dominate much of modern university culture.)

As we were warned by Norbert Wiener some fifty years ago, in the not too distant future, machines will be the best clerks.[32] None of us can afford to compete with machines. But, as it happens, it seems that we are entering a new era where many of us will need to develop new forms of education and work-based visual talents and skills that were long important but seldom acknowledged. And the changes may be greater and more rapid than any of us can now imagine.[33]

NOTES

1. Plato, *Phaedrus*, quoted in Donald A. Norman, *Things That Make Us Smart: Defending Human Attributes in an Age of the Machine* (Reading, MA: Addison-Wesley, 1993), pp. 45–46.

2. Larry Smarr, e-mail to author, August 6, 1994. Smarr is now director of the California Institute for Telecommunications and Information Technology at the University of California, San Diego. See also William J. Kaufman III and Larry L. Smarr, *Supercomputing and the Transformation of Science* (New York: Scientific American Library, 1993).

3. This chapter, originally prepared as an article at the request of the editor of the ACM SIGGRAPH journal *Computer Graphics*, is based on an invited lecture included in the German-language conference proceedings: "Rückkehr zum visuellen Denken" (A Return to Visual Thinking) in *Science and Scientific Computing: Visions of a Creative Symbiosis, Symposium of Computer Users in the Max-Planck-Gesellschaft, Göttingen, Germany, November 1993*, ed. Peter Wittenburg and Theo Plesser, Max-Planck-Gesellschaft Berichte und Mitteilungen, Heft 1/94. Some of the material summarized here has appeared previously in *In the Mind's Eye* and other presentations and articles by the author.

4. Gina Kolata, "Computer Graphics Comes to Statistics," *Science* 217 (September 3, 1982): 919–20.

5. James Gleick, *Chaos: Making a New Science* (New York: Viking, 1987), pp. 38–39.

6. Larry Smarr, e-mail to author, June 1995.

7. "Seeing Is Believing," *Economist*, August 19, 1995, p. 71.

8. Howard Gardner, *Frames of Mind: The Theory of Multiple Intelligences* (New York: Basic Books, 1983), p. 177. It should be noted that broad definitions of

"verbal" and "visual" (and, closely related, "spatial") capabilities are used here, referring in part to the varied but apparently antithetical thinking styles generally believed to be embodied in the left and right hemispheres, respectively. Gardner distinguishes several major forms of intelligence but argues for the special status of visual-spatial intelligence in contrast to verbal intelligence: "In the view of many, spatial intelligence is the 'other intelligence'—the one that should be arrayed against and considered equal in importance to 'linguistic intelligence.'" Although Gardner does not subscribe to the dichotomization of intelligence into separate hemispheres, he says, "Still, I would admit that, for most of the tasks used by experimental psychologists, linguistic and spatial intelligences provide the principle sources of storage and solution."

9. Karl Pearson, quoted in E. S. Pearson, "Statistics," in *The Selected Papers of E. S. Pearson* (Berkeley and Los Angeles: University of California Press, 1966), p. 252.

10. E. S. Pearson, ibid., p. 253.

11. Walter Zimmermann and Steve Cunningham, eds., *Visualization in Teaching and Learning Mathematics* (Washington, DC: Mathematical Association of America, 1991), p. 3.

12. Lynn Arthur Steen, "The Science of Patterns," *Science* 240 (April 29, 1988): 616.

13. Kyungmee Park, "A Comparative Study of the Traditional Calculus Course versus the CALCULUS & *Mathematica* Course" (PhD diss., University of Illinois Urbana-Champaign, 1993), p. 162. Some italics have been left out of the quoted text.

14. W. Davis, H. Porta, and J. Uhl, *CALCULUS & Mathematica* (Reading, MA: Addison-Wesley, 1994), p. 11. Remarkably, at the time of writing, in the spring of 2004, there seems to be substantial agreement among mathematics teachers and textbook writers that the approach used by Davis, Porta, and Uhl is the best way to teach these subjects. This observation is especially remarkable because only a short time before, their approach appeared to many to be the most radical departure from conventional teaching methods.

15. See Norman Geschwind and Albert M. Galaburda, *Cerebral Lateralization: Biological Mechanisms, Associations and Pathology* (Cambridge, MA: MIT Press, 1987); N. Geschwind, "Why Orton Was Right," *Annals of Dyslexia* 32 (1982) (Orton Dyslexia Society Reprint 98); N. Geschwind and P. Behan, "Left-Handedness," in *Proceedings of the National Academy of Sciences* 79 (1982): 5097–5100; Howard Gardner, *Intelligence Reframed: Multiple Intelligences for the 21st Century* (New York: Basic Books, Perseus Books, 1999).

16. See Thomas G. West, *In the Mind's Eye* (Amherst, NY: Prometheus Books, 1991), pp. 29–40, 101–75.

17. See ibid., 1991 and 1997 editions.

18. Quoted in John Tyndall, *Faraday as a Discoverer*, new ed. (London: Longmans, Green, 1870), p. 55.

19. Joseph Agassi, *Faraday as a Natural Philosopher* (Chicago: University of Chicago Press, 1971), pp. 128–29.

20. Ibid.

21. Richard P. Feynman, Robert B. Leighton, and Matthew Sands, *The Feynman Lectures on Physics* (Reading, MA: Addison-Wesley, 1963).

22. See Lewis Campbell and William Garnett, *The Life of James Clerk Maxwell* (London: Macmillan, 1882; reprint, New York: Johnson Reprint, 1969); Ivan Tolstoy, *James Clerk Maxwell: A Biography* (Chicago: University of Chicago Press, 1981); C. W. F. Everitt, "Maxwell's Scientific Creativity," in *Springs of Scientific Creativity: Essays on Founders of Modern Science*, ed. Rutherford Aris, H. Ted Davis, and Roger H. Stuewer (Minneapolis: University of Minnesota Press, 1983); West, *In the Mind's Eye*, 1991 and 1997 editions.

23. Everitt, "Maxwell's Scientific Creativity."

24. Gerald Holton, "On Trying to Understand Scientific Genius," *American Scholar* 41 (1972): 104–106.

25. Albert Einstein, *The Collected Papers of Albert Einstein*, vol. 1, trans. Anna Beck, Peter Havas, consultant (Princeton, NJ: Princeton University Press, 1987), pp. xviii–xxi.

26. Banesh Hoffman, *Albert Einstein: Creator and Rebel* (New York: New American Library, 1972), p. 25.

27. See Holton, "On Trying to Understand Scientific Genius"; West, *In the Mind's Eye*.

28. Holton, "On Trying to Understand Scientific Genius," p. 102.

29. Quoted in Jacques Hadamard, *An Essay on the Psychology of Invention in the Mathematical Field* (New York: Dover, 1954), pp. 142–43.

30. A. P. French, "The Story of General Relativity," in *Einstein: A Centenary Volume* (Cambridge, MA: Harvard University Press, 1979), p. 111. (Quoted from Constance Reid's biography of Hilbert, 1970.)

31. Abraham Pais, *"Subtle Is the Lord": The Science and the Life of Albert Einstein* (Oxford and New York: Oxford University Press, 1982), p. 172.

32. Norbert Wiener, *Cybernetics; or, Control and Communication in the Animal and the Machine*, 2nd ed. (New York: MIT Press, 1961), pp. 27–28.

33. In spite of the slowdown of the general economy evident in the SIGGRAPH conference of 2003, it is clear that scientific visualization, information visualization, and computer graphics, in all its many forms, are all still very much alive and well—and moving forward. SIGGRAPH 2004 showed a clear upswing in this trend. It is also clear that the SIGGRAPH organization, conferences, and members continue to be major forces in this development. In a recent issue of ACM SIGGRAPH *Computer Graphics*, Kwan-Lui Ma (University of California at Davis) begins his new series of columns on visualization with the title "Visualization: A Quickly Emerging Field," vol. 38, no. 1 (February 2004): 4–7. He notes, "While in the early years most of the research was largely driven by medical and supercomputing applications, visualization research is increasingly benefiting new applications such as industrial nondestructive testing, business decision making and bioinformatics." After reviewing a number of issues and continuing debates, Ma concludes, "Visualization will not be like computer graphics, which has created a huge industry of video games and films. It will, however, gain widespread use in all fields of study as it becomes more accessible. It is therefore imperative to develop not only novel techniques but also truly usable tools."

CHAPTER

We have Hawaiian names for the houses of the stars—the places where they come out of the ocean and go back into the ocean. If you can identify the stars, and if you have memorized where they come up and go down, you can find your direction. The star compass is also used to read the flight path of birds and the direction of waves. It does everything. It is a mental construct to help you memorize what you need to know to navigate. . . .

We use the best clues that we have. We use the sun when it is low on the horizon. . . . When the sun gets too high you cannot tell where it has risen. You have to use other clues. Sunrise is the most important part of the day. At sunrise you start to look at the shape of the ocean—the character of the sea. You memorize where the wind is coming from. The wind generates the swells. You determine the direction of the swells, and when the sun gets too high, you steer by them. And then at sunset we repeat the observations. . . . At night we use the stars. . . .

When I came back from my first voyage as a student navigator from Tahiti to Hawai'i the night before he went home, [my teacher] . . . said, "I am very proud of my student. You have done well for yourself and your people." He was very happy that he was going home. He said, "Everything you need to see is in the ocean but it will take you twenty more years to see it." That was after I had just sailed 7,000 miles.

—Navigator Nainoa Thompson of the Polynesian Voyaging Society

USING THE BEST CLUES WE HAVE

The words of navigator Nainoa Thompson provide a wonderful description of using the best of what is ready at hand to do a most important job—on which rests the survival of the culture of a whole people. Indeed, during the past twenty-five years, the successful voyages of the *Hokule'a* and other long-distance canoes have become cultural milestones, and Nainoa Thompson has become a major hero among Polynesians.[1] These voyages and revived navigation skills have much to teach us all. We are shown a highly refined example of the observational and visual-thinking skills needed to navigate across the Pacific. If we had not known better, most of us would have thought that it was not possible to do.

Perhaps we are just now mature enough in our modern culture to fully appreciate what these navigators accomplished in an earlier culture with the simplest of tools and the most sophisticated use of their brains—and to see that such feats rank with the highest accomplishments of human beings, in any field, at any time. We can now see that it is not a matter of developing complex mathematics or the most modern tools and technologies. Rather, it is a matter of using well what is available in the particular situation—developing techniques to train the brain and the senses through close observation, long practice, and sensitive teaching—making the best use of what is at hand, using the best clues that we have.

Feats such as these draw heavily on visual and spatial abilities and "intelligences" that have been generally underappreciated in modern culture. But all this is changing and the newest technologies are taking us back to some of our oldest and most essential abilities—teaching us that in some fields, the further forward we proceed, the more we reconnect with our ancient roots.

THINKING LIKE EINSTEIN

Visual thinking is a continuing puzzle. It seems to come up more and more these days—but few seem to understand its deep roots and larger implications. The human brain is indeed wonderful, the way it permits us to use all forms of natural systems and subtle information to do rather unbelievable things and still survive—or, rather, in the long run, *in order to* survive.

To navigate across thousands of miles of open ocean while feeling the long-distance swells (not simply sailing past tiny unseen islands just over the horizon), to adapt to amazing extremes of heat and cold; using with great sophistication only those tools and resources that are readily at hand—all without modern technologies or distant supports and hidden subsidies (always a major advantage for modern travelers)—all this is accomplished without a book of written instructions or "full" scientific knowledge. But it is accomplished with enough knowledge to hunt food, find a home, build shelter, fend off enemies, cooperate with a group, and raise a family—for thousands and thousands of years.

Strangely, the farther ahead we go, the more our future is seen to be like our distant past. The more modern we become, the more we come to appreciate (belatedly) the long-earned wisdom of traditional cultures. The more we understand the brain's deep resources for creativity and pattern recognition, the more we come to respect the accomplishments of our distant ancestors and appreciate the problems they solved—the solutions that have secured our survival and allowed us to be. The more we move into unfamiliar territory, without map or guidebook, the more we admire traditional knowledge, long discounted by bookish education.

This is not mere romanticism but level-headed respect. The more our technologies change (and also change us), the more we can see that the newest computer data visualization technologies draw on some our oldest neurological resources—more like those of the hunter-gatherers than those of the scribes, schoolmen, and scholars of more recent times. Albert Einstein tells us, as we have seen previously, that all his really important and productive thinking was done by playing with images in his head, in his imagination. Only in a secondary stage did he translate—with great effort, he says— these images to words and mathematics that could be understood by others. We now have technologies that can deal with the images directly—so the laborious translation may often not be necessary or even desirable.

Some believe that visualization technologies are already in evidence everywhere. They think the battle is over. Others, myself among them, think that visualization technologies have a very, very long way to go and that they have hardly begun to have substantial impact in the full range of fields they will transform over time. We think, with the exception of a few specialists, that the process of deep change has not yet really begun. We think that gaining insight and new understanding through the sophisticated use of visualization technologies and techniques, in time, should be as pervasive as reading and writing.

But there can be little debate that we already have tools that can help us think the way Einstein thought—and it is striking how old and traditional these ways of thinking were. In many ways, Einstein thought and worked more like a craftsman than a scholar. And, indeed, the more proficient he became at the sophisticated science and mathematics of his peers, the less visual he became—and, more importantly for our purposes, the less creative and innovative he became. It would seem that the traditional Polynesian navigators were drawing on some of the same neurological resources that were so very useful to Einstein when he was a young man— before, as we are told by other scientists, he became corrupted by excessive familiarity with sophisticated mathematics. As he became more expert as a scientist and mathematician, he accomplished less. He had abandoned the modes of thought that had given him his best insights.

It is notable that two physicists, Richard Feynman and Abraham Pais, both observed independently that as Einstein grew older, he became less visual in his approach and more adept at conventional mathematics. As pointed out in chapter 16, Feynman believed Einstein became much less productive when "he stopped thinking in concrete physical images and became a manipulator of equations."[2] Pais also noted in his scientific biography on Einstein that Einstein's increasing dependence on mathematics in later life also involved a reduced reliance on the visual and intuitive approaches he used so heavily and so productively in his earlier work. As mentioned in the previous chapter, Pais acknowledged the danger in relying on formal mathematical arguments, a danger Einstein did not escape in his later years.

When I was giving talks to teachers and school administrators in Fairbanks, Alaska, several years ago, I was told that the Athebascan students in the villages along the Yukon River were natural visual thinkers and natural scientists. This should make us think. We may well wonder whether they would have substantial advantages if they were to be educated in the visual world of Einstein's imagination and modern computer graphics, rather than the old, academic world of facts and dates, words and numbers. Shortly afterward, when I had given talks in Honolulu, others there told me that traditional Polynesian culture quite naturally promotes highly visual and hands-on approaches over verbal approaches to the communication of knowledge.[3]

If we were to fully and deeply understand the roots of knowledge in our own new world, we might see that Einstein's way of thinking is far more like those used in resurrected traditional cultures than it is like the academic conventions of the distant and recent past. We might see, again, that Einstein's way of thinking is more like that of the artisan or craftsman or traditional navigator and less like that of the conventionally trained scholar or mathematician or scientist.

SMASHING IMAGES, BLASTING BUDDHAS

There seems always to have been a certain tension between the world of the word and the world of the image. In March of 2001, a whirlwind fanned the fires of this ageless conflict. As the world watched in horror and disbelief (foreshadowing much greater horrors the following September), leaders of the Taliban government in Afghanistan decided that it was time to finally destroy all images in their country. No more playing on international sympathies or bargaining for foreign funds and support: they just declared that the statues were idolatrous and gave the order, and the giant, ninth-century Buddha statues of Bamiyan were blasted to rubble. "It took us four days to finish the big statue. He was very strong," said one soldier.[4]

Thus here we have the two extremes of a global and philosophical continuum: on one side, the image haters, those who would destroy all art in all forms out of a strict obedience to an ancient and narrow prescription; on the other side, those who would have art harnessed to shape and serve larger interests.[5] For a long time (it is not often observed), many Christian denominations have embodied this split as well. Some churches have always used the image to teach church doctrine and Bible stories—especially to those who were not able learn it through written text. Other Christian groups have tried to avoid all images and decoration—indeed, some of their Protestant forbears smashed stained glass windows and pulled off the heads of sculptures of saints in similar fashion to the Taliban in recent times. In some parts of England, even today, they are still discovering stained glass window sections that were buried long ago to save them from the enraged, puritanical Christian destroyers of images.

The story is not always simple. In fact, there is more to the story of the smashed Buddhas that did not come to light until months afterward. Not all the Afghans, or even all the Taliban, were happy about the destruction of the Buddhas. The thoughts of one Afghan Taliban defector might represent the thoughts and feelings of many in that country, especially in the Bamiyan area. Uncovered records of the minutes of meetings indicate that the smashing of the Buddhas was largely the idea of the foreign al Qaeda members, not the Afghan Taliban. According to press reports, Taliban defector "[Mohammed] Khaksar became especially disgruntled . . . when the Taliban leadership decided to destroy two ancient Buddha sculptures at Bamian, saying they offended Islam. Documents unearthed since the Taliban's retreat from Kabul suggested that al Qaeda pushed the Taliban into the action that earned international opprobrium."[6] "'It's a historic sculpture; they should not have destroyed it,' Khaksar said. 'I felt like I lost a member of my family when they destroyed this sculpture.'"[7]

NOTES

1. Dennis Kawaharada, "Wayfinding, or Non-Instrument Navigation," Polynesian Voyaging Society, http://leahi.kcc.hawaii.edu/org/pvs/L2wayfind.html (accessed June 23, 2004). See also Nainoa Thompson, "Voyage into the New Millennium," *Hana Hou!* February–March 2000, pp. 41ff; Harriet Witt-Miller, "The Soft, Warm, Wet Technology of Native Oceania," *Whole Earth Review*, Fall 1991, pp. 64–69.

2. Richard Feynman, quoted in James Gleick, *Genius: the life and science of Richard Feynman* (New York: Pantheon Books, 1992), p. 244.

3. Personal communications to author from C. Marshall (Fairbanks, AK), D. Preble (Honolulu, HI), and K. Smith (Madison, WI), all 2001.

4. Afghan soldier quoted in Kathy Gannon, "Afghan Soldiers," *Wisconsin State Journal*, March 27, 2001, p. A5.

5. See Leonard Shlain, *The Alphabet versus the Goddess: The Conflict between Word and Image* (New York: Viking, 1998).

6. "Al Qaeda Training," *Washington Post,* November 22, 2001, p. A35.

7. Peter Baker, "Defector Says Bin Laden Had Cash, Taliban in His Pocket," *Washington Post,* November 30, 2001, pp. A1, A25. This chapter was first published as an article in *Computer Graphics* in August 2002, nearly a year after the terrorist attacks of September 11 and the anthrax attacks in October of 2001. It is with some circumspection that I note that two of my earlier *CG* columns seem, to some extent, to foreshadow each event: "Smashing Images—A Review" (August 1999) and "When the World Plague was Stopped by a Digital Artist" (November 2000). This notable circumstance might suggest that, for good or ill, focusing on the broader range of visualization issues in a larger context can sometimes draw us toward ever more timely contemplation of our near future. Who would have thought that the consideration of an eighth-century Christian sect (the image-smashing iconoclasts in Shlain's prescient 1998 book, *The Alphabet versus the Goddess*) would so nearly characterize the thinking of a twenty-first-century fanatical religious group—one that has moved to the center of current US and world policy and concern (becoming increasingly important in 2003 and 2004)? Similarly, who would have thought that linking a science fiction story from *Wired* magazine with a Nobel Laureate's essay on infectious disease from *Science* would have raised a topic that is of grave concern and, at this writing (even in 2004), still unsolved?

CHAPTER

3   VISUAL THINKERS AND NOBEL PRIZES

RECOGNITION IN THE OLD TRADITION

"I didn't expect' a Nobel Prize 'at all,' he said, 'in part because of the nature of the work. There was less science [and more engineering] in it than the things customarily honored by the prizes." This is the observation of Jack S. Kilby of Texas Instruments, co-inventor of the integrated circuit, on being notified of his award in October 2000. The Nobel Prize for chemistry awarded at the same time to Alan J. Heeger (University of California, Santa Barbara) and Hideki Shirakawa (University of Tsukuba, Japan) for their work on conductive polymers also reflected the recognition of broad effects rather than pure science. "We're very excited," said Daryle H. Busch of the American Chemical Society, "because this award is in the old tradition. That is, it was given for work that has a very substantial impact on society."[1]

The shift back to an earlier tradition by the Nobel Prize committee may reflect a growing recognition in the larger world of the deep value of applied work of broad impact as opposed to the highly theoretical work of relatively low impact, which has commanded such high prestige in recent decades. Thus these changes might be read as the small beginnings of a larger and more gradual swing back toward a greater respect for hand and eye and image building in the brain.

For some time the major contributions of visual thinkers have been eclipsed in many fields by theoretical approaches that did not lend themselves to pictures, images, or imagined models and hands-on manipulation. For a long time, we have been told with confidence that visual approaches were old-fashioned and somehow primitive. Modern scientists and mathematicians, we have been told, did not need images—pictures and diagrams were for nonprofessionals and laypersons.

But we may now see that things may be going back the other way. With new visualization technologies and a new sense of missed opportunities with the old narrow methods, researchers in many fields are becoming aware that in order to do really creative work, they may need to go back to visual approaches once again. So perhaps we come back again to the place where much of the most advanced and creative work is carried out by visual thinkers using visual methods and technologies. Once again, pictures are not only for children.

REASSESSING VISUAL ROOTS AT GREEN COLLEGE

Quiet indicators of these powerful changes are beginning, here and there, to gain broader attention. In one instance, on a bleak and rainy Saturday in November 2000, a small but historic conference took place at Green College, Oxford University. With observations that will gladden the hearts of many strong visual thinkers, the conference presentations focused on high-level achievements in the arts and the sciences within families over several generations. Titled "Genius in the Genes?" and sponsored by the Arts Dyslexia Trust, the conference included an associated exhibition of art and scientific work from eight families. All these families showed evidence of a high degree of visual and spatial talents coupled with troubles with words. Several members of each family were also dyslexic.

In a view that is contrary to most of the generally held beliefs in educational testing and recent educational reform, the speakers indicated that very high-level and creative achievement in the sciences has often come from the neurological resources linked to success in the arts. The speakers indicated that some of those who have excelled most in their scientific achievements are from families with varied visual and spatial talents—ones that often have troubles with words. As we are becoming increasingly aware, there does seem to be a kind of trade-off between the two capacities: very early brain development, largely controlled by genetic factors, seems to gain unusual visual and spatial proficiencies at the cost of some lack of proficiency in some language systems.

Consequently, there may be various family members who have special strengths in art, design, computer graphics, visual mathematics, mechanics, or engineering, yet may have unusual difficulties with reading, spelling, arithmetic, rote memorization, or foreign languages. It is all part of a familiar pattern—that is continually repeated, with variations, generation after generation. The pattern continues through families, parents to children, always different in details but frequently similar in the overall pattern of visual strengths and notable language difficulties.

The pattern has often been observed but little studied in any systematic way. Many strong visual thinkers and their families are familiar with this sort of pattern. But this should not be surprising: their chosen occupations become a kind of filter. For example, the pattern is not uncommon among artists and designers, craftsmen and mechanics, surgeons and radiologists, architects and engineers. Even when the occupation may not be a giveaway, the hobbies often are.

FOUR NOBEL PRIZES

One of the speakers at the Green College conference was Patience Thomson, the former head of Fairley House School for dyslexics in London and later a founder of Barrington Stoke, a publisher of "books for reluctant readers." Thomson spoke of her family, where there are many visual-spatial occupations in the arts and the sciences and no fewer than four Nobel Prize winners. She explained that all of the prizewinning achievements have a substantial visual component. In a most remarkable example of the larger pattern, in this extended family the exceptional visual and spatial capabilities that have contributed to so much creativity and innovation seem to be balanced by problems in other specific areas.

On her side of the family, the Nobel laureates are her grandfather Sir William Bragg (1862–1942) and her father, Sir Lawrence Bragg (1890–1971). They received a joint prize for x-ray crystallography. In the family of her husband, David Thomson, the Nobel laureates are his grandfather Sir Joseph Thomson (1856–1940), for the discovery of the electron, and his father, Sir George Thomson (1892–1925), for the discovery of electron defraction.

She spoke of her famous father and the other outstanding scientists in her remarkable family, her gifted children, and the way the power of visual-spatial thinking has colored their lives and has contributed to many of the considerable achievements in the family. Along with the scientists among the Braggs and the Thomsons, there have been several artists, architects, television producers, and computer experts and one actor along with a number of other occupations where the role of visual-spatial proficiencies is not so obvious.[2]

However, through five generations of these families, with many children and grandchildren, there have been a number who have been mildly to significantly dyslexic. There are many great-grandchildren who are "too young to tell." Along with the award medals and family photographs, the exhibition showed drawings and paintings by family members, including a self-portrait by Sir Lawrence Bragg.

An indicator of the enduring importance of Sir Lawrence's work is that when James Watson wrote *The Double Helix*—the story of his discovery of the structure of DNA with Francis Crick—he asked Bragg to write the foreword to his book. The use of x-ray crystallography pioneered by the two Braggs was fundamental to understanding the structure of this molecule, which carries all genetic information.[3]

THE ART IN MEDICINE

Another speaker at the Oxford conference was Dr. Terence Ryan. Ryan described what turned out to be his own life story, as a man who was a leader in his field of medicine (dermatology) but who had unusual difficulties with his early education and his medical education because of his dyslexia. For example, with exams, he would usually recognize accurately symptoms and conditions but would sometimes come up with the wrong Latin names.

However, in his practice and clinical observations, he found that he could be a leader and innovator because he could recognize disease patterns that his medical colleagues could not easily see. He suspected that he had greater powers of visual observation than many of his associates. He also thought his dyslexia helped him to be more flexible and innovative in his thinking, coming up with theoretical approaches quite different from others in his field.

As an example of the creative, inverted thinking that dyslexics sometimes exhibit, he described one of his own theories that is still controversial. Generally it is taught that skin grows as its lowest layers and older cells allow themselves to rise to the top layers to slough off at the surface. He explained that from his point of view, cells would be unlikely to allow themselves to automatically rise to the top layers—as they would thereby be moving further and further away from their food supply in the bottom layers. Consequently, he uses the novel alternative explanation that the cells that rise to the top are in fact inadvertently pushed out of the way by other cells that are in fact making their own way down toward the nutrient supplies in the bottom layers. In many ways the final results are the same, but the actual process is quite different. Consequently, his associates see him as one of the important "lateral" thinkers in the field.

In spite of his extensive educational difficulties, his medical career has been highly successful. Now retired, he was clinical professor of dermatology at Oxford University and vice warden of one of the Oxford colleges. He has been president of many of the national and international professional societies in his field as well as being active in establishing regional dermatology training centers in Africa and Central America. He is "not easily confined by definitions," which has helped him break new ground and produce now nearly six hundred publications. As a hobby, Dr. Ryan does colorful flower paintings—often exploiting visual ambiguities in which it may not be clear whether a garden stair goes up or down or whether a flower is inside or outside a frame.

A VILLAGE OF MILLERS AND CLOCK MAKERS

The Green College exhibition also included information about a family from the village of Blockley, Gloucestershire, England. Blockley was the home of small industries and craft workers long before the Industrial Revolution. Most of the town lies along the spring-fed, "never-failing" Blockley Brook, "once a very vigorous stream, which, for a thousand years or more, drove many mills."[4]

This family showed remarkable continuity over many generations of involvement with occupations that require a high degree of visual and spatial talent—construction and operation of these small leased mills in the village over hundreds of years as well as barrel and clock making. One clock made by a family member was in use in a church in a nearby village from 1695 until 1962.[5]

In 1658, one member of the family (William Warner) emigrated to America, settling in the Philadelphia area, where his descendents continued for generations in occupations and businesses that required talent in mechanics, invention, engineering, art, and craft. For example, Joseph Warner was a silversmith in the middle of the eighteenth century.

It happens that I am a descendent of this family on my mother's side. Although at the conference I spoke mainly of the visual-thinking scientists who preceded the Braggs and Thomsons, the Green College exhibition did include oil paintings by my artist parents (Anne and Charles West) and sculpture by my son Jonathan. It may be no surprise that within this visually oriented extended family, there are several possible or diagnosed dyslexics, including myself.

SEEKING FAMILY PATTERNS

I have to admit that when I was originally urged to submit samples of family art for the Green College exhibition, I was interested—but also reluctant. I thought it would be interesting to look at our immediate family and then go back several generations to see what I could find. I think many families with high visual talents, with or without dyslexia, wonder about this sort of thing.

As we noted previously, neurologist Dr. Norman Geschwind said that the dyslexia trait would not be so common and would not persist generation after generation (in its varied forms) if it were not good for something. So, I wondered, did it persist in our own family? What was it good for?

My own parents were both artists. They met in art school. Some would expect (not entirely seriously) that this alone might be a strong predictor of some degree of dyslexia in their children (as well as visual talents). I wondered what form it might take in each generation. So I thought I would provide a few examples in the exhibition to provoke discussion about the possibilities. Perhaps it provoked discussion among other visual thinkers and their families as well. (In the process, I realize that my book *In the Mind's Eye* is in some ways an attempt to answer the question, what is it good for?)

ALWAYS AT THE LEADING EDGE

Viewing visual strengths and verbal difficulties over many generations (through many changes in technological and economic context) can be remarkably instructive. Accordingly, we may be led to ask whether it is true, as some believe, that many of the early dyslexics and strong visual thinkers with language problems quit their schools and conventional towns as quickly as they could and headed for the sailing ships and water-powered mills, the railroads and telegraph lines, the gold mines and oil fields.

Did they mostly leave places like London, Boston, and Philadelphia to seek their fortune (in disproportionate numbers) in places like Australia, New Zealand, Canada, Texas, Alaska, and California? Did all the Swedes who could not read (and so were not permitted to marry) really immigrate to America (as one Swedish researcher speculates)?

We may ask how varied strong visual traits have contributed over time to both school difficulties and to remarkable innovations and inventions, within a shifting technological context. Why do these individuals always seem to be out in front of everyone else, especially when they can move forward with a minimum of book learning and paper credentials while using their special visual-spatial abilities, creative imagination, and hands-on skills—often taking great risks?

Why do so many of today's technologists and entrepreneurs seem to fit this pattern? Why do there seem to be so many of these individuals in places like Silicon Valley? Whatever the time or place, some individuals seem to find ways to get away from the traditional books and the old ways by creating things that are entirely new. It seems to be a pattern that would be familiar to individuals and families where strong visual thinking is common. Perhaps it is worth looking at some of these families over time to see whether there is evidence of these enduring traits over generations—visual thinkers doing the things they can do best in whatever technological context is made available by their time and place. The patterns may be more clear and enlightening than we expect.[6]

NOTES

1. Quoted in Curt Suplee, "Six Awarded Nobel Prizes in Chemistry, Physics— 'Information Age' Contributions Honored,'" *Washington Post*, October 11, 2000, p. A2.

2. See G. M. Caroe, *William Henry Bragg, 1892–1942: Man and Scientist* (Cambridge: Cambridge University Press, 1978).

3. See James D. Watson, *The Double Helix: A Personal Account of the Discovery of DNA*, foreword by Sir Lawrence Bragg (New York: Atheneum, 1968).

4. Cotswold Wardens and the Ramblers Association, *Country Walks around Blockley* (Gloucester, UK: Gloucestershire County Council, 1991), p. 1.

5. H. E. M. Icely, *Blockley through Twelve Centuries* (Alburgh, Harleston, and Norfolk, UK: Erskine Press, 1996), p. 275.

6. This chapter is based on a column that appeared in *Computer Graphics* in February 2001 and, in a different form, on the Internet at the Web site LDOnLine (http://www.LDOnLine.org) in April 2001.

CHAPTER

4

WORD-BOUND
THE POWER OF SEEING

Until the 1960s, a student in an American engineering school was expected by his teachers to use his mind's eye to examine things that engineers had designed—to look at them, listen to them, walk around them, and thus to develop an intuitive "feel" for the way the material world works (and sometimes doesn't work). . . . By the 1980s, engineering curricula had shifted to analytical approaches, so that visual and other sensual knowledge of the world seemed much less relevant. . . . As faculties dropped drawing and shop practice from their curricula and deemed plant visits unnecessary, . . . working knowledge of the material world disappeared from faculty agendas and therefore from student agendas, and the nonverbal, tacit, and intuitive understanding essential to engineering design atrophied.

—Eugene Ferguson, *Engineering and the Mind's Eye*

In his book *Engineering and the Mind's Eye,* Eugene Ferguson provides an overview of developments in engineering education and practice over long periods and in recent times—providing an assessment of some of the larger implications and consequences of progressively abandoning visual and nonverbal approaches.[1]

Ferguson asserts that the dominant trend in engineering education and practice in recent decades has been "away from knowledge that cannot be expressed in mathematical relationships." The "art of engineering" has been put aside, producing engineers who are well suited to do esoteric mathematics but poorly suited to producing well-integrated engineering designs.

PRECISION WITHOUT INTEGRATION

Accordingly, Ferguson says, this trend tends to produce designs like the Hubble space telescope, where some parts (such as the mirrors) are extremely precise (beyond all previous accomplishment), yet the overall device initially would not work—because the parts were never fully integrated (in reality or in the imagination), requiring early repair at enormous cost and delay. He notes that "these blunders resulted not from mistaken calculations but from the inability to visualize realistic conditions."

Ferguson makes reference to points made by engineering teacher and writer Henry Petroski: in the old days, the use of the slide rule to perform calculations made the design engineer constantly aware of the limits of his accuracy. However, with early simplified computer models, having apparent precision of six or more significant figures, the design engineer could have "unwarranted confidence in the validity of the resulting numbers."[2]

With this kind of false confidence and lack of an integrated view, Ferguson points out that the resulting design errors can have tragic results: stadium roofs that collapse, bridges that fall, nuclear power plants that run out of control, missile systems that shoot down the wrong aircraft. What makes it worse is that often such failures are ascribed to "operator error," deflecting attention from the fundamental design flaws—flaws that can overwhelm operators with more information than they can assimilate to make rapid and critical decisions. In addition, occasionally, design errors can result from the failure of the engineering profession to see the relevance of other disciplines to a particular design (such as the relevance of aerodynamics to the behavior of a suspension bridge in high crosswinds).

SMART SPECIALISTS WITHOUT A LARGER VIEW

In an especially troubling passage, Ferguson observes that design problems may be expected to become more and more common in the future—because of the spread to the highest levels of these design philosophies. He notes that "the magnitude of the errors of judgment in some of the reported failures . . . suggests that engineers of the new breed have climbed to the tops of many bureaucratic ladders and are now making decisions that should be made by people with more common sense and experience."

Overall, the problem often comes down to an excessive enchantment with highly specialized, mathematically oriented academic attainments that are at once abstract, difficult, and prestigious—all resting on an unstated assumption that people who are good at doing these difficult and demanding tasks are somehow fundamentally "smart"—and are therefore also capable of coming up with the best solutions to large and complex problems. A look at Ferguson's examples and arguments would suggest, on the contrary, that we need to reconsider widely held ideas about "smartness."

Instead, we should perhaps begin to have a higher respect for visual and hands-on approaches, the long-denigrated methods of the artisan, the craftsman, the artist, and the senior skilled workman—learning by doing, learning by hand and eye rather than by formula and book, as our newest technologies take us back in that direction. (In this context, by contrast, one cannot help but be reminded of the career of the extremely "smart," high-IQ "whiz kid" Robert MacNamara and the long-term disasters that he created, in the view of many, in Vietnam and the World Bank.)

The Competitive Advantage of Hand and Eye

Sometimes a longer view is instructive. Ferguson notes that some economic historians see the richer mode of learning by hand and eye as a major factor in the early superiority of British industry over that of the French and other Continental countries. The French pursued a century-long attempt to duplicate steel made in Britain. However, after many failures, a disappointed French official noted in 1752 that "the arts never pass by writing from one country to another, eye and practice alone can train men in these activities."[3]

Ferguson does not see the visual understanding and nonverbal knowledge of the skilled workmen as the only determining factors in the Industrial Revolution. However, he does see them as "essential components." Accordingly, he suggests that young engineers should, in spite of their current training, spend time observing "experienced workers in their expert, unselfconscious performances." Doing this, the engineer can hope to "avoid the surprises that too often result from an engineer's ignorance of the nature of manual skills."

Back to Visual Roots

Of course, in a sense, Ferguson's argument is rehearsing an age-old story—the contrast between the classical scholar and the practical worker, between the urban sophisticate and the country person, the bookish college student and the can-do, hands-on mechanic. It is such an old story, indeed, that we might wonder how we could ever have gone so far down one path, largely losing track of the considerable advantages of the other.

But there is a twist to the story that seems genuinely new—and essential to our perspective. Just now, we can see that the latest computer-graphic technologies seem clearly, in many ways, to be taking us back to our visual and nonverbal roots, not further into unfamiliarity and abstraction (as was largely the case before). Members of the computer graphics community, as major actors in the field, seem now to be in an odd position. Perhaps without being fully aware of it, they are in the process of recasting the computer tools that originally helped to destroy the perceived value of visual, hands-on approaches—in order to resurrect these approaches once again.

However, there clearly is a deep and pervasive lack of understanding of the long-lost of power of seeing, and unfortunately this seems especially prevalent among the highly educated. For example, one member of SIG-GRAPH recently had to move to another state—mainly because her college had a new president. The president wanted to "improve" the standard of the college program, so she eliminated all studio arts because they were mere "craft." Art history, however, was kept in the program because it was sufficiently scholarly and verbally oriented.

In another example, a computer graphics staff member at a major software company told of a presentation from a senior company officer, who described with gestures a new software package that would be able to do everything from graphics and image processing "down here" to advanced mathematics and programming "up here." Reading the gestures, one graphics staffer said to the other, "I think we have just been insulted." This graphics staff member observed that one of his main duties was to try to bring other staff around to properly and fully appreciating the importance of visual literacy.

WORD-BOUND

Part of the problem of having underdeveloped visual-literacy skills stems from our long-held high regard for verbal literacy skills. For a long time the latter were rare and therefore valuable. Long ago, these were the skills with which priests and clerks and some kings held power. It is a very old habit of thought. But, in spite of these long-held habits, we need to see that reading and writing are only a form of technology. (A very successful technology—but a form of technology nonetheless.) Thus, at times, we may find that someone who is surprisingly slow with certain verbal tasks—making them appear to be of low intelligence—may be strikingly fast and proficient in certain high-level, visual-spatial, nonverbal tasks. Some people easily recognize this pattern. But for many others—schooled to assume, deep down, that intelligence is unitary and largely verbal—this is a new and revolutionary observation.

Of course, I am not trying to underrate the value of the written word. Its power is obvious and pervasive in history, politics, literature, religion, and science—indeed, almost every area of human knowledge—and in every mode of transmitting knowledge between generations. Its power is so great, however, that many believe that it is all that there is. The role of language will always be important, whether written or transmitted in some other manner.

But the case I am trying to make is that the new visual technologies are likely to promote a greater balance between words and images—involving a gradual transition to using nonverbal capacities in doing high-level and high-value work. With this transition, words will be used to comment on, to point out, to debate. However, the real core of the work will be in understanding the images, not the words. If my expectations are correct, those who wish to do this kind of high-level work will need to be as comfortable with images as they are with words.

Hiring the "Supersmart"

In a book excerpt published in *Fortune* magazine some years ago, Randall Stross asserted that hiring the "supersmart" is Microsoft's big competitive advantage: "Following policies set by brainy Bill Gates, recruiters at the world's favorite software company seek high-IQ candidates and worry about teaching skills later."[4]

But brains alone, it seems, are not enough. Stross observes that Microsoft seeks a particular kind of smart person—"one who is pragmatically inclined, verbally agile, and able to respond deftly when challenged." Stross recounts the story of a senior vice president from a leading computer company who was interviewing for a job at Microsoft. She told Gates that she would have to do some research to come up with answers to several of his questions.

According to Stross, "he is said to have demanded of her, 'Why don't you have an answer? Are you stupid?' This exchange appeared in the press and provided yet another example of why Microsoft has acquired an image of a company with a macho culture. . . . But the heart of Gates's displeasure was not a lack of smarts but lack of another attribute he sought: verbal facility."

And so we come, once again, to the central issue of what it means to be seen as really "smart." Verbal quickness is, of course, a long-established indicator of a certain kind of intelligence. But is it an indicator of overall intelligence? Or, is it an indicator of the kind of intelligence and abilities wanted in every case? Certainly the theory of multiple intelligences, set forth some time ago by Howard Gardner and others, would suggest that the idea of general, innate, and unified intelligence is somehow missing the point.

Perhaps we just have to be specific about what is wanted—and not lump everything together under the term "smart." Sometimes it is highly desirable to have people around who are verbally quick—especially in the short run. However, if we want to look into things really deeply, perhaps then we ought to be ready to deal with people who are slow to answer—

those who hesitate long enough to formulate a response. James Clerk Maxwell often had to have twenty-four hours or more to prepare his response to an original and unexpected question.

A SENSE OF TIME

There was a time when skill in reading and writing was relatively unimportant—for weavers, merchants, farmers, sailors, ship builders, mothers, warriors, craftsmen, and kings. Now we assume that the need for conventional verbal literacy is almost universal. However, we may soon need to consider the growing need for a new form of literacy—visual literacy—a literacy that may reawaken in a range of fields the ability to see the larger, more integrated overall perspective. It may not be long before visualization technologies and techniques spread into many areas that formally were thought to be the exclusive domain of words and numbers. Thus, in this new more advanced and balanced world, we might expect a higher regard for a broader range of abilities—and a higher value placed on the needed contributions of people who are unusually good with images, although they may lack a quick facility with words.

NOTES

1. Eugene Ferguson, *Engineering and the Mind's Eye* (Cambridge, MA: MIT Press, 1992).
2. Henry Petroski, quoted in ibid., p. 179.
3. Quoted in ibid., p. 59.
4. Randall E. Stross, "Microsoft's Big Advantage: Hiring Only the Supersmart," *Fortune*, November 25, 1996, pp. 159–62.

CHAPTER

5   WHEN THE WORLD PLAGUE WAS STOPPED BY A DIGITAL ARTIST

The future of humanity and microbes likely will unfold as episodes of a suspense thriller that could be titled Our Wits Versus Their Genes.
—Dr. Joshua Lederberg, "Infectious History"

Our initial hope was to find some weakness in [the] Mao [plague virus] that we could exploit. But what we found scared the living daylights out of us. . . . What we discovered [was that] . . . in hours, it converted the entire immune system into an ally. We were devastated. [But in time we realized that] we had the human genome nailed, and we had the Mao genome nailed. And we had that marvelous [broadband Internet virtual reality] system for communicating among scientific minds. We used the system to design a new human killer T-cell—the Mao [plague virus] Killer T. . . .

How did you do that?

Actually, it wasn't me; that was Javier's idea.

But I thought Javier was a graphic designer, not a scientist.

Which is probably why he cracked it, and we didn't. He worked out the simulation routines that showed how [the] Mao [virus] did the cell intrusion and subversion. And he became fascinated with membrane geometry, not knowing anything about protein electrochemistry or synthesis. For him it was just a graphics puzzle, and he played around with the simulations until he found a surface that would turn the probe back on itself. All we'd asked him to do was modify the program. . . . We thought . . . he would just create a simple command. Instead, he solved the problem of armoring, because if you can simulate it, you can order it up in wetware. When we saw the demo, the [lab] went silent. Absolute silence for perhaps 30 seconds. Then everybody started talking frantically.
—Interview excerpt from the story
"Savior of the Plague Years 1996–2020," *Wired* magazine

OUR WITS VERSUS THEIR GENES

It is our wits against their genes—and their fast evolution. And it will always be so.

We now understand that we can never live without microbes. We used to think they were the enemy; now we can see clearly that they are essential supports for our lives and our world. Finally, we have learned to think more in terms of ecology than warfare, interdependence rather than elimination. Yet we now also know that we can never stop finding new ways to protect ourselves from their occasional pathological outbreaks (and, worse, our own stupidity). We can never adapt through our own genes as quickly as they can—so we must find other ways. We must use our wits and learn to use all the different kinds of cleverness and inventiveness that we have among us. And we can never stop.

When I read Joshua Lederberg's wonderful short essay in *Science* on how we have come to understand the fundamental nature of infectious disease,[1] I was immediately reminded of the *Wired* short science fiction story excerpted above. This story has stayed with me, recurring to mind from time to time, since I first read it years ago—the sign of a good piece. I thought there might be a special connection between the two that would be of interest to those who know something about the short- and long-term prospects for computer graphics.

Initially, it is a bold and almost silly idea—the world being saved by a digital artist, during a fictional time of global plague where small surviving colonies were linked by a diminished but still-functioning Internet. Yet the way the story is told, the idea gained unexpected credibility. And behind the story there is a greater question and possibly a deeper understanding— one that we have been dealing with for some time in its various aspects: that is, of course, does the skill, the technology, the kind of mind and the special experience of the digital artist actually lend itself distinctly to solving certain kinds of problems better than others? And might these solutions (one day) have an unexpectedly broad impact? Perhaps we have a short story here that could be making a statement that has greater weight than many volumes of science, policy, or procedure. Considering the enduring importance of the topic, it would appear that it could be of special interest to many beyond the comparatively small world of computer graphics. And, considering the more recent history of global threats from SARS, anthrax, mad cow disease, and bird flu, it would seem that all of us should have a deeper and more enduring interest.

JUST A GRAPHICS PUZZLE

I had long admired the *Wired Scenarios* story because it seemed to capture in a few words (and provocatively doctored photographs) my own long-held belief that the visual approach has a special power for seeing patterns and solving problems that society does not properly or fully appreciate. Too often it is assumed that what is wanted is to know a lot of facts and to recall them quickly and accurately, on demand. The training and selection for most of our professions, from law to medicine, is based mainly on this narrow idea.

However, the literature on creativity has long observed that the most important thing is *seeing* the big patterns and *seeing* the unexpected connections and novel solutions. For this, it is often the outsider who has the advantage of seeing the unexpected pattern, which the well-trained professionals within the field somehow miss. The story of the less-than-fully-trained and less-than-fully-informed outsider making the big discovery is in fact a commonplace in the history of science.

By his own report, as we have already noted, Albert Einstein relied more on his mental images than the kinds of mathematics used by his associates. It is striking that both Richard Feynman and Abraham Pais noted Einstein's diminishing creativity as his approach turned away from the visual and toward the mathematical. Even his own contemporary David Hilbert, a mathematician who came close himself to some of the early basic insights involved in general relativity, pointed out that Einstein's fresh ideas were not a result of his mathematical skill.

I was pleased to see the authors of the *Wired* story acknowledge these observations. But I was even more pleased to see them focus on the skills and approach of a computer graphics artist—one who saw the solution to the disease process as "just a graphics puzzle" involving "membrane geometry." Since (in the story) they were all using virtual reality (VR) simulations of the microbes, he could visualize directly the various structures. Because of the VR images, he did not have to rely on years of training and experience to build a crude personal mental image of what was going on at the surface of the molecule.

It is quite easy to imagine that someday soon, discoveries such as this may be routinely expected with powerful graphic computers and as high-quality VR and high-bandwidth Internet connections become more and more widely available. With such technological developments, a lot of previously unrecognized talent could come quickly and unexpectedly into play. In the end, of course, we need both the experts and the outsiders. We also need a large and varied team with many kinds of training and innate talents in order to find solutions as well as implement remediation programs. In the not-too-distant future, with the widespread use of new visualization technologies, perhaps we will all grow to have a greater appreciation of what each person, and each kind of brain, can bring to such a problem, whether in medicine or in other areas (thus avoiding "groupthink").

AROUND THE WORLD IN 80 HOURS

In his *Science* essay, Dr. Lederberg pointed out that in our competition with microbes, many of our recent technical and economic advances play right into the strengths of the fast-adapting, tiny creatures. We live longer and world population grows, doubling twice in the last century, fostering "new vulnerabilities." There is greater crowding, facilitating disease transmission among individuals. Continued destruction of forests brings greater contact with disease-carrying animals and insects. Increased freedom in travel and trade further compound these problems. "Travel around the world," he says, "can be completed in less than 80 hours (compared to the 80 days of Jules Verne's 19th-century fantasy), constituting a historic new experience."

Everywhere this long-distance travel has become frequent and routine: "Well over a million passengers, each one a potential carrier of pathogens, travel daily by aircraft to international destinations. International commerce, especially in foodstuffs, only adds to the global traffic of potential pathogens and vectors [carriers]. Because the transit times of people and goods are now so short compared to the incubation times of disease, carriers of disease can arrive at their destination before the danger they harbor is detectable, reducing health quarantine to a near absurdity."

Dr. Lederberg also points out that when it comes to the pathological development of microbes, we may be our own worst enemies. He observes that "the darker corner of microbiological research is the abyss of maliciously designed biological warfare (BW) agents and systems to deliver them. What a nightmare for the next millennium! What's worse, for the near future, technology is likely to favor offensive BW weaponry." The events of the years since 2000 have, of course, made Lederberg's words even more troubling.

BRILLIANT FLASHES

Consequently, in both the long run and the short run, we can see that it is indeed our wits against their genes. And it will always be so. Mostly, as Dr. Lederberg explains, we now see that microbes are essential supports for our lives and our world. They are everywhere—and mostly they are on our side, more or less. However, we do need to be aware that in spite of medical successes and a wiser understanding of ecological perspectives, serious problems probably lie ahead.

We know more, but our economic and political successes may create enormous future problems. However, we may take some heart in expecting that the spread of new visualization technologies (among other things) may help to promote a more comprehensive view of our whole situation—promoting strong visual thinkers to make wiser decisions about the future for us all. And, with some luck, we may learn to explicitly appreciate the full value of digital artists (and those like them)—and their real-life potential to be true global heroes if the worst were to happen.

While we have learned to think more in terms of ecology than warfare, we all now know that we can never stop searching for new ways to protect ourselves. We can never adapt through our own genes as quickly as the microbes can. We must find other ways. So, we have to use our wits and we must learn to use all the different kinds of cleverness and inventiveness that we have among us—especially among those who might be best suited to seeing patterns and structures that might be missed by the experts. We need to search a broader field with greater success. Because we can never stop.[2]

NOTES

1.   Joshua Lederberg, "Infectious History," *Science*, April 14, 2000, pp. 287–93. Lederberg is a Sackler Foundation Scholar heading the Laboratory of Molecular Genetics and Informatics at Rockefeller University in New York City. He received the Nobel Prize in 1958 for his research on genetic mechanisms in bacteria.

2.   This column first appeared in *Computer Graphics* in November 2000. Much has happened since then to underscore the relevance of Dr. Lederberg's essay and the *Wired* story.

CHAPTER

6   SMASHING IMAGES

In the eighth century, a sect arose from within the ranks of its highly literate clergy that so despised images that its members declared an all-out war against statues and paintings. . . . At first, they sought out only religious images to smash. Church mosaics, painted icons, and stained-glass artistry fell to their savage assaults. Later their targets also included painters, sculptors, and craftsmen. They even murdered those whose crime it was to love art. Monks who resisted were blinded and had their tongues torn out. The iconoclasts beheaded the Patriarch of the Eastern Church in 767 for refusing to support their cause. The iconoclast movement never spread to illiterate Western Europe; its madness consumed only the segment of Christendom that boasted the highest literacy rate. Artists fled for their lives from Byzantium, heading for the western court of Charlemagne whose largely illiterate courtiers welcomed them with open arms.
—Leonard Shlain, *The Alphabet versus the Goddess*

RECONSECRATED SHRINES

When we are trying to understand something fundamental about human beings and the human brain, it seems wise to look, as much as possible, to other ages and other cultures to see the full range of what we need to consider. This is effectively what has been provided by Leonard Shlain in his book *The Alphabet versus the Goddess: The Conflict between Word and Image.*

Shlain, a surgeon from Mill Valley, California, spent seven years drawing together elements from many cultures and thousands of years of history to weave a narrative and an argument about the sometimes catastrophic interplay of image, alphabetic writing, religion, gender relationships, and human history. For the vast sweep of the topic, Shlain's achievement is astonishing—although it is not always entirely convincing. One does not have to accept all of Shlain's argument, however, to be persuaded that he is dealing with a topic that is well worth our attention. His view is bold, and he delivers new insights and information that substantially enlarge our understanding of important historical dynamics—as well as helping us, strangely, with developing a better understanding of some of the main issues of our time.

While on a tour of Mediterranean archaeological sites years ago, Shlain was told that many shrines had originally been consecrated to a female deity. Then, later, "for unknown reasons, unknown persons reconsecrated" the shrines to a male deity. After some consideration, Shlain "was struck by the thought that the demise of the Goddess, the plunge in women's status, and the advent of harsh patriarchy and misogyny occurred around the time that people were learning how to read and write."[1]

He wondered whether "there was something in the way people acquired this new skill that changed the brain's actual structure." Shlain points out that in the developing brain, "differing kinds of learning will strengthen some neuronal pathways and weaken others." Applying what is known of the individual brain to that of a whole culture, Shlain "hypothesized that when a critical mass of people within a society acquire literacy, especially alphabet literacy, left hemispheric modes of thought are reinforced at the expense of right hemispheric ones." This change resulted, he proposed, in "a decline in the status of images, women's rights, and goddess worship."[2]

USING BOTH SIDES

In developing this approach, Shlain points out that his own occupation as surgeon (and as an associate professor of surgery) probably has contributed in significant ways. By selection, training, and daily work, it is often observed that surgeons have to move constantly back and forth between right- and left-hemisphere modes of thought. Accordingly, Shlain observes that his "unique perspective led [him] to propose a neuroanatomical hypothesis to explain why goddesses and priestesses disappeared from Western religions."[3]

The experience of surgeons is thus unlike that of many scholars and historians. The latter are expected to use mainly one side only—the left side of the brain, the world of words, grammar, logic, and highly specialized analysis. Less weight is given to pictures, images, and the large-scale, global view so characteristic of the right side of the brain. It is widely recognized in some circles that there is often a trade-off between verbal and visual skills; this trade-off is recognized in the half-serious joke sometimes told by neuroscientists: "Never trust a surgeon who can spell." If you are too good with the mechanics of writing, perhaps you may not be good enough with the mechanics of visualizing, locating, and removing a dangerous tumor. Unlike many others, surgeons need to be both "bookish" and "hands-on."

Two Hemispheres through History

Years ago, when I was researching my earlier book, *In the Mind's Eye*, I found that always in the background, behind and under every story and every neurological observation, was my own awareness of the larger implications of the dual nature of the two hemispheres of the human brain. I was aware that this then relatively new understanding of the brain provided the larger context for most of the things I was writing. (Although we have since learned that the roles of the two hemispheres are more complex than previously thought, the contrasting functions are still useful ways of thinking about the brain and cognitive processes.)

Along with this awareness, however, came a persistent series of questions. If we are now in fact moving from a present world largely based on words to an emerging new world increasingly based on images, has this happened before in other periods of history and how did it happen? In the past, were there whole societies and cultures largely based on right-hemisphere kinds of knowledge—as ours seems to be based largely on left-hemisphere forms of knowledge and understanding? What would be the main consequences of following one approach over the other? What is gained and what is lost in each direction? And what happens to various factions and power groups within these societies when there is a substantial change in one direction or another?

I wondered why certain religions and certain cultures seem to revere the written word and the book so very highly (two relatively new technologies in the long history of the human race)—and seem so ready, from time to time, to explode with a destructive force full of fear and hatred for images and everything linked to them? And what might all this mean for us today if we are, in fact, beginning to go through such a major change once again? I knew just enough of history to suspect that there was a major story to be told. But these questions were outside the scope of my own research—and I had no time to look into them further.

Years later, Shlain's wide-ranging analysis has provided a rich and thought-provoking series of possible answers to these questions. His observations show some of the wonderful possibilities but also some of the frightening prospects. It is the kind of book that holds your attention long after you have put it down—turning the evidence and arguments over in your mind, returning to passages, trying to see whether or not the pattern holds—and trying to sort out what it might mean for our own times. It is a very different picture from what we are usually given. It is full of ideas that many will find very hard to accept. Sometimes he seems to push his material too hard to make it fit his thesis. However, in the end, his perspective may prove to be far more perceptive and pertinent than many more conventional interpretations.

In a series of thirty-five tightly constructed chapters, Shlain surveys an enormously broad territory: "Image/Word," "Hunters/Gatherers," "Right Brain/Left Brain," "Hieroglyphs/Isis," "Abraham/Moses," "Athens/Sparta," "Taoism/Confucianism," "Jesus/Christ," "Muslim Veils/Muslim Words," "Mystic/Scholastic," "Protestant/Catholic," "Sorcery/Science," "Page/ Screen." With example after example, he attempts to show that, in general, the old goddess-linked, polytheistic religions are more concerned with the cycles of life, more tolerant, and less given to religious warfare, tending to exhibit the values and perspectives of the right hemisphere. The newer, literacy-linked, monotheistic religions, on the other hand, are more given to single-minded pursuit of narrow-group goals, are often intolerant and self-righteous in the extreme, can be extraordinarily savage in extended religious warfare (in spite of peaceful religious teachings they pretend to follow), and tend to exhibit the values and narrow perspectives typical of the left hemisphere of the brain.

Shlain argues that these changes were brought about, remarkably, by learning to use alphabetic writing systems. "Aside from obvious benefits that derived from their ease of use, alphabets produced a subtle change in cognition that redirected human thinking. . . . Alphabets reinforced only half of the dual strategy that humans had evolved to survive." Each part of this "duality perceived and reacted to the world in a different way; a unified response emerged only when both complementary halves were used." "All forms of writing increase the left brain's dominance over the right." Learning to read and write "supplants *all-at-once* gestalt perception with a new, unnatural, highly abstract *one-at-a-time* cognition."[4]

NEW THOUGHTS ABOUT THE NEW WORLD

Consequently, according to Shlain, the rapid spread of literacy and inexpensive printed materials with Gutenberg's press in 1454 had mixed results. "The rapid rise of literacy rates wrought by the printing press was a boon to European science, literature, poetry, and philosophy. And yet it seemed no country could escape the terrible religious upheaval that inevitably followed the march of the metal letters." Shlain provides detailed descriptions of the religious wars of this period.

The possibilities inherent in one predisposition versus another is probably most clear in Shlain's speculations about the discovery of the New World. If the Old World discoverers had been more tolerant and less single-minded, he argues, this sad period of history might have been very different. "Had the discovery and invasion of the New World been undertaken by a culture other than sixteenth-century Europeans driven mad by the printing press, a different scenario might have ensued. In the fourth century BCE, Alexander the Great made peace treaties with Dravidian tribes in India and Scythians in Thrace; people as exotic as any he would have encountered in America. Unencumbered by the intolerance that comes with alphabet monotheism, Alexander did not feel compelled to eradicate the local religions and enslave the native populations." Alternatively, "If Julius Caesar had discovered the New World, would he have destroyed the local population, stolen their lands, and rooted out their culture? Likely not. This wise pagan would have forged alliances, fostered trade, and treated the people with respect." This should be expected, according to Shlain, because this is the policy he actually pursued with the "blue-painted Celts and Picts."[5]

It is noteworthy that in Shlain's view, the most dangerous historical times appear to be soon after the growth and establishment of widespread literacy. The more people learned to read, the more likely they were going to find good and authoritative reasons to begin slaughtering each other. It is doubtful whether this will be a popular view among the growing numbers of well-intentioned literacy programs. However, perhaps we can be grateful that in the United States and other advanced economies we are now mostly working on the last few percentage points in the literacy rate—rather than the first burst of widespread literacy, as in other parts of the world, especially certain developing countries. For the advanced economies, the dangerous period has largely passed; for the newly developing, the dangerous period has just begun (giving us a new and troubling perspective on the rising militancy of fundamentalist religions in certain countries).

HOPING FOR A NEW BALANCE

Shlain gives us an unsettling picture of what can happen with the rapid spread and deep effects of a powerful technology—reading, writing, and the book. In his epilogue, however, he apologizes for his criticism of the books he loves so dearly. "Throughout, as a writer, as an avid reader, and as a scientist, I had the uneasy feeling that I was turning on one of my best friends." However, he felt that he had to point out the "pernicious side effect" of literacy that "has gone essentially unnoticed."[6]

What is most important is finding a new balance once again. He notes that "even when we become aware that literacy has a downside, no reasonable person would . . . recommend that people not become literate. Instead, we seek a renewed respect for iconic information, which *in conjunction with* the ability to read, can bring our two hemispheres into greater equilibrium and allow both individuals and cultures to become more balanced."[7]

The promise of this new balance leads Shlain to foresee a brighter future. "I am convinced," he asserts, "we are entering a new Golden Age—one in which the right-hemispheric values of tolerance, caring, and respect for nature will begin to ameliorate the conditions that have prevailed for the too-long periods during which left-hemispheric values were dominant. Images, of any kind, are the balm bringing about this worldwide healing."[8]

As a group of people interested in the image in its many forms, we may hope that Shlain is correct in his future expectation of a new balance. However, we may also hope that we will not see a revival of those who are single-minded in their love only for the written word, smashing images on every side in their passionate intensity.

PASSION OVER *THE PASSION*

A relatively short time ago we might have wondered whether the actions of historically distant Christian reformers or Islamic fundamentalists would ever bear on our personal interests today. However, it has become increasingly clear that these issues are becoming more relevant with each passing month. Indeed, I sometimes wonder whether we may be going through one of those portentous periods where world events and mass media will be dramatically shaped once again by the age-old battle between the image haters and the image lovers.

At this writing, in the spring of 2004, it is clear that images still stir deep passions—now, however, with a curious reverse twist of which many seem to be unaware. In an article on Mel Gibson's film *The Passion of the Christ*, art critic Paul Richard points out that the film depends heavily on the literal and bloody depictions of the crucifixion of Christ characteristic of Counter-Reformation art from within the Catholic Church. Indeed, Richard observes that the great irony here is that the avowed target audience for the film, consisting primarily of evangelical Christians, seems to be attracted to the same literal and bloody depictions that were used as a weapon against their own theological ancestors long ago. Such images were hated by the leaders of the early Reformation, yet their theological descendents have come to embrace them with enthusiasm.

How did all this come to be? In Richard's words, "Martin Luther's Reformation was a theological rebellion. No longer would the rebels accept the pope in Rome, or the hierarchy he led, or the Latin of the Mass and of the Vulgate Bible, which most of them could neither read nor understand."

They wanted their own Bible, in their own language so they could understand and interpret the scriptures for themselves. "They didn't need the pope, they didn't need his saints, they didn't need his priests, and—as some began insisting—they didn't need his art."[9] They realized that the art of the Catholic Church, and especially the art of the Counter-Reformation, was a counterattack on their own call for an end to all image making (as they believed was required by Scripture) and for extreme simplicity in all things. As Richard notes, this desire for simplicity is still evident among American Protestant buildings. "That plainness is still seen in the clean, white clapboard churches scattered through New England, in the Quaker meeting houses of Pennsylvania, all the way to the Crystal Cathedral in Orange County, Calif. No Catholic paintings taint these sanctuaries."[10]

Reminding his readers of the historical events, Richard gives some detail about the Reformation's role in destroying many works of art through a hatred of images of all kinds. "On Aug. 10, 1566, at Steenvoorde in Flanders, a Calvinist preacher named Sebastian Matte told his listeners to go and smash the art of the Catholic churches. Ten days afterward, the cathedral at Antwerp was methodically trashed." Although Richards does point out that "later, under Catholic rule, Rubens was commissioned to re-do [the cathedral's] splendor," the fate of most churches and cathedrals in Protestant areas was grim indeed. "Such spasms of enthusiastic image-breaking erupted in the British Isles for most of the next century. 'Lord, what work was here!' lamented the Bishop of Norwich in 1647. 'What clattering of glasses! What beating down of walls!'"[11]

Eventually, after years of civil war, the image haters came to be in full control of England and in time found reason to chop off the head of their king, Charles I. Later, after years of puritanical and repressive rule by Oliver Cromwell and his supporters, the English people had had enough of it. They then brought back the king's son and restored him to the throne—releasing a rebirth of creativity and vitality rarely seen before or since. As Kenneth Clark observed, the restoration of Charles II in 1660 "ended the isolation and austerity which had afflicted England for almost fifteen years. As so often happens, a new freedom of movement led to an outburst of pent-up energy. There are usually men of genius waiting for these moments of expansion, like ships waiting for high tide."[12] So came a rebirth of English accomplishment in art, architecture, and science.

A MORE ANCIENT AND KINDLY ISLAM

The surprisingly central role of the image in current world events is strikingly evident in a recent book about problems of democracy by Fareed Zakaria. Zakaria argues, "If there is one great cause of the rise of Islamic fundamentalism, it is the total failure of political institutions in the Arab world. Islamic fundamentalism got a tremendous boost in 1979 when Aya-tollah Ruhollah Khomeini toppled the staunchly pro-American shah of Iran. The Iranian Revolution demonstrated that a powerful ruler could be taken on by groups within society. It also revealed how in a developing society even seemingly benign forces of progress—for example, educa-tion—can add to the turmoil."

Zakaria observes that over past centuries Islam was more adaptable and flexible than what we see today. "Until the 1970s most Muslims in the Middle East *were illiterate* and lived in villages and towns. They practiced a kind of village Islam that had adapted itself to local cultures and to normal human desires. Pluralistic and tolerant, these villagers often worshiped saints, went to shrines, sang religious hymns, and cherished art—all tech-nically disallowed in Islam."

All this was changed by more recent historical forces (of course, in some measure not unlike the Protestant Reformation in the West hundreds of years ago): "By the 1970s, however, these societies were being urbanized. People had begun moving out of their villages to search for jobs in towns and cities. Their religious experience was no longer rooted in a specific place with local customs and traditions. At the same time *they were learning to read* and they discovered that a new Islam was being preached by a new generation of writers, preachers, and teachers. This was an *abstract faith* not rooted in historical experience but *literal and puritanical*—Islam of the high church as opposed to Islam of the street fair."[13]

It is striking how well this brief aside in Zakaria's book seems to fit Shlain's main argument. (For emphasis, I have added italics.) It is fair to assume that Zakaria may know little or nothing about Shlain's book and argument. Yet there is a persuasive convergence. Whether Taliban or al Qaeda, Islam's puritanical fundamentalists are intent upon destroying images in all forms, just as they are intent upon destroying all tolerant and progressive institutions—in a manner strikingly similar to the puritanical Protestant Christian fundamentalists of long ago. This passage reveals how much these patterns still dominate our times and how modern political commentators, however well informed, seem to be unaware of a larger pat-tern of which their current concerns are but the most recent manifestation. We might hope that over the longer term, unfolding conditions might be more favorable to image lovers, as well as tolerance in general. However, in the short run, it would appear that the image haters and image smashers will be shaping world events in the familiar age-old pattern. And we can wonder how long it will go on before people will have had enough of it— and will want to restore a former balance.

NOTES

1. Leonard Shlain, *The Alphabet versus the Goddess: The Conflict between Word and Image* (New York: Viking, 1998), p. vii.

2. Ibid., p. viii.

3. Ibid., p. xi.

4. Ibid., pp. 66–67.

5. Ibid., pp. 350–51.

6. Ibid., p. 430.

7. Ibid., p. 429.

8. Ibid., p. 432. It is worth noting a possible alternative variation of Shlain's theory. As we have seen, Shlain argues that the new development of literacy has a strong tendency to change people's brains, emphasizing left-hemisphere modes of thought. Such effects may be subject to debate. However, there is an alternative dynamic that Shlain does not mention but is implicit in his argument and may be an important contributing factor. Just as individual brains might be changed, so whole populations might be changed as well. Perhaps it is not so much that the brains of individuals are changed (so quickly) but that with the spread of reading those individuals (and factions) with a certain skill and talent mix suddenly achieve, because of the new importance of reading, a status and power that they never had before—bringing along their mainly left-hemisphere (i.e., one-dimensional and single-minded) view of the world. In other words, in a new reading-based culture and power structure, those with natural inclinations toward reading proficiency come to prosper, rising quickly to the top ranks. As a consequence, left-hemisphere values and views of the world become an increasingly dominant part of this new culture. (Right-hemisphere values of balance and tolerance are overwhelmed, at least for a time.) Thus, alternatively, it may not be that all brains are quickly changed, but rather that the whole population comes to be dominated by those with a certain kind of brain.

9. Paul Richard, "So Much Irony in This Passion," *Washington Post*, February 29, 2004, p. B5.

10. Ibid.

11. Ibid.

12. Kenneth Clark, *Civilisation: A Personal View* (New York: Harper and Row, 1969), p. 213.

13. Fareed Zakaria, *The Future of Freedom: Illiberal Democracy at Home and Abroad* (New York: W. W. Norton, 2003), p. 143.

PART

2 VISUAL TECHNOLOGIES

CHAPTER 7

IS VISUALIZATION NO LONGER A "NEW NEW THING"?

THE WORLD ACCORDING TO JIM CLARK

For most people in the computer graphics field, the idea of visualization is really old hat. They can hardly remember a time when it was not obvious that computer visualization and computer graphics could be used for nearly everything—from feature films to product design to physical science to understanding stock market trends. The concept is so incredibly self-evident. Mostly, the important barriers have always been related to hardware power, speed, and cost. (According to some observers, these barriers largely melted away in 1999 with dramatic increases in computer power.) Otherwise, the basic idea was never in dispute—not at least among those who really understood (in a deep and fundamental way) the power of images and their wide applicability.

However, it is useful to be reminded—as in *The New New Thing,* Michael Lewis's book about Jim Clark—that this was not always so.[1] "'Computer graphics is as fundamental to computers as vision is to humans,' Clark wrote back in his teaching days. That thought, strange at the time, soon became commonplace." Lewis notes that "a lot of people who should have seen the importance of Clark's Geometry Engine thought it was a useless toy. Half the venture capitalists on Sand Hill Road who made their money, in theory at least, financing the future had failed to see its potential. So had the enormous gray corporations of the late 1970s. Clark had offered to license his invention to IBM, Apollo, Hewlett-Packard, and DEC. All turned him down."

This was over twenty years ago. The money people didn't see it; the corporate people didn't see it; even the technical people didn't see it:

Even people whose work would be transformed by his invention were slow to grasp its importance. . . . An engineer from Lockheed visited Silicon Graphics (SGI) soon after the company was founded. The SGI engineers offered him a demonstration: an automobile depicted and manipulated in three-dimensional space. . . . "That might be good for designing cars," said the man from Lockheed, "but I design airplanes. . . ." He did not understand that Clark's new company had made it possible to design *everything* inside a computer. And every new Lockheed airplane from now until eternity would be created by Silicon Graphics' technology.

However, it was no surprise to many in the field that even though the money people, the corporate people, and the technical people didn't see it, the entertainment people were quick to see what the possibilities were. "The Hollywood people were shrewder about the possibilities, and it wasn't long before Steven Spielberg and George Lucas were banging on Clark's door and asking to be his first customers."

Limits of Vision

Once the "new new thing" became commonplace in many fields, it is hard indeed to understand how it was not obvious to all when it was first presented. What did Clark and his associates see that others took so long to see? Why couldn't the Lockheed engineer make, in a flash, the (rather small) conceptual leap? What deficiency of training and nature would make him so literal-minded, so limited in vision? Who were the decision makers at IBM and Hewlett-Packard who did not immediately see the potential for a profitable new product line—if not a technological revolution? We might wonder—do these individuals still wince when they remember the role that they played?

The situation would now seem to be quite different. Some leaders in the visualization field were expecting soon after 1999 a "shower of products" using new visualization technologies. With ever cheaper and more powerful computers, they argued that "information visualization will pass out of the realm of an exotic research specialty and into the mainstream of user interface and application design."[2]

However, Clark moved on some time ago. And we may wonder about this since Clark's ability to spawn major innovation and see new trends from afar has indeed been impressive. Jim Clark has been responsible for starting four "new new things." With Silicon Graphics he played a major role in the initial widespread acceptance of computer graphics and visualization. With Netscape, he brought the public to the Web and created the dot-com stock boom—which, in turn, created revolutions that still reverberate in the worlds of the stock market and venture capital. With Healtheon, according to Lewis, Clark developed a vision of getting computing to move toward the center of the health care business—and he succeeded in getting Wall Street interested even at a difficult time. And, subsequently, with a company called MyCFO, he was finding ways to tap into the "grievances" of new wealth, seeking to take advantage of "cartel" status to gain preferential services and rates.[3]

EARLY WARNING

I myself can recall with some amazement and bafflement that I had my own early warning of the "world according to Jim Clark" some time ago. Out of curiosity and a concern to keep current, I had attended a presentation given at the National Library of Medicine by a sleepy young programmer who had been up most of the previous night preparing a new project for release. He was talking with delight about the large number of downloads of new software, something he called a "browser," that he and his associates had developed at the National Center for Supercomputing Applications at the University of Illinois, Urbana-Champaign. His name was Marc Andreessen, and he was talking about the new Internet browser called "Mosaic."

It seemed not too long afterward that I was planning a small visualization conference at the Aspen Institute in Colorado. I wanted to invite Jim Clark, but I was told that he had left SGI, and I was given the number of a new company then briefly called Mosaic Communications. The name Netscape came soon thereafter. He was too busy. I still ask myself how was it that I did not understand at this early stage what the possibilities were. But of course, in those days, there were no similar precedents—so it was hard for me to imagine (as for most people) what might happen. Then why, we might ask, was Jim Clark able to see the possibilities?

ROCK OFF A CLIFF

Clark's first big venture, Silicon Graphics, has long had a special position at computer graphics conferences—indeed, for years it held the actual central position at the front door of the SIGGRAPH exhibition floor. Over the years, many of the most impressive demonstrations of new technologies were shown first in the SGI exhibition space. For a time SGI was expanding rapidly, and hiring activity went into high gear at SIGGRAPH. Clearly, for a time, both SGI and SIGGRAPH were on a roll. Yet, in the middle of its boom, Jim Clark saw that the company he had created was doomed. After a motorcycle accident, "in bed waiting for his leg to heal . . . he wrote a paper. It summarized his thinking of the past few years, as he groped for a solution to what he viewed as Silicon Graphics' inevitable doom."

Clark understood that in time "Microsoft would one day overrun the high end of computing where Silicon Graphics made its money." Clark saw that "Microsoft had made it clear that the only way to preserve your station in [Silicon] Valley life was to create a monopoly. If you created a monopoly, you were at least partially exempt from the ordinary rapid cycle of creation and destruction. In computing, a monopoly took the form of a toll booth. Bill Gates had his toll booth, the PC operating system. Jim Clark wanted his own toll booth."

So Clark developed a paper for the SIGGRAPH conference and the SGI Board on an idea he called the "telecomputer." The ideas he developed were first intended for the television but proved to be perfectly adapted to the Internet. Here we see that Clark was remarkably successful in getting whole industries to follow him, even when it was down a blind alley—as with Clark's telecomputer. As soon as the big companies (SGI, Microsoft, Sun, Oracle, and AT&T) had geared up, competing with each other to make Clark's vision a reality, they realized all at once, as one of Clark's engineers put it, "that the next big thing was not the television set but the personal computer hooked up to the Internet." Lewis observed, "thousands of people had more or less wasted billions of dollars and, whether they knew it or not, had been *following his lead*. Then, just as they all ran as a herd in one direction, he took off in another. And within six months [with Netscape] he made them all look like fools. It was one of the great unintentional head fakes in the history of technology."

Indeed, the whole Microsoft antitrust trial that received so much attention years ago started because Jim Clark made a phone call. By the time the trial opened, "pretty much everyone, including Clark, had forgotten about the phone call . . . that had set the trial in motion. Certainly no one saw the Microsoft antitrust trial for what it was: yet another rock Clark had pushed off the side of a cliff, and watched with godlike detachment, as it became an avalanche."[4] Toward the end of Lewis's book the author notes that one of Silicon Valley's leading venture capitalists has long had a special admiration for Jim Clark and his ability to see the "new new thing" well in advance of others: "Even in the dark periods of their relationship, [John Doerr] spoke of Clark, behind his back, as 'a national treasure.'"

LIMITED SUCCESS

As successful as visualization technologies and techniques have been in many fields, there are still vast areas that remain untouched. Technologies and techniques that have become standard in some fields are still virtually unknown in others. It is some time ago that Boeing's 777 jet was designed entirely on computers (mostly SGIs). Computer images in three dimensions of real, 3-D airplane parts may not be hard to handle for most. However, abstract visualizations of large complex data sets may be quite another matter.

What can traditional accountants or stockbrokers make of numbers that are shown as clouds in space or as complex, pulsing histograms? Or what of traditional physicians who are happy with imaging that extends the microscope or x-ray machine—but who have remarkable difficulties with sophisticated information visualization techniques that are indeed truly novel? Or how do we understand traditional architects or geologists who are so tied to the old methods that they cannot take advantage of the benefits of visualization (in their inherently visual fields)? Whether visualization is directly or indirectly useful, convention still serves as a strikingly powerful barrier for many. For others, however, the new visualization technologies seem as natural as breathing.

LEFT IN THE DUST?

Considering Jim Clark's career, we might wonder whether his first venture has already rightly been left in the dust—whether the visualization revolution is already over before the technology has become really big. If Clark is so prescient, why has he moved on? If visualization is so important, why did Clark leave it behind some time ago? An obvious answer is perhaps that Clark (as portrayed by Lewis) is mainly interested in making a lot of money, not necessarily following a technology through to its fullest application, however radical and revolutionary the consequences. And, in Silicon Valley, as he says, that means developing an idea and making a lot of money out of it—before Microsoft swallows up the business and takes it for its own.

So we might argue that perhaps Clark's instincts are correct for making lots of money but that they have little relevance for understanding the longer-term possibilities for computer graphics and information visualization. Indeed, we might speculate that Clark would agree that these technologies still have a very long way to go—but he is personally not interested. They may have an interesting future, but it will be as a mass market for Microsoft as well as game companies and others—with many competitors, including a slimmed-down SGI, serving even smaller niche markets. Perhaps there is less fast money to be made, but a bigger technological revolution is yet to unfold, as these technologies and techniques move into many new and ever more specialized application areas. Or are we just part of another unintentional head fake?

NOTES

1. Michael Lewis, *The New New Thing* (New York: W. W. Norton, 1999). All quotations in this chapter are from this source unless otherwise indicated.

2. Stuart Card, Jock MacKinlay, and Ben Shneiderman, eds., *Readings in Information Visualization: Using Vision to Think* (San Francisco, CA: Morgan Kaufman, 1999), p. xiii.

3. In more recent years, Jim Clark has continued to move on, but his success rate has not continued to be so impressive. He sold MyCFO and Healtheon and moved on to other ventures. MyCFO was sold in 2002 for "one-third of its total funding." Business reporter Paul Festa wrote that industry sources complained that "MyCFO is just the latest of Jim Clark's ventures to collapse despite generous funding and high profile stewardship. Clark walked away from Silicon Graphics to found Netscape. . . . Clark two years ago . . . pulled the plug on his teen-centered site Kibu, shortly after resigning from his health care venture Healtheon/WebMD"; see Paul Festa, "Netscape Founder Sells Start-up MyCFO," CNET News.com, October 3, 2002, http://news.com.com. However, WebMD still survives, having dropped the "Healtheon" part of the name; see Karen Southwick, "Diagnosing WebMD: Ultimate Dot-com Survivor Faces New Challenges," CNET News.com, May 11, 2004 (both articles accessed June 28, 2004).

4. At the time of writing, in the spring of 2004, the avalanche caused by Jim Clark's stone (his forgotten phone call) has not yet run its course. For some time it looked like the US government would limit Microsoft's market dominance. (Among many books and magazine articles, see Ken Auletta, *World War 3.0: Microsoft and Its Enemies* [New York: Random House, 2001].) The story is complex, but in the end, the US government more or less backed off and Microsoft got mostly what it wanted. However, in Europe, the case against Microsoft is still very much alive, and the company could face fines as high as $3 billion (although lesser fines are more likely): "European regulators moved closer yesterday to forcing Microsoft Corp. to offer two versions of its dominant Windows operating system—one with media-playing software and one without—to satisfy antitrust charges"; see Jonathan Krim, "EU Likely to Order Microsoft to Unbundle: Putting Media Player in Operating System Said to Stifle Competition," *Washington Post*, March 16, 2004, pp. E1, E5.

CHAPTER

8 TALK LESS, DRAW MORE

We should talk less and draw more. I personally would like to renounce speech altogether and, like organic nature, communicate everything I have to say in sketches.

—Johann Wolfgang von Goethe

The idea that one would rather not speak at all and simply communicate in sketches is indeed strange and remarkable coming from a famous writer—in this case, the great German poet and author of *Faust*, Johann Wolfgang von Goethe. Goethe's words are quoted by essayist Stephen Jay Gould, who explains that it is quite notable that words occupy such an important place in human culture, in spite of the fact that we are highly visual by nature. "Primates are visual animals," explains Gould. "No other group of mammals relies so strongly on sight. Our attraction to images as a source of understanding is both primal and pervasive. Writing, with its linear sequencing of ideas, is a historical afterthought in the history of human cognition. Yet traditional scholarship has lost this root to our past. Most research is reported by text alone, particularly in the humanities and social sciences. Pictures, if included at all, are poorly reproduced, gathered in a center section divorced from relevant text, and treated as little more than decoration."[1]

Gould touches on a matter that I expect will become more and more important over time. It seems inevitable, as new visualization tools are applied effectively in more and more fields, that visual talents and skills will have greater and greater value. However, during the transition, I would expect some debate about the proper roles of visual versus verbal ways of thinking. Accordingly, we might ask, what then can be gained by following Goethe's advice—so much in line, in Gould's view, with our own deepest nature? Of what use, then, is visual literacy? What can be gained by talking less and drawing more?

THINKING IN PICTURES, MODELS IN THE MIND

Some wonder whether it is really useful or even possible to think in pictures. Indeed, if you want to think clearly and precisely about something, they ask, doesn't it have to be done in words? Isn't visualization just a lot of pretty pictures, as they say, smoothed and textured and colored to be pleasing—useful for laypersons perhaps but never for hard-headed, serious professionals? These prejudices have long been evident in Western culture—varying from field to field, more or less—for decades or for hundreds of years. From ancient times, often the highest prestige has been reserved for occupations associated with written language and the book—for the small elite who had an academic education and proximity to power, the priests and the clerks who had control of the technology of writing and the book.

But, as we have been saying, all this seems likely to change in fundamental ways. The enduring prestige of the written word, we can now see, is wrapped up in the power of writing and reading as a technology. This technology changed forever the transitory and ephemeral nature of ordinary speech and the long-standing oral tradition. In a similar fashion, I expect the new technology of computer graphics and data visualization to deeply transform our own culture, gradually shifting from a world based largely on words to one where images will have a much more important role: a new world where the real action will be in learning to develop deep and sophisticated understandings of complex systems by internalizing complex, moving three-dimensional images—that is, by building models in the mind.

But how can we be confident that these new changes will take place? Sometimes it is most useful to stand back a distance (using a visual-spatial metaphor, of course) in order to see the whole picture. In his highly innovative book *Timescale: An Atlas of the Fourth Dimension*, British science writer Nigel Calder talks of learning "how to be a Martian"—learning how to see Earth and all that is on it as a distant and "dispassionate" being would see it. This is a way of sorting out what is really important—and what is really happening over time, separated from the presumed "serious business" of "pots, kings, and battles."[2]

Calder points out that it is really quite difficult to cultivate this disinterested view. He notes that "even the most skeptical historians seem barely able to distance themselves from the assumptions of their culture." Accordingly, nearly "everyone takes it for granted that reading and writing are blessings," but our education provides us with little awareness of the "high levels of sophistication" attained by illiterate peoples—such as reading the stars and ocean currents well enough to navigate the Pacific (as we have seen in chapter 2). He notes that "skill in archery may have been as important as writing in shaping the course of history."

It is to be expected, Calder notes, that there should be some self-promotion among the makers and users of books. Schools, in their own limited view, he says, measure the "worth of young citizens" based on their "facility in the cumbersome information technology displayed on the wafer of wood pulp in your hands." Our education gives us little awareness that "most humans have lived and died unable to read or write, and some bright individuals are dyslexic." However, Calder observes that "new technologies may soon make the art as outmoded as oarsmanship for galleys." So, he concludes, the "emphasis laid upon literacy by scholars who earn their living with written words appears self-serving." If we take a really long view, then perhaps we can see how even those who appear to be well educated may have special difficulty in seeing what is actually taking place. It may be too close to home.

Of course, the usefulness of words, in whatever age or setting, is not being challenged. What is being argued here is that the center of gravity may shift in substantial ways—and the really important work, the comparative advantage, will often involve the sophisticated interpretation of images by those who have special talent and experience in this area. In fact, I would expect not so much a shift to the other side but a new balance between the two—an uncommon symmetry, perhaps—that is, the restoration of a balance and interdependence between two modes of thought that have generally been rare.

(It may be a sign of a broadening maturity that, for example, more recent editions of the works of English poet William Blake now include his illustrations and illuminations along with the text of his poems—which were long published alone.)

QUESTIONS ABOUT FUNDAMENTAL CHANGE

Taking the longer view, then, it seems clear that what many take as a given could really be something that is changing in fundamental ways. The "new technologies" Calder refers to might very well involve computer graphics and information visualization. Once started, the general trend seems clear enough. When the technology is available to amplify and extend some important human attribute, one can guess that it is only a matter of time before these possibilities are manifested in real outcomes that reverberate through our culture. (However, as we have seen, convention can be a powerful block to this kind of change.)

I think it is a good sign, however, that some are skeptical within the computer graphics field. It is good that we are not entirely buying our own predictions and promotions. For example, I received an e-mail message from a student who had just read my article "Forward into the Past: A Revival of Old Visual Talents with Computer Visualization" in the

November 1995 issue of *Computer Graphics* (appearing in this book, in adapted form, as chapter 1).

She said she found there were too many words and too few pictures: "The subject at hand is visual literacy, is it not? Why then, . . . the glaring omission of . . . graphics in your article? . . . I keep reading all these articles stressing the potency of the visual image and that its time has come, but most of these articles are exactly like yours (flip through the rest of this issue) in that they don't practice what they petition. Maybe visuals aren't that important after all. You seem to have done just fine without them."

"You are absolutely right," I replied by e-mail. "I am . . . aware of my role in using words to tell how limited they are. But I am also aware of the reality of irony—and its usefulness. Gandhi was skillful in using the British law and the British press against British power in India. Accordingly, important changes often use the power of the old to help along the power of the new (which is really older)."

However, defending myself, I noted that when I give talks, "I use lots and lots of visuals and short . . . videos from the SIGGRAPH Electronic Theater and elsewhere. Finally, I am most often talking about stories of what people have been able to do with visual thinking and visual tools. I . . . rarely talk about how they do it—which is a very different topic—and I suspect the most interesting aspects are not . . . understood by those who do it well. But this may change over time."

"Thanks for trying to keep me honest," I concluded. "Anyway, I don't want to give up the words. . . . I just want to balance things out a bit and mainly persuade a lot of word-bound people that something very important is just beginning—using the only means they are likely to understand."

Of course, this is indeed the right time to try to keep ourselves honest in these matters. Many in this field saw the possibilities long ago. The last ten or twenty years have seen enormous changes in the technical capacity to deliver what was promised. After all, the ACM SIGGRAPH *Computer Graphics* special issue titled "Visualization in Scientific Computing" was published in November 1987. Those who have long been advocates for the potential of scientific visualization are now quite rightly asking themselves if it is really turning out as they hoped and expected—asking themselves what is really happening when they say they gain new insights from the images.

It is the right time to apply a more rigorous standard. But the technology is now out of the box. The whole business is less in the control of the computer graphics community and the practitioners of scientific visualization. Finance and business users as well as others are now picking up and adapting the techniques and are retesting the reality of these assertions, using new and exacting scales. A new stage of development is under way. But I expect these new users will teach us a lot about the potential as well as the limits of this powerful new medium. Nonetheless, it seems clear that there are many fields that will be deeply changed by talking less and drawing more.[3]

NOTES

1.   Stephen Jay Gould, *Eight Little Piggies: Reflections in Natural History* (New York: W. W. Norton, 1993), p. 427.

2.   Nigel Calder, *Timescale: An Atlas of the Fourth Dimension* (New York: Viking, 1983).

3.   This column was first published in *Computer Graphics* in August 1996. There has been a certain amount of exchange between these columns and my book *In the Mind's Eye*. In this case, parts of this early column and others were used in different form in the epilogue of the updated edition of *In the Mind's Eye*, published in 1997. Here and elsewhere I have taken the advice of a friend who encouraged me not to leave out important and pertinent material just because it appeared in the other book, or vice versa. This column also provides an early example of reader response, indicating the lively debate that sometimes occurs among those within the field.

CHAPTER

9   UNINTENDED, UNEXPECTED CONSEQUENCES

THINGS THAT BITE BACK

As we are sometimes painfully aware, each technological change creates difficulties and dangers as well as advantages and opportunities. But sometimes the unintended consequences and adverse impact can be much greater than we might have imagined. The best intentions can sometimes yield horrifying results. Thus, claims Edward Tenner, some of our greatest successes can lead to enormous new problems: "Antibiotics marshaled against disease have spawned new varieties of highly virulent drug-resistant bacteria that pose new threats to human health." Similarly, in another area, "methods for preventing forest fires have been so effective in preserving the dry underbrush that wildfires are now enormous conflagrations, destroying forests that survived lesser flames for centuries." Or the solution to one problem creates another: "Chlorofluorocarbons, introduced as refrigerants to replace potentially explosive chemicals, eventually wreak havoc when they float to the stratosphere and deplete the ozone layer."

The persistence, pervasiveness, and seeming perversity of such unintended consequences is the subject of Tenner's book *Why Things Bite Back*, reviewed in *Science* by Langdon Winner.[1] Members of SIGGRAPH and other professionals in the computer graphics field are often so caught up in the ever-mounting excitement of rapidly unfolding technological potential that we perhaps stop too rarely to think of the longer-term adverse consequences—whether unintended or unexpected. However, now may be just the right time to consider which of our current great successes may lead to substantial problems. As the real power of these new technologies and techniques are just now beginning to be widely recognized and used, this may be the time when we should expect to see unwanted patterns emerging.

Whereas Tenner's book provides many tales of unintended disasters, Winner notes that it is weak in trying to identify future problems. Of course, he acknowledges that these may not be easy to anticipate because they often come without warning: "Unhappy results usually come as bolts from the blue." Winner points out that "troubles arise . . . when noble but narrowly focused goals enter the complex interactions that make up nature and society."[2] Accordingly, if we want to anticipate problems, we need a larger view, a less narrow focus (although, admittedly, this still may not ensure success). Tenner also acknowledges that we should not think that the problems we see are temporary—that they are only problems of transition, that they will eventually be sorted out—especially in areas of modern technology. On the contrary, they never stop. They never go away. As some problems are dealt with, others emerge. Accordingly, they require continuing vigilance. Thus Tenner notes that "technological optimism means in practice the ability to recognize bad surprises early enough to do something about them."

It is not so hard to see that we need to monitor the "traffic in bacteria and viruses," for example. But we may need to consider also, as the reviewer does, "what lies in store for a society bound and determined to saturate homes, schools, and personal lives with digital technology." There can be little doubt that the computer graphics and visualization revolution now under way will have something of this character as its real power unfolds. (And I suspect that computer graphics professionals may be better placed than most to see what the possibilities on both sides might be.) But perhaps we may hope—with a large number of strong visual thinkers using these powerful new "big-picture" technologies—that we might be in a better position this time around to anticipate some of the problems in sufficient time "to do something."

BIGGER PICTURES, LONGER VIEWS

So much of our modern culture has focused on specialization and the mastery of minute analysis, with relatively rigid barriers between areas of knowledge and study. Of course, as is often noted, much has been gained through such a strategy. But such an approach rarely considers the big picture or the long view. Visual thinkers and visualization technologies, on the other hand, seem to be constitutionally predisposed to the very modes of thought carefully avoided by this old, analytic approach. The more these new technologies succeed in entertaining, educating, and informing—showing patterns in nature and society not seen before—the more their very success is likely to be seductive and lead to a range of unwanted consequences along with those that are desired.

It may not be too much to hope, however, that the new tools (that we are just now beginning to learn how to use) may over time help to shift the larger culture toward new ways of thinking about our many growing problems—indeed, shifting our thinking perhaps to new scales in time and space in the process. Some perspectives need to be very broad and very long-term indeed. This deep change in ways of thinking and working may be far more powerful than we might now expect or intend.

RESURRECTION AND CARPAL TUNNEL IN THE BAYOU

In the Digital Bayou exhibit at the SIGGRAPH conference in 1996, we did indeed see the leading edge of several new technologies—sometimes with consequences that were both unintended and unexpected. I certainly was surprised to be impressed and intrigued with a new version of a very old arcade game. San Francisco Rush, from Atari Games Corporation, using new fast processors, provided surprises of several kinds. Racing cars we have seen. But something really does change when you have lots of processing power. What happens on the racecourse is close to being physically correct. It is less of a game and more of a simulation. (And this trend has progressed greatly in the years since.) I asked why the cars were sometimes transparent. I was told that in order to allow beginners easily back onto the track while other cars continued the race, the designers had to develop a ghost car that was slowly reincarnated as the car approached the proper speeds once again. In order to bring back the car from death, the designers found that they had to invent this ghostly resurrection. But there were other unexpected consequences. Even the deadly crashes took on a whole new aspect with this new power and speed. Indeed, the crashes were so numerous and fascinating that I guessed that in time one of the unintended consequences of such a powerful new game would be a competition for the most elaborate or artistic or elegant crash scenes. In the old games, all crashes led to the same canned crash sequence. All were exactly alike. With a more reality-based model, however, each crash is different, reflecting all the complex circumstances of the individual car and its surroundings.

The designers themselves were clearly intrigued with the new possibilities from these extraordinarily powerful new processors. Such unexpected complexity and variety—indeed, a bit like the real world. With such a remarkably sophisticated simulation of reality, I wondered whether it might eventually attract a larger audience than the older models. With such variety, these new games might also hold the attention longer. With the possibility of a larger market and longer "shelf life" (if my speculations proved to be correct), then one might consider these new games a great success. But much depends upon whether machine sales and rental fees are considered, or whether the players' lost time (however enjoyable) is considered. Much depends on point of view and perspective.

A bit further along in the Bayou, I was drawn to what seemed to be an extraordinarily original conception, inhabiting a setting both ordinary and familiar. "Plasm: Yer Mug" seemed to be a plain 1950s diner counter with stools, menu holders, and suitably attired waiters. But in time the breakfast foods on the screen in front of me transformed themselves into rotating faces. Slowly, I became aware that I was responsible for the transformations, owing to a hidden elbow- and buttock-driven interface. The images were responding not to hand manipulation but to shifting weight on the counter and the stool. I wondered how far one could go with such an idea and what it might mean for countless carpal tunnel syndrome sufferers.

LEGOS AT SPEED AND TUMBLING TYPE

A bit further along in the Digital Bayou, I encountered Virtual Lego Village, which held my attention (here and on the exhibition floor) in ways I could not quite understand. There seemed something quite marvelous about the moving images. Was it the lighting, the color, the ease of moving through the space? I was told by the MultiGen engineer that much came (once again) from the great speed of the processors. I wondered whether a similar sort of setup could be used to model financial markets and economic trends, weather patterns and ecological systems.

As I wandered further through the darkened space with fishing nets and crab traps, I thought what a great idea it was to project each Bayou exhibit randomly on big screens to ensure multiple exposure. On these big screens, it seemed almost impossible not to pay full attention, each time it came by, to Scott Kim's "Watch Your Language: Typography in Motion." The tumbling and transforming fonts and typefaces with shifting perspectives—all linked to important individuals in the history of computer graphics—seemed a powerful statement about what it is like to really think visually, transforming and manipulating models of reality in the mind's eye.

THE HITCHHIKER'S GUIDE TO CREATIVE SOLUTIONS

In another form of unintended consequences, the late science fiction author Douglas Adams (*The Hitchhiker's Guide to the Galaxy*) advised, "Exploit your problem." Make use of your technical limitations "while you've still got 'em." In art and life, he said, what you cannot do makes you more creative. In computer graphics, as with any other art form, Adams thinks that genuine creativity often flows from turning technical limitations into opportunities. Accordingly, he thinks the artist and the programmer should not be separate. Any really creative artist must get into the "grain" of the material deeply enough to see what can be done in order to do something original and unexpected, discovering new possibilities. Keynote speaker at the SIGGRAPH conference in 1996, Adams used his characteristic humor to cut to the core of many concerns of the computer graphics community.

He told the story of Starship Titanic, the CD-ROM being produced by his company, Digital Village. The technical problems they learned to exploit highlighted the trade-off between picture quality and speed of navigating through a virtual space. Adams noted that the game Myst "raised the bar on graphic quality." But at the time, players could not navigate quickly with such high-quality images. (Nowadays, this is no longer true.) Consequently, he and his group saw the necessary solution: to fly quickly through the ship's systems in a kind of "wire frame" mode, thus avoiding the need for high-quality graphic images while in motion. The problem forced them to develop a feature that eventually came to be seen as an unexpected advantage.

Pacing back and forth, Adams commented on a range of topics. He noted the stages of development from the expected to the unexpected in the history of uses for the computer. First, it was a better adding machine. Then, a better typewriter. Now, for commercial interests on the World Wide Web, it is "a better brochure!" However, he feels that what we are coming to understand is that the computer is really a modeling machine—vastly superior to and more flexible than any produced before, giving us the opportunity to work and think differently, doing things that before were not really possible. Because some of the new uses are so different from the old, he noted that it is especially hard for certain groups to understand what is really going on. They understand the old uses but find it difficult to imagine the potential of the new. Adams observed that this may be especially true in Britain, where the opinion makers in journalism, law, and politics are often those with a literary or liberal arts background. Because British education is based on early specialization, generally this group knows very little about science or technology. Consequently, he notes, in Britain, science has to "come in through the tradesman's entrance."

It is a curious fact, Adams observed, that with so many professional writers largely ignorant of science, some of the best writing being done today is in fact science writing. He gave the books on evolutionary biology and artificial life by his friend Richard Dawkins as examples. Adams found himself greatly influenced by this line of investigation, especially the work of the Santa Fe Institute, with Chris Langton and others working on artificial life, where computers are frequently used as modeling machines. (Although I was serving as reporter for SIGGRAPH at this event, I found myself putting Adams in touch with Karl Sims so that they could exchange information and videos related to the evolution of Karl's block creatures; see chapter 12 for more on this topic.)

Despite the troubles of Apple Computer and the Macintosh at the time, Adams asked for support of this alternative machine—and not only because he himself was a long-time Mac user. He explained that companies like Apple are needed for the computer design "gene pool" and should not be allowed to be overtaken and driven out by the bigger players. He also called for greater activism among computer users. He said that we should not be content now that most hotels allow us to plug our laptops into their telephone systems—about ten years after we really needed it. He urged a large audience to call their hotel managers en masse and insist that the hotels provide more bandwidth now—and not make us wait another ten years for reasonable Internet access. We might wonder, however, whether one of the unintended consequences of this greater bandwidth would be to make us less creative. What limitations would we then be unable to exploit?[3]

NOTES

1.   Edward Tenner, *Why Things Bite Back* (New York: Knopf, 1996).

2.   Langdon Winner, review of *Why Things Bite Back*, by Edward Tenner, *Science*, August 23, 1996, p. 1052.

3.   This chapter, based on a column that first appeared in *Computer Graphics* in November 1996, provides a slice in time, a window on a period of great growth and experimentation with high hopes in the field.

CHAPTER

10 ARTIST DISCOVERIES AND GRAPHICAL HISTORIES

The idea was to make something that was so large that it could not be readily seen as a whole and force the viewer to scan the image in a Brobdingnagian way, as if they were Gulliver's Lilliputians crawling over the surface of the face, falling into a nostril and tripping over a mustache hair.
—Chuck Close

BROBDINGNAGIAN VISIONS

In an interview, artist Chuck Close explained that the reason he painted his portraits with large blocks with colored circles on enormous canvases was that he wanted the viewer to be forced to view only a part of it at any one time. He did not suggest, however, that at the same time he was also discovering aspects of perception that scientific researchers were only to become aware of much later. Computer graphics technologists and digital artists have long been concerned with the interrelationships of art, technology, and science. They are aware, perhaps much more than others, how new paths are often opened by the artists. But the artists frequently are not credited with their accomplishments (not at least since the Renaissance, anyway). A welcome exception to this pattern is the cover article in a recent issue of *Science* magazine. In "Close Encounters—An Artist Shows That Size Affects Shape," Chuck Close is credited with "discovering [the] size-dependent breakdown of our ability to extract shape from shading."[1]

Researcher Denis Pelli, from New York University's Center for Neural Science, observes that "we easily recognize objects of all shapes and sizes, yet no one knows how we do it." It would appear obvious that we recognize shapes regardless of size, he notes. If this were not true, "we would recognize our friend or the letter 'a' differently at each size or viewing distance." However, he notes that the portraits by Close show "vividly" that this is not so. Rather, when one looks at the portraits, or "heads" (as Close calls them), done in the years 1987 to 1997 (in their actual size), "one can move forward and back, again and again, and the face, solid from afar, always collapses into flat marks when seen from near." Pelli explains that it is this pattern of change with distance that indicates "size affects the perception of shape, disproving the popular assumption that shape perception is size-independent." According to Pelli, careful measurement of observers while viewing these "heads" has shown that "the effect is visual (perception) not optical (physics)."[2]

Pelli notes that we might erroneously view Close as merely a "naïve artist, obsessed by grids, who innocently produced the coarsely gridded paintings." However, Pelli notes that the artist knew exactly what he was doing. Indeed, Pelli asserts that Close was "more thorough than his scientific colleagues." In his experiments from 1973 to 1997, Close increased his grid size in a strikingly regular fashion (15 percent per year). Also, he made sure that all exhibitions of his work satisfied the necessary observational requirements; he cancelled a "retrospective that could not provide long viewing distances." Accordingly, Pelli finally asserts, "So credit Chuck Close with discovering this size-dependent breakdown of our ability to extract shape from shading." So, we may observe that this time, the artist has led the way and gotten the credit, too. But it probably will not be the last. We can imagine that in the near future, there will be many opportunities for digital artists to lead the way in new directions—as the growing practical craft of graphics and visualization illuminates new corners of the human brain.

CATCHING THEIR ATTENTION

Dealing with groups with limited vision is not, of course, seen only in science and art. At the beginning of the 1999 SIGGRAPH conference, many of us had the opportunity to see the first theater showing of a film titled *The Story of Computer Graphics*. We were delighted with the production and grateful to the many contributors. It was great to see flashes of the early classics and to hear pioneers talk about developing the basics—in obscurity and with growing excitement—during the time when no one took digital technologies and techniques seriously. Ed Catmull, one of the two founders of Pixar, was delightful as he said, with a twinkle in his eye, that the days of doubt, when no one was interested in computer graphics, are now past and that digital artists had finally "caught the attention" of traditional animators and filmmakers.

(More recently, we can see that the enormous success of the Pixar computer-animated films distributed by Disney has enabled a role reversal.

Before, Pixar was glad to be distributed by the mighty Disney marketing and distribution machine. Recently, however, in the spring of 2004, it seems clear that Disney is upset that Pixar computer-animated films have done much better than those produced directly by Disney—and it is Disney that would like Pixar to renew its contract. However, Pixar has announced that it will strike out on its own. It is a familiar but still surprising story: in spite of the lessons from the boom-and-bust years, it has been shown that it is possible for a "high-tech" company to succeed in a big way, from complete obscurity—"no one would listen"—to full market dominance of a major new field in a few short years.)

Many conference attendees were eager to get copies of *The Story of Computer Graphics* to show to students and lay audiences—to tell the story that is still widely unknown. However, many of us were concerned with the weight given different aspects of the history. Some complained of the too heavy emphasis on cold war talk and devices at the beginning of the film. Others thought there could have been more emphasis on contributions from groups outside the United States. Personally, I was pleased with the time given to observations by the founders of Pixar (Ed Catmull and Alvy Ray Smith) and Industrial Light and Magic (George Lucas). However, I would have liked to see much more from people like Donna Cox (National Center for Supercomputing Applications) and Dan Sandin (Electronic Visualization Laboratory and co-inventor of the CAVE virtual reality system) talking about scientific and information visualization. The general public is now accustomed to digital special effects in feature films, but they still know almost nothing of the information and scientific visualization technologies that may be expected to have a major impact over the coming years.

LET THERE BE LIGHT

The other major theater event at the 1999 SIGGRAPH conference was, of course, the Electronic Theater, where all the best computer graphics work for the year is shown to a large and enthusiastic audience. The program had a beautiful start with *Fiat Lux* from Berkeley (nicely covered by Paul Debevec in the August 1999 issue of *Computer Graphics*).[3] But on the whole, the program seemed unusually disappointing. There was a disproportionate share of time given to digital special-effects samples from feature films, some of them relatively old. In addition, several of the pieces exhibited a preoccupation with violence that had not been seen in recent memory.

Personally, I am mainly interested in examples of new innovations that convey, to a nonprofessional audience, the unfolding power of computer graphics. In previous years we have seen many pieces that have since become enduring classics: the flocking behavior of birds and fish in *Stanley and Stella: Breaking the Ice*; the complex thunderstorm simulation from the National Center for Supercomputing Applications (NCSA); the pulsar with planets from Wayne Lytle of the Cornell Theory Center; the sophisticated whimsy of Pixar's *Luxo Jr.* or *Tin Toy*; the clever and amusing inversion of the sphere from the Geometry Center (which was joined by a different inversion technique two years later); Jim Blinn's brilliant Voyager fly-by and *Story of Pi*; the first six minutes in the creation of the universe, prepared for IMAX by Donna Cox and others (NCSA); the American Indian archaeological site reconstructions for *500 Nations* from Santa Barbara Studios; and the moving drawings of *Leonardo's Deluge* from Karl Sims, Mark Whitney, and others. Each year, more or less, we have been treated to another unfolding in an ever more self-assured repertoire of wonderful things. New digital artists finding more and better ways of amusing us, delighting us— or of imitating nature, once again, as in the Renaissance—but with greater depth and breadth than ever before, as they imitate not only appearance and form but also accurate physical motion, patterns of growth, and believable behavior. In 1999, however, I found it more difficult to identify such examples. With a few exceptions, throughout there seemed to be mainly a harder edge and a darker view. Of course, there were delightful pieces such as *Tightrope, All Is Full of Love, Spatial Frames*, and *Fishing*. Even the breaking of bricks showed convincing simulations, with a bit of humor.

However, the only piece I saw as a major innovation of the kind I am interested in was the spectacularly convincing computer graphic face in *The Jester* by Pacific Title/Mirage Studio. It is unclear to me whether the most important technical device is mainly a highly detailed form of motion capture, but I found the final results quite astonishing, making all previous such experiments appear wooden, waxy, or puppetlike. (It has often been said that the most difficult of all computer graphic challenges is to be able to create a convincing human face. Our brains seem to be wired for high levels of face interpretation, so we are all sophisticated and demanding experts in this area. Thus success in this area is a magnificent accomplishment indeed.) It was my hope that the following year the submissions and the screening process would yield more light once again, in the form of a long list of further innovations destined to be future classics as well.

A Shower of Products Delayed?

The relationship of art to technology and science may soon take on vastly new dimensions in the world at large if the editors of a new collection of readings are correct. According to Stuart Card, Jock MacKinlay, and Ben Shneiderman in their 1999 book of articles on visualization titled *Readings in Information Visualization: Using Vision to Think*, "The foundational period of information visualization is now ending" and very shortly "there will be a shower of products using its techniques." The authors argue that "the absorption of . . . advanced interactive graphics capabilities into the standard PC computer platform at the end of the 1990s" was virtually complete by the time their book was published. Thus they believe that "the path is now clear for information visualization to be used in mass-market products." And as this fifteen-year foundational period drew to a close, "in the next period, information visualization will pass out of the realm of an exotic research specialty and into the mainstream of user interface and application design."[4]

If they are correct, the long-predicted broad effects of these new visualization technologies and techniques may now, finally, be at hand. And perhaps it is not only sales talk (or desperation) that prompted Apple Computer to promote its (then) new G4 computer as "the first supercomputer on a chip." Picturing a Cray and claiming sustained performance of over one gigaflop or more, they explain in a *Fortune* magazine ad to their audience of senior corporate leaders, "Chances are you've never heard of a gigaflop before. But very soon you won't be able to live without at least one on your desktop."[5] Many of us have been anticipating these trends for some years. We cannot be sure that the broad awareness of these technologies—and the new forms of visual literacy that go with them—will occur as rapidly as we expect. It surely will not happen quite as rapidly as the sudden media awareness of the Internet and the World Wide Web. However, one wondered at the time whether it might break upon an unsuspecting world with similar speed sometime in the following twelve months. (Five years later, we can say with confidence, with certain limited exceptions, that it did not—and that it still has not.)

Of course, much will depend upon the speed with which mainstream computer users and software designers develop applications of immediate usefulness to a large audience. Applications like Adobe's PhotoShop did suddenly increase the processing demands far beyond those required for word processing and spreadsheets. Much will depend upon how quickly a clear need is seen for sophisticated information visualization applications. But it is worth noting that the corporate culture in many places is still remarkably deficient in awareness of the power and potential of visualization tools and visual proficiencies. As Alvy Ray Smith noted in the May 1999 issue of *Computer Graphics*, for example, "Microsoft . . . , frankly, just does not get it about artists. The technically creative people here are awesome and Microsoft is the best-run company I've ever seen, but the people here don't respect artists. . . . They seem to believe the really good talents in the world are technical and if you can't cut that then you do other things, like art. In other words, the culture here doesn't (not yet anyway) welcome in 'the other side.' I'm trying to change this, but it isn't so yet."[6]

Accordingly, much may depend upon how rapidly companies like Microsoft come to really understand the potential of these technologies and techniques—and the potential of the artists and visual thinkers who have been in the forefront of their use. Perhaps smaller companies will need to take the lead, allowing the artists and visual thinkers to show the world what they have discovered and what can be done. Then, we might see another future Pixar turning the tables on a future Disney, as we are seeing now. It has not happened yet, but it will happen. The factors are right. The technology is powerful, and the links to deep human capabilities are strong. But for most people it is very, very new. So, it is not easy. But it will happen. It has happened before.

NOTES

1.   Denis G. Pelli, "Close Encounters—An Artist Shows That Size Affects Shape," *Science*, August 6, 1999, p. 846. The description provided for the cover of *Science* is "COVER: Chuck Close's *Maggie* (1996). Oil on canvas. 30 by 24 inches (76.2 by 61.0 cm). Reduced to 44 percent of actual size and cropped. This painting demonstrates that the perception of shape depends on the size of the image. Compare its appearance from far to near, as the solid face collapses into flat squares. [Photograph of painting Ellen Page Wilson. Courtesy of PaceWildenstein]" A photograph of the Close painting and the Pelli article can be found at http://www .psych.nyu.edu/people/faculty/pelli/Pelli1999Science/Pelli-Science-285-844.html (accessed June 28, 2004). See also Robert Storr, "Interview with Chuck Close," in *Chuck Close* (New York: Museum of Modern Art, and London: Hayward Gallery, 1999), pp. 85–101.

2.   It is worth noting that in my lectures, I have used one of Close's "heads" in my PowerPoint presentations, especially at art schools, and have found that the audience seems to see the expected effect quickly as I shift back and forth between various sizes on the screen. It is remarkable that this holds true for my PowerPoint slides, because even my largest slide is nowhere near as large as Close's canvases.

3.   Descriptions of classic computer graphics videos and scientific visualizations mentioned here and elsewhere are provided in the appendix, along with contacts, Web sites, and information on obtaining VHS, CD, or DVD versions where available.

4.   Stuart K. Card, Jock D. MacKinlay, and Ben Shneiderman, eds., *Readings in Information Visualization: Using Vision to Think* (San Francisco: Morgan Kaufman, 1999), p. xiii.

5.   Foldout ad in *Fortune* magazine, October 11, 1999, after p. 88.

6.   Alvy Ray Smith, interviewed by Jessica Sances and Danielle Antonini, "About the Cover," *Computer Graphics* 33, no. 2 (May 1999): 8.

CHAPTER

11   Transforming Spheres— In Three Parts

> More than 40 years ago, a University of Michigan graduate student named Stephen Smale laid down a challenge for future mathematicians. He proved an abstract theorem that had a startling corollary: An elastic sphere can be turned inside out, or "everted," without tearing or creasing it—providing the sphere can pass through itself, ghostlike.
>
> —Dana MacKenzie,
> "Sphere Does Elegant Gymnastics in New Video"

According to a 1998 article by Dana MacKenzie in *Science* magazine, the problem in higher mathematics known as Smale's challenge came to be solved by the technology of computer graphics, still new at the time. "Demonstrated in a 6-1/2-minute video tour that [premiered in the August] International Congress of Mathematicians in Berlin and was shown [first] in an abbreviated form [in July at the] SIGGRAPH 98 convention in Orlando, Florida, [a new solution] provides the most satisfying answer yet to Smale's challenge." MacKenzie notes futher, "It also shows how topologists are turning to computer graphics to solve some of their hardest problems." "'In a real sense . . . the eversion question has become the benchmark for the use of computer technology in attacking problems of surfaces in three-dimensional space.'"[1]

SPHERES COMING TOGETHER—RETURNING TO IMAGES

The annual SIGGRAPH computer graphics conference often scoops other conventions and conferences in other fields. But it is not too often the case that SIGGRAPH scoops (however briefly) professional mathematicians—who seem always to be, in one way or another, way out in front of the rest of us. Years ago, I first became aware of the annual SIGGRAPH conference when I noted that the best computer graphic work I saw elsewhere had appeared six, twelve, or even eighteen months earlier at a conference held by this strangely named group called SIGGRAPH. However, after my first brief exposure in Boston in 1989 (on a day trip visit from my vacation on Martha's Vineyard), I quickly realized something really important was happening at this meeting, and I have attended nearly every SIGGRAPH meeting since. As SIGGRAPH old-timer Jim Blinn rightly observed in his keynote address in July 1998, computer graphics as an area of interest, once an exotic academic curiosity, indeed became in later years a mighty engine of change and transformation in field after field, sphere after sphere—as most of the world still understood little about the new technology or its unfolding power.[2]

Four years earlier, a more complex version of the everted-sphere problem was shown at SIGGRAPH, in a film called *Outside In*. (It is indeed noteworthy that SIGGRAPH seems to have a continuing relationship with such innovations, even in higher mathematics.) Several people remarked that it was "best of show" for the Electronic Theater that summer. I especially was interested to attend a workshop a year later with detailed discussions about the making of this earlier video—when mathematicians, in typical SIGGRAPH style, spoke of how much they relied on the artists, choreographers, and filmmakers working with them to find ways to effectively communicate complex mathematical ideas to a wide audience, with effective motion, pacing, color, and form—and not a little humor.

It is a commonplace for other fields, disciplines, and spheres of knowledge to become progressively more and more specialized, mutually disdainful, and mutually unintelligible. In vivid contrast, SIGGRAPH conferences seem to have harnessed a powerful countercurrent, bringing together in effective interaction a range of diverse talent unthinkable in most spheres. In this way and others, for over twenty-five years SIGGRAPH has helped, again as Jim Blinn noted, to redefine the range and content of the technical meeting in many different fields.

It is perhaps not surprising that SIGGRAPH and certain forms of higher mathematics seem to have a special relationship. Both have been going through major changes in recent years, in somewhat parallel fashion. Some observers note that it is only fairly recently that the real nature of mathematics has come to be fully appreciated. Fundamental developments in higher mathematics during the last two or three decades have changed the discipline itself as well as the mathematicians' view of themselves. According to one professional observer, Lynn Arthur Steen (quoted in chapter 1), mathematics should no longer be seen as the study of number, or even of space—it should now be seen as the science that studies patterns.[3]

In time, says Steen, the tools that serve the discipline begin to transform the discipline. "To the extent that mathematics is the science of patterns, computers change not so much the nature of the discipline as its scale: computers are to mathematics what telescopes and microscopes are to science. They have increased by a millionfold the portfolio of patterns investigated by mathematical scientists." No longer is mathematics seen as mainly the domain of number and rigorous logical proof (with just a little geometry on the side for historical interest). The long-term trend is reversing itself, as geometry and related visual-spatial forms move to the center of interest once again. "Historically, geometry, the study of space, has been one of the major pillars of core mathematics. For various reasons, its role in the mathematical curriculum has declined over the . . . years, so that even those with university degrees in mathematics often have little acquaintance with geometry beyond . . . high school [levels]. In sharp contrast to this curricular decline is the renaissance of geometry in research mathematics. In a very real sense, geometry is once again playing a central role on the stage of mathematics, much as it did in the Greek period."[4]

Steen points out that an indicator of this reversal of trend is that two out of the three Fields Medals (the equivalent of the Nobel Prize in mathematics) awarded in 1986 went to researchers for fundamental advances in mathematics related to geometry. A similar trend in mathematical research seems to have continued to the present day. The Fields Medals, given once every four years, were presented at the same International Congress of Mathematicians meeting in Berlin mentioned above. Of the four medals presented, one was awarded to a researcher who "investigated the Mandelbrot set, which compactly summarizes the chaotic behavior of certain equations, including those often used to describe phenomena such as flowing liquids and changing weather systems. His research provided a precise characterization of the Mandelbrot set's convoluted boundary." Other awards served to indicate the shift back to geometry, involving elliptic curves, string theory, and mathematical knots.[5]

WITHOUT COVER: SPHERES INTERSECTING

An inevitable consequence, perhaps, of the vast diversity encompassed within SIGGRAPH is the occasional clash of differing conventions and expectations. In the midst of high technical proficiency, a certain zaniness is expected—indeed, insisted upon. (Certainly a contender for "best of show" in 1998 was Jim Blinn's chart of name tag ribbon length over the years—with the rapid growth of the SIGGRAPH tradition of linking ribbon after ribbon on the bottom of conference name tags. A tall man with a long beard, long hair, and a name tag almost reaching to the floor was one of the delights of the old SIGGRAPH experience.) One can see that occasionally a super-straight engineer and a way-out artist may have trouble figuring out what to make of each other—although it is frequently the case that the two may come to rely on each other and respect each other's contributions in ways that would rarely happen in other conferences and other disciplines.

At the Orlando conference in 1998, however, the introduction of the first live nudes in the Digital Pavilions with Enhanced Realities and Touchware Art seemed to test the tolerances and interactions of the various groups somewhat. Those from the worlds of art and design were unaffected. But technical folks and others unfamiliar with fine art, life drawing, performance art, and five hundred years of the nude in painting and sculpture were not entirely sure what to make of these new innovations.

The "bar code guy" was more serene, just lying there in his plastic foam form (with a small electric heater on the side) as observers swiped the various bar codes on plexiglass over different parts of his uncovered anatomy—bringing up corresponding parts of visible-human digitized medical data and other, more whimsical images on monitors nearby.

However, "Project Paradise," from the Centre for Metahuman Exploration—with its two distant line-them-up booths and strangely familiar telephone controls, its Garden of Eden in a metal drum room, the uncovered models with robot camera arms, and the twin television monitors open to passersby—generated a quiet but continuing buzz of puzzlement. "Is someone else controlling this?" "What's this for?" "Is that her boyfriend?" "Where are they?" "Is that weird?" "Can they hear us?" "They will never believe me if I don't take a picture of it." "He looks really bored." "This has got to be hard work."

The artists managing the Digital Pavilions had wondered whether there might be complaints—but they were surprised to find that the only one they did receive finally was from a staff member of a computer company who complained of a nude in a slide show during an artist lecture. That was all.

The "collective" of five who devised and performed "Project Paradise" were on the whole much encouraged. After development in the Robotics Institute at Carnegie Mellon and several gallery and television performances, they were readying themselves for a showing at Ars Electronica in Europe in the autumn. They felt that they had succeeded in using familiar, simple, "transparent" technologies of the telephone and television to make their art accessible to a broader audience. Too often, they explain, the technology itself is the piece being shown, not what it does. It is, they said, like putting a radio transmitter in a glass display case rather than having it transmit radio broadcasts.[6]

Other exhibits in the Touchware area became favorites with repeated visitors, each promising to transform spheres of their own. A source of instant recognition and fun was "Thirteen Sketches for an Incompetent User Interface"—where various commands resulted in various catastrophic events on the screen. Those who sat on the sofa in front of the blue screen wondered whose hands were behind them, although no one was really there. A compact and hidden marvel was the "Lost Worlds" exhibit, with moving images projected on a tiny model of ruined buildings in a dark corner. Others wondered at the cones on the floor that, when touched, released flights of birds and other marvels in patterns that were hard to predict.

SPHERES IN FLUX: CELLS LOCATING BY SMELLS

Since this chapter deals with quirky innovation and other early trailblazing work, I will take the liberty of discussing some work by a user of scientific visualization and self-described strong visual thinker, William J. Dreyer, a molecular biologist from Caltech who may eventually be recognized as being responsible for a scientific scoop of his own. (This is the same William Dreyer to whom this book is dedicated.) Like SIGGRAPH itself, this work might at first seem academic, remote, and esoteric. But in time—if it is in fact proven to be correct over time—this work may come to be seen as a major factor in all biology, genetics, and embryology.

Dreyer's radical new theory was published August 4, 1998, in the *Proceedings of the National Academy of Sciences* and summarized in an August 15 article in *Science News* by John Travis. According to Travis, "Dreyer lays out the provocative idea that the cell surface proteins in the nose that detect odors also help assemble embryos. He argues that these olfactory receptors and related proteins act as identifiers, much like the last few digits of a telephone number, that help cells to find their intended neighbors in a developing embryo."

"'I've been searching for these last digits for 20 years,' says Dreyer. . . . 'No one can say for sure [whether the new theory] is true, but I'm up to 90 percent confident. . . .' [One scientist] who studies development of the vertebrate olfactory system . . . admits he was ready to reject Dreyer's theory but found he couldn't. 'One experiment could tell us that the theory is totally impossible, . . . but I haven't found that experiment yet. I don't know of any one thing that unequivocally says it's wrong,' he says. As for Dreyer, he has faced skepticism before . . . but later [has been] proven correct. [He] is now hoping history will repeat itself."[7]

NOTES

1. Dana MacKenzie, "Sphere Does Elegant Gymnastics in New Video: A Tour de Force of Computer Graphics Gives the Simplest Solution Yet to the Venerable Problem of Turning a Sphere Inside Out," *Science* 281 (July 31, 1998): 634; also

available at *Science* Web site, http://www.sciencemag.org (accessed July 1, 2004). This column indicates the range of topics covered during a particularly diverse SIG-GRAPH conference in 1998—giving the flavor of many SIGGRAPH conferences with highly innovative ideas distantly associated.

2.   A full transcript of Jim Blinn's keynote address at SIGGRAPH 1998 can be found at http://www.siggraph.org/s98/conference/keynote/blinn.html (accessed July 1, 2004).

3.   Lynn Arthur Steen, "A Science of Patterns," *Science* 240 (April 29, 1988): 616. Steen is professor of mathematics at St. Olaf College and has served as chairman of the Conference Board of the Mathematical Sciences. (Part of this discussion appeared in different form previously in "Forward into the Past," *Computer Graphics*, November 1995.)

4.   Steen, "A Science of Patterns," p. 616.

5.   I. Peterson, "Math Prizes: Moonshine to Quantum Logic," *Science News* 154 (August 22, 1998): 117.

6.   For further information on "Project Paradise" from the Centre for Meta-human Exploration, see http://www.metahuman.org (accessed July 1, 2004).

7.   John Travis, "Dialing Up an Embryo: Are Olfactory Receptors Digits in a Developmental Code?" *Science News* 154 (August 15, 1998): 106–107. See also William J. Dreyer, "The Area Code Hypothesis Revisited: Olfactory Receptors and Other Related Transmembrane Receptors May Function as the Last Digits in a Cell Surface Code for Assembling Embryos," *Proceedings of the National Academy of Sciences* 95, no. 16 (August 4, 1998): 9072–77; also available at http://www.pnas.org (accessed July 1, 2004).

PART

3   VISUAL BRAINS

CHAPTER

12   MAKING ALL THINGS MAKE THEMSELVES

> *The reaction to the Darwinian theory was . . . diverse when it first exploded onto the Victorian scene. . . . For Charles Kingsley, a deity who could make all things make themselves was far wiser than one who simply made all things.*
> —John Brooke, "Science and Religion: Lessons from History?"

Computer graphics has always been about making things, whether making three-dimensional images of real objects, making images of imagined visions, or making models of the "unseen" in visualizations of scientific data. During the Renaissance, the goal of art was to imitate nature, to make true and accurate images of the real world. Even in the poetry of the period, the "prime aim . . . was to make an imitation" in order to "grasp the essential meaning and value."[1]

Although this goal fell away some time ago, we can now see that our newest tools make it possible to imitate nature once again—but this time at much deeper levels. The imitation can be not only of images of surfaces but also imitation of nature's growth, its physical motion, its processes, its inner workings, its unfolding instructions according to a simple code—imitating the immense complexity generated by variation of a simple code within a context of meaningful selection. And it is already becoming clear that part of this imitation is developing some understanding of things that "make themselves."

VIRTUAL CREATURES

Years ago, when I first saw the short silent movies of Karl Sims's block creatures—walking, swimming, seeking light, and guarding their food— I was thunderstruck. I felt immediately that something very powerful indeed was afoot. And I imagined that what I was seeing was really only the very beginning.[2]

Of course, Sims's work is in many ways mainly a highly sophisticated extension of Richard Dawkins's Blind Watchmaker program, developed for the early Macintosh. With this program (included with Dawkins's book of the same name[3]), two-dimensional, static, monochrome stick figures varied their form in random ways. This allowed the player to select among an array of mutations for different kinds of shapes and traits, play after play, generation after generation—until a new and wonderful centipede, starfish, or complex crystal was produced. This piece of software showed the potential of a modest interactive game to reveal a deeper concept, a fundamental process of nature. However, for me, although the stick figures were fascinating, it took the more lifelike motions and behavior of Sims's virtual creatures to drive the point home.

WHAT WORKS

Accordingly, I think our new tools and our new toys are bringing us face to face with a deeper understanding of how nature's system really works—how truly dazzling adaptations to a particular environment can be generated with a relatively simple mechanism, constantly interacting with a particular and changing environment. This deeper understanding also belies the idea of fixed superiority, since so much depends upon one form of environmental context for any particular form of superiority. The system may evolve an amazingly superior swimmer, but this does not make for a superior walker.

With such models, we can see what an effective mechanism evolution is, partly because of this intense and constant interaction between the expression of genetic code and its outside environment. Indeed, we might reflect that even if there were overt intention by a "maker," this might not be a good thing. We humans are constantly designing things by intention. But how often do we come up with the "unintended consequences" that are so often observed and lamented? (See chapter 9 for more on this.) It becomes clear that making things that make themselves may be a much more practical strategy in an ever-changing world.

But there is a rub here—for many people, an enormous change of metaphor. We now have to view the maker's role not as a craftsman or designer or engineer, but as a maker of things over which the maker has only limited control. Over time, the vast complexity generates a freedom of form and function well beyond the power of the maker. And often, I would argue, this is a good thing.

EARLY DISCOVERIES

One of Sims's creatures in particular stands out in my mind. The design specified walking as forward motion. One creature found that by simply building itself very tall (with an appropriately placed weight), it could fall and tumble head over heels so that it could generate ample forward motion and thus satisfy the selection criteria. Sims observed that this was a strategy that had never occurred to him—the programmer, the arm-length designer.

What is no less remarkable is that Sims also found that other creatures took advantage of the bugs and the programmer's mistakes in specifying the physical world: "It is important that the physical simulation be reasonably accurate when optimizing for creatures that can move within it. Any bugs that allow energy leaks from non-conservation, or even round-off errors, will inevitably be discovered and exploited by the evolving creatures. Although this can be a lazy and often amusing approach for debugging a physical modeling system, it is not necessarily the most practical."[4]

Unexpected innovation and relentless exploitation of possible advantage—these are impressive indeed and show the amazing power of nature's engine of adaptation. If these striking innovations are so easy to observe in a synthetic universe, in only a handful of generations, how much more should we expect in the real world of nature?

Of course, when viewed in this way, ample evidence can be seen in every direction. A 1999 article in *Science News*, for example, noted that a graduate student found a kind of bacteria living on ants that proved to be highly beneficial to the ants. The ants "farm" a certain kind of fungus for their own food. However, this fungus would be easily killed by another pest fungus—if it were not for the antibiotic secretions of the ants' bacterial ride-along buddies. Thus the graduate student, "who once mused about funny-looking patches" on the ants, found that the insects have "a microscopic partner species overlooked despite about a century of study."

"What's interesting from an evolutionary perspective is that once again the ants hit on something before we did. Ants beat humans in developing agriculture by some 50 million years. Now, says [one scientist], it looks as if the same ants came in ahead on bacterial antibiotics by millions of years."[5]

LEARNING FROM THE LOWLY

Such stories take us to a place where we should be prepared to have much higher respect for apparently ordinary and humble creatures. What we are not sufficiently aware of is that these creatures are the beneficiaries of a system capable of innovation far beyond our own small imaginings.

Perhaps it is time to reconsider centuries of human self-congratulation on our own cleverness and begin to look at the cleverness—indeed, the wisdom—of humble creatures. These creatures have used an elegant process not only to produce clever innovations but to produce clever innovations that are proven to work again and again, over millions of years. Such accomplishments should teach us a great deal about the possibilities for "sustainable development."

We have built an elaborate maze of justifications and explanations for our behavior. Modern culture has sophisticated arguments to explain why human beings are at the top the pecking order and why human language is a supreme evolutionary achievement. Accordingly, it is very hard for us to fully appreciate the accomplishments of the humble ant, the unsavory fungus, and the insignificant microbe. Yet, our newest technologies—as the microscope and telescope did centuries ago—are slowly opening up these worlds so that we may see clearly once again what we should have known all along.

However, learning from such lowly creatures is not easy. Our whole culture, for most of us, has trained us not to think such thoughts. Certainly there is very little in the modern Western tradition to cultivate such an appreciation. Generally, there has been little respect for the intelligence of animals. Intelligence is not seen as manifest in nature; rather, it comes in spoken words and in writing. Respecting the intelligence of animals and creatures that make themselves would seem to be more consistent with the worldview of our very distant ancestors.

It would indeed be curious if our new visualization technologies and computer simulations were to take us back in time to a place where we can admire—once again, as our distant ancestors did—the high intelligence of lowly creatures. These creatures learn and innovate not from words and logic but from relentless experimentation and selection over long periods of time, thus showing the deep wisdom of making "all things make themselves."

NOTES

1.   Leonard Dean, *Renaissance Poetry* (New York: Prentice-Hall, 1960), p. 1.

2.   Karl Sims, "Evolving Virtual Creatures," *Computer Graphics Proceedings,* Annual Conference Series, 1994, pp. 15–22. More information about Sims's work can be found at "Karl Sims Retrospective," http://www.biota.org/ksims/. Several movies of his creatures can be downloaded from http://alife.ccp14.ac.uk/ftp-mirror/ alife/zooland/pub/research/ci/Alife/karl-sims/ (both sites accessed July 1, 2004).

3.   Richard Dawkins, *The Blind Watchmaker: Why the Evidence of Evolution Reveals a Universe without Design* (New York: W. W. Norton, 1987).

4.   Sims, "Evolving Virtual Creatures," p. 18.

5.   S. Milus, "Farmer Ants Have Bacterial Farmhands," *Science News* 155 (April 24, 1999): 261.

CHAPTER

13 ENORMOUS EYES AND TINY GRASPING HANDS

The 6-mile-wide meteorite that struck Yucatan 65 million years ago caused the earth to be enveloped in a huge cloud of dust and debris that blocked sunlight for many months. This event destroyed the dinosaurs and many other groups of animals. The mammals, however, were well equipped to survive this cold, dark period because they were active at twilight or at night, they were warm-blooded, and they were insulated with fur. When the dust finally settled the mammals found a world in which most vertebrates larger than themselves were dead: the meek had inherited the earth.

—John Allman, *Evolving Brains*

In his book *Evolving Brains,* biologist John Allman describes with some detail the changes that led to the complex of distinctive features seen in primate brains—features that in turn provide the fundamental neurological foundation for all the work done by visual thinkers and those using computer graphic technologies.

WHY BIG BRAINS?

Allman's book is a treasure of observations and comparisons between different kinds of animals. I was especially interested to see how one survival strategy plays off against another. For example, in the really big picture there seems to be a trade-off between investments in building the brain and investments in building the digestive system. Accordingly, in a manner of speaking, the animal can "choose" to eat plentiful, low-quality food like leaves and grass. But then the animal will have to invest in "plumbing" and complex chemical processing in its digestive system to turn this low-quality food into something useful. In this case, the animal does not need to invest much energy and substance into its own brain since there is really not so much for a brain to do—at least with respect to food. The food of choice is everywhere, so the animal does not have to go to much trouble to find it.

But there is another strategy. The animal can choose higher-quality food such as ripe fruit. This survival strategy requires a good deal more brainpower—to find the right kinds of food in the right places and at the right times. However, these higher-quality foods require a good deal less sophisticated chemical processing by the body to render the food useful. Accordingly, Allman explains, "Because of the high nutritional quality of ripe fruit and its easy digestibility, there is often intense competition from other animals for these scarce resources. . . . Fruit-eaters must plan their foraging expeditions carefully if they are to survive. By contrast, leaves are ubiquitous and can be easily harvested with little competition for these abundant resources. . . . Ripe fruits are a much rarer and more variable resource in space and time than are leaves. The existence of larger brains in fruit-eaters than in leaf-eaters supports the hypothesis that the brain helps the animal to cope with environmental variation."[1]

THE ENERGY COST OF THOUGHT

Similar principles apply to digesting food as in finding food. It takes more energy to digest leaves than it does to digest ripe fruit. "These costs are incurred because the complex carbohydrates in leaves must be fermented and broken down into usable simple sugars, a process requiring a large specialized gut (stomach and intestines) and a considerable amount of energy." Researchers have found that "the size of the digestive organs is negatively correlated with brain size." Accordingly, in comparisons among different animals, "the brain tends to expand at the expense of the digestive organs, and vice versa."

Thus, on the one hand an animal may choose (again, in a manner of speaking) to expend its energy on digestion of widely available but hard-to-digest foods (leaves). Or, as Allman notes, "on the other hand, the animal may use a larger portion of the available [energy budget] to support an enlarged brain with the capacity to store information about the location and cognitive strategies necessary to harvest food (ripe fruit) that is scarce and hard to find, but these foods are less costly to digest."

DECISIONS, DECISIONS

Similar considerations and trade-offs apply to eyes, hands, brains, and visual processing. For example, as early mammals gained greater visual capacities, they gave up some of their sense of smell. There was a reduction in the capacity of their olfactory communication. Similarly, animals with front-facing eyes gain much depth perception, so useful for hunting, but then they may more easily be attacked from behind. Accordingly, it then becomes advantageous to live and hunt in groups. But this, in turn, promotes the need for an "expansion of the system for emotional communication via facial expressions."

One change implies another—or a cascade of related alternatives. Of course, no such decisions are really made, but the consequences of each strategy imply corresponding changes elsewhere. Although it all happens through variation and selection in backward fashion, it seems not unlike the trade-offs that human designers have to deal with.

Small Beginnings

After "the meek had inherited the earth," in Allman's phrasing, the global environment became much warmer than it is today, and "tropical rain forests covered a much larger portion of the planet than they do now." The forests became the home of the early primates, who became abundant about 55 million years ago. Allman explains that these early primates "weighed only a few ounces" and clung with their "tiny grasping hands" to the smallest branches of trees in the tropical rain forest. They were closely related to a group of primates still living called prosimians (meaning "before the monkeys"). Here and elsewhere Allman reminds us of the fundamental interdependence of eye, hand, and brain. Indeed, perhaps this is one of the core lessons that Allman has to teach us—that there is something extraordinarily special about the interaction of these three.

For a long time, the SIGGRAPH organization has explicitly stated that it deals with computer graphics and "interactive technologies." However, we may need to be reminded that the interactive aspect should not be incidental or occasional but instead should be treated as essential in nearly all aspects of computer graphics. It is something to think about. Given the deep importance and long history of these interrelationships, we might consider where these technologies can be employed in places not thought practical before. And we might also want to consider how our newest technologies can move us closer to this end.

Deeper Integration

The other core lesson we can learn from Allman is how many subcomponents of the eye, hand, and brain system depend upon each other. As noted, the changes in the early primates were accompanied by a cascade of interlocking changes. With their large eyes facing forward, the resolution of their visual system was greatly improved by a richer density of "photoreceptors at the center of their retinas." With this change also came increases in the corresponding parts of the brain—and a split into two functional systems: one "exquisitely sensitive to motion and small differences in contrast" and the other responsive to "shape and form." Another notable improvement seen in the early primates was a special brain cortex area "devoted to the visual guidance of muscle movement." Allman asserts that these functionally related changes in the visual and motor coordination systems became "the basic defining features for primates" and "served to differentiate them from other groups of mammals."

Given these interconnections and special innovations, it is indeed extraordinary and remarkable that our culture has succeeded in narrowing the focus of these traits toward mainly eye and hand in reading and writing rather than some more vast repertoire of associated behaviors. But, as observed before, perhaps the new visual (i.e., spatial, interactive) technologies will allow us to correct this imbalance.

METAPHORICAL FINE BRANCHES

There is another aspect of Allman's observations that should not escape our attention. Just as the early primates seemed well adapted to waving tiny branches, perhaps our new information visualization systems could take advantage of similar capabilities in a metaphorical sense. We might wonder whether complex information trees from Xerox PARC and elsewhere might be more purposefully adapted to take advantage of this basic neurological architecture—changing detailed specialist data into a metaphorical framework of fine branches to be "grasped" and understood by metaphorical creatures with enormous eyes and tiny grasping hands. No more flat screens. To find the best use for long-standing human capabilities in our newest computer systems, we need to find more and better ways to probe and grasp.

DANCES WITH WOLVES

Allman ends his thought-provoking book with observations about man and wolf that might furnish a somewhat similar metaphor or analogy. He notes that about 150 million years ago, the one mammal most prevalent in most parts of the world was the wolf (*Canis lupus*), living throughout most of Eurasia and North America. At that time, the ancestors of modern man were restricted to Africa. Allman argues that it is likely that the mutual advantage from human interdependence with wolves, many of which became domesticated dogs, allowed the ancestors of modern man to move out of Africa and spread around the globe. The superior senses of smell and hearing of dogs would have complemented "the early human's keen vision in detecting both prey and predators." Dogs would be faster in running down and seizing prey. However, "from the dog's point of view, humans were pack members who brought food to the pups." Indeed, convincingly, help from humans "enabled dogs to have two litters of pups per year instead of the single litter in wolves."

Curiously, however, the success of this teamwork in reducing environmental variation and stress has led to reduced average brain sizes in both dogs and human beings. Domesticated dogs have brains that are about two-thirds the size of the brains of wolves. With domestication, human beings have accepted the responsibility to provide food and shelter. Consequently, the "dog's necessity for maintaining a larger brain is decreased." In a similar fashion, human brain size has also been reduced over the past thirty-five thousand years. According to Allman, "early humans had brains that averaged about 1,450 grams, whereas the average for contemporary humans is about 1,300 grams." It is argued that with the rapid development of agriculture and every other aspect of culture during the past thirty-five thousand years, environmental variation has been reduced sufficiently to allow humans to get along with smaller brains. "Perhaps humans," observes Allman, "have domesticated themselves."

A Newer Domestication

The implied question is, of course, whether mankind's new relationship with the computer will ultimately have effects similar to the relationship with wolves. Clearly, we have already moved a long way in the complementary interdependence of humankind and machines.

But will the analogy become more apt and the relationship more powerful with the new generations of interactive-graphics machines—so different in essence from the old text-and-number machines? Will we be able to break out of areas to which we have been confined up to now? However, in so doing, will we reduce environmental variation and stress once again—and thereby domesticate ourselves that much more once again? If this were to happen, who would then have the big brains, and why?

Note

1. John Morgan Allman, *Evolving Brains* (New York: Scientific American Library, 1999), p. 165. All other quotations in this chapter are also taken from this source.

CHAPTER

14 BRAIN DRAIN
RECONSIDERING SPATIAL ABILITY

Some years ago, a friend told me of a television program shown in Canada about the French "brain drain." Earlier, I had seen newspaper articles about scientists and engineers leaving France because of apparently limited opportunities—coupled with their belief that they would always be known for the schools they attended rather than for how well they could perform in their work.

But this new story was of special interest to me because it involved a young computer graphics artist, Valerie Delahaye, who could not find work in France because of her dyslexia. However, as Delahaye told the story on television, she found that she was warmly received by computer graphics companies in the United States. They were interested in her artistic skills and thought the dyslexia was not a problem—since they already knew that many digital artists are dyslexic to some extent. She has since worked on many projects, including the films *The Fifth Element* and *Titanic*.

She told me that her personal estimate is that about half of all computer graphics artists are probably dyslexic. Some readers may think her estimate is rather large until we recall that the rate was given at fully 75 percent in the only systematic study undertaken so far on the matter—that is, the study of first-year students in a London art school.[1]

In France, Valerie's difficulties with writing and working under pressure had kept her from passing exams—even those required to enter art school. In the United States, however, she was able to have accommodations with exams so she could finally receive a professional education in her areas of strength. She was not judged in areas that were largely irrelevant to her work and talent. She expressed concern that the educational system in France still has done very little to address these problems.

This story highlights for us, once again, the great changes we seem to be going through—and the increasingly evident differences between the skills valued in the old verbal technological context and the skills more highly valued in the emerging technologies of images and visualization. The old world of the book and writing requires one set of talents and skills, whereas the expanding world of moving images and visualized information (as noted in previous chapters) seems to require quite a different set.

Some might argue that the move to images is really quite superficial—even retrograde, indeed, as it would appear to shift attention and time from basic verbal literacy. However, we can argue that, especially for the young, visual literacy will be as important, or more important, than verbal literacy. (Of course, it's best to have proficiency in both as much as possible, but we should not allow real visual talent to fall by the wayside just because of verbal difficulties.)

In contrast to the differences noted above, we can also make a case that the experience of this digital artist may be very similar indeed to the experience of scientists and engineers. More and more groups are coming to see that there is a common thread between areas that were formerly thought to be quite different—in the arts as well as the sciences, mathematics, and related disciplines. And, in this case, the common thread is a newly rediscovered awareness of the importance of visual and spatial abilities. In spite of strong conventions of thought and common belief, we are seeing a gradual reawakening of interest in spatial abilities that were formerly thought to be relatively unimportant in most areas.

REDISCOVERING SPATIAL ABILITIES

For some time, the assessment of abilities other than verbal and mathematical have been widely neglected in most educational settings. They simply were thought to be unimportant. Fortunately, this has begun to change, as research groups are gradually rediscovering the real value of assessing visual and spatial capabilities. Researchers at Johns Hopkins University, for example, can provide us with a small window into what a few researchers are doing—and how views are changing in a few institutions in ways that would seem sympathetic to the perspectives of strong visual thinkers. These researchers have been trying to improve methods of identifying scientific talent at various educational levels and to better predict performance in science education before college. They saw that the conventional verbal- and mathematical-reasoning measures were not enough, and they determined that what was needed was a good way to assess spatial reasoning as well. In their words, "Spatial ability has been given only token attention as an important dimension of cognitive functioning. Research on the structure, identification, and development of spatial ability has been conducted by a few researchers spread around the world and often ignored by the psychological and educational community. In addition, spatial ability has played only a modest role in educational assessment and instruction."[2]

The Hopkins researchers are aware that they are to some extent breaking new ground. Of course, assessments of spatial abilities have been around for a long time, but they have never occupied center stage. They have nearly always been treated as tangential to the more conventional measures of academic abilities. The researchers note that although there are other research programs similar to theirs, they are the only ones so far using measures of spatial ability in a serious way.

One area of concern with spatial tests is that they have long been thought to be biased in favor of men. However, the Hopkins researchers have shown that the truth is more complex and perhaps more balanced. They have found that whereas males do better with mental rotation tasks, females are significantly better at visual memory. Some studies indicate that there is a convergence to the point that male and female spatial skills are less dissimilar than had been formerly believed.[3]

The use of computers in the Hopkins testing program is of special interest. One obvious benefit of computer use in spatial testing is that it allows the actual rotation of objects on the screen—objects such as blocks, twisted cables, or molecular structures. Another benefit is that computers also allow a form of testing that can respond to the ability level of the students. The test can drop off unnecessary questions in response to right answers. It is interactive, or, in the researchers' terminology, "adaptive." As they explain, "adaptive tests respond to students' correct and incorrect answers. The computer program chooses questions at the last second, based on whether or not the previous item was answered correctly. This process leads to more precision in measurements with less time required for testing." The researchers have also found that tests on computers are especially helpful to many students with learning disabilities, since there is only one question on the screen at a time. And finally, with computers, the test taker receives an immediate score.[4]

MIXED TALENTS

It is noteworthy that the Hopkins researchers have also found that to deal effectively with the most highly talented students, one must be ready to deal with dyslexia and other learning disabilities as well. This idea is especially hard for many conventional educators to handle. By training and shared experience, they find it hard to believe that the smartest people quite often have dyslexia or some form of learning disability. It is to the credit of the Hopkins researchers that they began to see clearly, early on, that they were seeing patterns of mixed abilities in their students—patterns that many thought could not and should not exist. "She is so bright," traditional teachers would say, "she must not be working hard enough." Or, "if he is dyslexic, he clearly does not belong in our highly demanding educational institution."

But the Hopkins researchers, along with a few others, are aware that some forms of learning problems are not uncommon among the most highly gifted. This is the reason that an explicit item on their six-point research agenda is to "explore the benefits of using spatial tests to identify academic ability in students with learning disabilities."[5]

Thus the Hopkins researchers explain that they are investigating "the relationship between the development of spatial reasoning and specific learning disabilities. Although there is much speculation about such a relationship," they point out, "little empirical research has been conducted to establish its existence. This line of research would help us to better understand individuals with learning disabilities and assist educators as they plan appropriate educational interventions." Accordingly, they feel that "one possibility is the development of teaching approaches that utilize a spatial orientation for . . . students who possess strong spatial skills and who have difficulty learning in other modalities."[6]

It is worth noting that the Hopkins researchers came out of a tradition started in the 1970s where they had been accustomed to dealing with only the most highly gifted students, in the beginning focusing on mathematical talent. Indeed, for some time they have dealt with, as they say, the "one-out-of-10,000" gifted, not the usual "one-out-of-20" gifted. In order to do this they have conventionally given the college entrance examination (SAT) to students five or six years early—testing students on a good deal of material that they had never been taught. Then they would accept into their program only those students who received the highest scores out of very large numbers of students nationwide.[7]

Consequently, the Hopkins researchers had as their early focus extremely gifted children. It is therefore all the more interesting that their research focus has moved, in time, toward spatial abilities, toward learning difficulties, and toward the integral use of computers. Perhaps they have been moving through a gradual learning process that might be reflected, over time, in our culture and our institutions at large. We may wonder how long it will take before conventional educational institutions begin to think similarly.

UNIDENTIFIED PROMISE

The Hopkins researchers think that their new spatial tests are timely. They note that "spatial tests have been around for years, but have not been as widely administered as are tests of verbal or mathematical reasoning."

However, "today," they observe, "some educators are intrigued by their potential. What if spatial tests were added to the regular program of standardized assessment? Could they flag abilities that currently go undetected? Could they identify promise in students who now pass more or less unnoticed?" That, at least, is their hope.[8]

Perhaps the greater use of spatial tests, coupled with a much broader understanding of the importance of rediscovered spatial abilities, might help prevent conventional educational systems from letting fall by the wayside those who are especially well suited to visual and spatial tasks—whether in creating grand illusions on film or in understanding visual patterns in the stock market or complex weather systems.

NOTES

1. "The Art of Being Dyslexic," *Independent* (London), Education Supplement, February 27, 1997, pp. 4–5.

2. "IAAY Research: Spatial Ability," unpublished overview, Institute for the Academic Advancement of Youth, Center for Talented Youth, Center for Academic Advancement, Johns Hopkins University, n.d., p. 1.

3. See "Perspectives: Dr. Heinrich Stumpf and His Spatial Test," *Imagine*, Institute for the Academic Advancement of Youth, Johns Hopkins Press, n.d., p. 10; Heinrich Stumpf and J. Eliot, "Gender-Related Differences in Spatial Ability . . . ," *Personality and Individual Differences* 19 (1995): 33–45; Heinrich Stumpf and E. Klieme, "Sex-Related Differences in Spatial Ability: More Evidence for Convergence," *Perceptual and Motor Skills* 69 (1989): 915–21.

4. "Perspectives," p. 10; personal communication with Carol J. Mills, head of IAAY research, May 1998.

5. "IAAY Research," p. 3.

6. Ibid., pp. 2–3.

7. Personal communication with C. P. Benbow, ODS conference, November 1993.

8. "Perspectives," p. 11. The list of suggested further reading provided by the IAAY includes John B. Carrol, *Human Cognitive Abilities: A Survey of Factor-Analytic Studies* (Cambridge: Cambridge University Press, 1993); John Eliot, *Models of Psychological Space: Psychometric, Developmental, and Experimental Approaches* (New York: Springer-Verlag, 1987); Howard Gardner, *Frames of Mind: The Theory of Multiple Intelligences* (New York: Basic Books, 1983); Roger B. Nelsen, *Proofs without Words: Exercises in Visual Thinking* (Washington, DC: Mathematical Association of America, 1993); Heinrich Stumpf, "Development of a Talent Search and Related Programs for Scientific Innovation among Youth," CTY Technical Report 12 (unpublished, IAAY, 1995); Thomas G. West, *In the Mind's Eye* (Amherst, NY: Prometheus Books, 1991).

CHAPTER

KNOWING WHAT YOU DON'T NEED TO KNOW

I saw mathematics was split up into numerous specialties, each of which could easily absorb the short lifetime granted to us. . . . My intuition was not strong enough in the field of mathematics to differentiate clearly the fundamentally important, that which is really basic, from the rest of the more or less dispensable erudition.

—Albert Einstein, *Autobiographical Notes*

In his *Autobiographical Notes,* Albert Einstein explains in a curious fashion the reason that he decided as a student to study physics rather than mathematics. In a sense, he tells the reader that his problem with mathematics was that he could not easily figure out what was comparatively unimportant.[1] He had difficulty knowing what he did not need to know. Fortunately, he had no such difficulty with physics.

As our knowledge economy grows ever more rapidly, it seems likely that we all will be increasingly confronted with problems akin to Einstein's. With so much specialist education required and so much information daily at our fingertips, how will we know what we need to know—and, more importantly, how will we know what we don't need to know? Computer graphics professionals have long been familiar with the problem of abundant information and especially the role of computer graphics and scientific visualization as powerful means for dealing with information overload in many fields. However, even computer visualization technologies and techniques cannot eliminate the problem. They may deliver the right information in a form that can be more readily comprehended and understood. But what is the right information?

These considerations are becoming more widespread as near-term developments are being recognized and discussed in the general media. An article in the *Washington Post*, for example, discussed the new ways of handling information that have been developed at Xerox PARC and other research organizations. The "cone tree," "perspective walls," and other graphic devices have heretofore required, of course, more powerful computers than those available to most PC users. However, at the time of the article there was a growing awareness that this would change in the near future. Indeed, the *Post* article quoted Stuart Card of Xerox PARC as saying that "over the next 18 months" computer hardware capable of supporting these types of demanding new graphics software "will be available to a mass audience."[2]

As we move in fits and starts from a world of words to a world of images, there are many ironies and paradoxes. One paradox is that visual thinkers— who, as we have discussed previously, often have difficulties with word-based educational systems—may find themselves to be among those best able to lead others in solving the increasingly pressing problem of our age, that is, quickly and effectively navigating oceans and oceans of information. Our technological culture is drowning in its own success; masses of data and information are accumulating everywhere. As time goes on, it is apparent that these problems are only likely to become much worse, not better—unless, of course, the entire system somehow collapses under its own weight.

SPECIALIST MYOPIA

Until now, the basic strategy for dealing with these growing masses of information has been long, mind-numbing education and reckless, blinkered specialization. That this strategy has been effective in many respects, so far, is hardly doubted. The problems we are discussing are a tribute to its ample and abundant success—up to now. However, it is becoming increasingly clear that this strategy may be entering a phase of diminishing returns. It has long been recognized that this approach has always had built-in problems. The more one knows in one's own increasingly narrow area, the more one is ignorant in other areas, the more difficult is effective communication between unrelated areas, and the more unlikely it is that the larger whole will be properly perceived, comprehended, or understood. Like the student who reads too much small print, the specialist's habitual near focus often promotes a myopic perspective that precludes the comprehension of larger, more important patterns. The view of the distant whole is blurred and unclear.

If an astronomer focuses only on a small group of stars at the edge of the Milky Way, he does not perceive the larger structure of the whole galaxy, of which the group is one tiny part. "He cannot see the forest for the trees," people would say. Sometimes it is not so much a matter of whether to specialize, but at what level and magnitude to fix the focus. Specialists who are expert in one area may not even have commonsense knowledge in other areas. This is sometimes recognized, of course, but often discounted. Instead, because of their success in the one narrow area, specialists are encouraged in an arrogant belief that they can make pronouncements in many other areas as well. The prestige of knowing a great deal, even in one limited area, carries great weight. It is an old story, really. Some time ago, philosopher and mathematician Alfred North Whitehead noted the danger of knowing a great deal: "Dead knowledge is the danger. It is the peculiar danger of scholarship, of universities; and it is considered quite respectable. If you 'know' a great deal, that is supposed to suffice. Now what is wanted is 'activity in the presence of knowledge.' Novel viewpoints; knowledge applied to experience."[3]

The specialist strategy breeds its own limits. Pieces of the puzzle in separate areas remain far apart or come together only after decades of specialist resistance. Or, sometimes success in one area can lead to great problems in another. As we look at the long-term consequences of progress in material wealth, transportation, or healthcare, for example, we see that wonderful technical successes in specialty areas lead, in time, to enormous, difficult, and intractable problems in other areas. Seemingly, spectacular success in one narrow sphere leads inevitably to major problems with the whole. Many consequences are easily predictable and are, to some degree, inevitable. Cars and aircraft produce wonderful mobility for many people, but these forms of transportation also deplete resources, produce accidental fatalities, and increase pollution; material abundance produces waste disposal problems; success in vaccination, hygiene, and healthcare lead to all the problems concentrated human populations. As the specialist strategy continues to be pursued, increasingly a sense of the whole is lost. Many are expert; few are wise.

GLOBAL THINKERS, GLOBAL TOOLS

But many visual thinkers have been outsiders or, at best, reluctant participants in this specialist culture—especially the energetic, global-minded ones who seem always to be interested in everything. They are often unable to settle on a highly specialized (and therefore considered "serious") area of study. Many, because of verbal difficulties, may be unable to complete years of disciplined study and intense examination. Others find it impossible to apply themselves to the dull repetition of a properly conducted specialist career. Or, even if they do settle on an acceptable specialty area, they (like Albert Einstein or James Clerk Maxwell) become known for addressing a wide variety of topics (from light particles to river courses, from cybernetic devices to the rings of Saturn).

While many of the "best and brightest" have taken comfort in their own successes, digging into the warm, insulated, safe shelter of their chosen specialty, the global, visual thinkers remain in the bracing, changeable winds on the plain. The minds of these visual thinkers are as restless and vibrantly alive as their transcripts and resumes are varied and erratic. The most successful do seem to learn how to still this restless curiosity to some extent—just enough, at least, for them to focus their passion for a time and finish a few of the many projects that emerge from their imagination. More than others, such people probably need to know how to manage and discipline themselves and their attention—when to rein in and when to let go.

But, in time, these same creative visual thinkers with verbal difficulties often have learned, by inclination and necessity, what their unaffected fellows cannot have learned: how to gain the most understanding with the least information, how to learn as much from what they see as what they read, how to be savagely selective in their reading, and how to guess what is inessential and focus only on the really important. Like Einstein, they may have a better chance to learn what they don't need to know. The more verbally proficient specialists may be able to work far more rapidly and retain more of what they have read, but too often the specialist is prone to wasting time without being aware of it. They do what the professor wants or what the employer expects them to do. They may be too well focused and disciplined to see what nature invites them to discover.

In any field, or any subfield, as Einstein said, there is so much to do and so much to know that one can easily squander a lifetime (career or material success notwithstanding) without results of real consequence. Specialists must develop some sort of inner guide to avoid the continuous acquisition of comparatively inessential information. Visual and global thinkers seem rarely to have the inclination or feel the temptation to stake their claim to one tiny hoard of knowledge, as specialists do—holding off all comers with a barrage of facts, minefields of technical language, and bulwarks of prerequisites and qualifications. Students in these specialties have to study for years and pass all these exams before they can even begin to think about or discuss the topic—or so their mentors say.

THE ADVANTAGES OF LIMITS

But visual thinkers, sometimes with verbal problems, often experience a different necessity. They learn the value of their own limits. Whether their particular difficulty is with reading or memory or something else, from the outset many of them have had to learn how to judge what is worth knowing and what should be left aside. They have had to learn how to select—first for teachers, but then for life and the world. Many have had to integrate knowledge with what they already know in order to learn and retain it—for unconnected knowledge quickly slips away. They have had to learn basic concepts well enough to be able to generate and regenerate factual material that would not alone remain still and accessible and unchanging in their minds. Often they have had to learn how to constantly check the validity of their imagination and the accuracy of their conclusions against some really reliable standard—and then check them again, remaining ever vigilant to ensure that yet another error does not creep in to spoil the result.

The specialist has long been comforted by knowing 95 to 99 percent of what he needs to know. No critic can reasonably challenge the completeness of this knowledge. In contrast, many visual thinkers have had to learn to survive being able to survey, absorb, and retain only, say, 20 or 30 percent of what they are expected to know. As information and knowledge grows by orders of magnitude and orders of magnitude again, in ever-decreasing periods of time, how long before the specialist will have to be content with 85 percent, then 75 percent, then 65 percent or less of an ever more narrowly focused specialty—an awareness of the larger whole constantly receding? Which experience is likely to be a greater help in coping in the coming years and in the coming decades? Visual thinkers with verbal or memory problems have had to develop methods to sift, sample, and select because they can never read and absorb at the rate that others are able to. One might be able to, say, digest a single article in the same time that the specialist can cover, say, ten or twenty articles. But what happens when the specialist has to cover one hundred, or one thousand, or even ten thousand articles in limited time?

Of course, in the long run, we will always need both the narrow specialist and the global visual thinker—or the rare individuals who somehow combine the strengths of both. The problem is not essentially with specialization itself. Rather, the problem is with the way education and work are organized—the way we are often led to believe that only the specialist knows anything, the way the specialist approach is believed to be adequate. "We are nearly there," they say. "We just need some more time and some more money."

But sometimes an entirely different approach is needed before the answer can be found. Sometimes we need to back off some distance, rather than burrowing in deeper. Sometimes the answer is sitting right in front of us, but we refuse to recognize it. Sometimes we would need a whole lot less money for research if we could just see the larger patterns. Long-standing tradition has often forced us to go the wrong way, toward greater specialization. It now seems, however, that we may soon observe a reversal in this trend. The new visualization technologies, coupled with the natural propensities of visual thinkers, may help to turn the flow so that we may begin to find ways of dealing with larger problems and with more enduring solutions.

In his book *The Image*, Kenneth Boulding pointed out that professors have always wanted students to learn as much as possible. The students, on the other hand, he says, have always been interested in learning as little as they could get away with. The irony of it all is that, in the end, the students, as Boulding points out, are clearly in the right—the more so now than ever before, and even more so in the future than now.[4] And the greatest irony may be that the path may be led by those who have been forced to excel in understanding more from knowing less—in other words, those who know what they don't really need to know.[5]

NOTES

1.   Albert Einstein, *Autobiographical Notes*, ed. Paul A. Schilpp (Chicago: Open Court, 1979).

2.   Elizabeth Corcoran, "Brain Teasers That Matter: Top Researchers on Five Questions Whose Answers Could Change Our Lives," *Washington Post*, December 21, 1997, pp. H1, H4. As it happened, the fast machines did come as predicted. But with the exception of a few specialists, most people, as we have seen, were not yet in a position to begin to use the new and powerful visual and graphical capabilities.

3.   *Dialogues of Alfred North Whitehead*, as collected by Lucien Price (New York: New American Library, Mentor, 1964).

4.   Kenneth Boulding, *The Image* (Ann Arbor: University of Michigan Press, 1956).

5.   This chapter is largely based on "Patterns, Implications, Possibilities," chap. 10 in my book *In the Mind's Eye* (Amherst, NY: Prometheus Books, 1991, 1997). Part of Einstein's observation was referred to briefly in the August 1997 "Images and Reversals" column, which dealt with unexpected discoveries in DNA research and inexpensive innovation by the Wright brothers (see chap. 17 of this book).

PART

4   VISUAL PEOPLE

CHAPTER

16 FEYNMAN DIAGRAMS, SPREADING ILLUSIONS

Schwinger's quantum electrodynamics and Feynman's may have been mathematically the same, but one was conservative and the other revolutionary. One extended an existing line of thought. The other broke with the past decisively enough to mystify its intended audience. One represented an ending: a mathematical style doomed to be fatally overcomplex. The other, for those willing to follow Feynman into a new style of visualization, served as a beginning. Feynman's style was risky, even megalomaniacal.
—James Gleick, *Genius: The Life and Science of Richard Feynman*

Those of us who have been following the gradual development of computer information visualization over the years may assume that its value is obvious to all. We may be unaware or forget how rare and revolutionary visualization has been (at least in relatively recent times). We may need to be reminded of how it has often been used by the most creative and innovative mavericks, those who have had to depart from both conventional concepts and conventional methods.

As we move further ahead with these technologies and techniques into newer fields and the wider workplace, we are likely to enter areas where many of the established practitioners do not take naturally to visualization. In this phase of development, we need to be reminded of the recurring pattern of resistance—as well as the remarkable power of this new approach.

ANYTHING IN THE UNIVERSE

James Gleick's book *Genius: The Life and Science of Richard Feynman* provides several delightful and illuminating portraits. In one passage, there is a classic illustration of the battle between two very different ways of thinking about a problem—ways that converge from different directions (more or less). Julian Schwinger and other physicists were trying to extend the conventional mathematical approaches—extending the known concepts and techniques just a little bit further. They wanted an incremental improvement. On the other hand, Feynman, not unlike the archetypal visionary, wanted a great deal more. In the words of physicist Freeman Dyson, Feynman "was searching for general principles that would be flexible enough so that he could adapt them to anything in the universe."[1]

Time and time again, Feynman provides us with wonderful examples of the working and thinking style of the strong visual thinker—and how different this is from that of colleagues and competitors who follow the more conventional verbal, logical, and mathematical approaches, approaches that have dominated physics and many other fields in recent times. Such stories can provide us with insights that will likely extend in many directions.

Whereas others used mainly mathematics, Feynman (like Albert Einstein, James Clerk Maxwell, and Michael Faraday) relied heavily on diagrams, pictures, and mental models. Indeed, Feynman once told an associate, "Einstein's great work had sprung from physical intuition and that when Einstein stopped creating it was because 'he stopped thinking in concrete physical images and became a manipulator of equations.'"[2]

MERE DEFINITIONS

Just as Feynman's style of thinking was in deep contrast to Julian Schwinger, so, too, was it entirely different in most respects from that of another important physicist, Murray Gell-Mann. As Gleick observes, "In so many ways these two scientific icons had come to seem like polar opposites. . . . Gell-Mann loved to know things' names and to pronounce them correctly. . . . Feynman . . . despised nomenclature of all kinds. Gell-Mann was an enthusiastic bird watcher; . . . Feynman's [belief] was that the name of a bird did not matter. . . ."[3] Repeatedly, we see Feynman making the point that simply naming a thing does not demonstrate that you really understand it in any meaningful way—a fundamental idea that is in opposition to basic education and testing at all levels, often especially in the sciences. (He was furious that his own young children were being taught not real science, as he saw it, but "mere definitions."[4])

Gleick cites comparisons of the visual Feynman and the verbal Gell-Mann at some length. "Physicists kept finding new ways to describe the contrast between them. Murray makes sure you know what an extraordinary person he is, they would say, while Dick is not a person at all but a more advanced life form pretending to be human to spare your feelings." Murray was interested in many things but was "openly contemptuous" of branches of science outside high-energy physics; "Dick considered all science to be his territory—his responsibility—but remained brashly ignorant of everything else."[5]

Their use of the body is important. "Feynman talked with his hands—with his whole body, in fact—whereas Gell-Mann, as physicist and science writer Michael Riordan observed, 'sits calmly behind his desk . . . hands folded, never lifting them to make a gesture. . . . Information is exchanged by words and numbers, not by hands or pictures.'" The power of these brief descriptions of very different styles of thinking should not be underestimated. "'Their personal styles spill over into their theoretical work, too. Gell-Mann insists on mathematical rigor in all his work, often at the expense of comprehensibility. . . . Where Gell-Mann disdains vague, heuristic models that might only point the way toward a true solution, Feynman revels in them. He believes that a certain amount of imprecision and ambiguity is essential to communication.'"[6]

With all their differences, however, both men are passionate in the honesty and directness with which they approach their subject. "Gell-Mann was no more likely than Feynman to hide behind formalism or to use mathematics as a stand-in for physical understanding."[7] Yet both men projected masks to the world that became important parts of their personal realities. "Murray's mask was a man of great culture. . . . Dick's mask was Mr. Natural—just a little boy from the country that could see through things the city slickers can't."[8]

VISUAL AND MUSCULAR TYPE

It is important for us to note that for Feynman and others like him, what is needed was not only or entirely visual. It is something just beyond the visual—as it extends naturally into the physical. These kinds of thinkers need "a kind of seeing and feeling" grounded in "physical intuition." We should note here that, as mentioned before, Albert Einstein made similar observations. Einstein pointed out that in his own thought processes, part of his "vague play" with "signs and more or less clear images" were "elements . . . of visual and some of muscular type."[9] Clearly, for some, there seems to a close association between moving images in the mind and moving muscles and parts of the body.

As Gleick observes, "Intuition was not just visual but auditory and kinesthetic. Those who watched Feynman in moments of intense concentration came away with a strong, even disturbing sense of the physicality of the process, as though his brain did not stop with the grey matter but extended through every muscle in his body. A Cornell dormitory neighbor opened Feynman's door to find him rolling about on the floor beside his bed as he worked on a problem. When he was not rolling about, he was at least murmuring rhythmically or drumming with his fingers. In part the process of scientific visualization is a process of putting oneself in nature: in an imagined beam of light, in a relativistic electron."[10]

Feynman tried to explain how his approach was not entirely or exclusively visual. "What I am really trying to do is bring birth to clarity, which is really a half-assedly thought-out pictorial semi-vision thing. I would see the jiggle-jiggle-jiggle or the wiggle of the path."[11] Gleick notes that "in seeking to analyze his own way of visualizing the unvisualizable [Feynman] had learned an odd lesson. The mathematical symbols he used every day had become entangled with his physical sensations of motion, pressure, acceleration. . . . 'When I start describing the magnetic field moving through space,' Feynman observed, 'I speak of . . . fields and wave my arms and you may imagine that I can see them. I'll tell you what I see. I see some kind of vague, shadowy, wiggling lines . . . and perhaps some of the lines have arrows on them—an arrow here or there which disappears when I look too closely. . . . I have a terrible confusion between the symbols I use to describe the objects and the objects themselves.'"[12]

SPREADING ILLUSIONS

Anyone who has experienced the NCSA CAVE virtual reality system or some other high-quality immersive environment will see immediately the close relevance of Feynman's descriptions to the kinds of tools we now have at our fingertips.[13] With Feynman's "wiggling lines" and disappearing arrows, I am reminded of my own immersion in the data of wind currents over Florida at a SIGGRAPH conference demonstration of the CAVE years ago. As I looked around the room with walls and floor made of computer screens, I saw yellow lines with arrows at about my waist height. Crouching down, I then saw all the streaming patterns of wind coursing over my head like a layer of thin yellow clouds. I was truly "immersed in the data," and it had a dramatic effect. I could imagine how strong visual thinkers, from Michael Faraday to Nicola Tesla, might have perceived their own data, their own world, whether imagined or real.

Such whole-body interaction with very high-quality imagery can have effects far beyond what might have been expected. Airline pilots frequently emerge perspiring and shaken from their computer-simulated near-misses and crashes. And car designers now know never to allow visitors to take coffee cups into their simulators—because they are likely to put their cups down on surfaces that are not really there. Remarkably, in such a display as the CAVE there is a persuasive illusion of concreteness and physicality that we might not expect. Visual material presented in the right way, it would seem, with the right speeds and at the right resolution may go very far toward activating and mimicking the kinesthetic along with the visual and the auditory.

When these kinds of technologies reach a certain level of sophistication, we may find that we rarely have to go so far as to add the complexity of force feedback or other cumbersome devices to generate a useful and persuasive illusion. Indeed, with the right speeds and with real ease of interaction we may move quickly beyond the merely effective and impressive to the frightening. (We must also be aware, however, that beyond certain limits our bodies sometimes do not take well to a confusing partial message—as with the strange symptoms and brief neurological shutdowns fighter pilots sometimes suffer as a consequence of simulator sickness, as they get all the visual information associated with being in a real fighter with only a small fraction of the g-forces they would normally encounter.)

As these technologies and truly new ways of working and thinking spread throughout the economy (even with painful slowness), at least in the short run, we should expect to see increased tension and a widening divide between new and traditional approaches. Some will take (or have already taken) to these new technologies and techniques like finding water in the desert. Finally, they realize, they have found a mode of communication that works the way their own minds work. But for most people, in most disciplines, it is more likely that their attitudes will be puzzled or even resistant. We see it all around us now, in different disciplines, at different stages. Initially, such people have said that the new visual technologies and techniques are not really serious or sophisticated. Later, they have said, well, of course we all use these things, but the benefits are limited and the applications are restricted. But, still later, they may come to realize how the deep power of these new methods can transform their world—making hostile and alien an area that once was theirs alone. Thus these changes may make their special talents less valued, their traditional approaches and skills less relevant. However, of course, in the end, both sides and both kinds of approaches will always be needed. But it may be some time before we have moved beyond all of this to circle back once again to an awareness and a genuine appreciation for a broad range of approaches and thinking styles.

AN EXTENDED TURNING POINT

Years ago, we expected much, but the rise of visual technologies has taken place astonishingly slowly. For example, in a 1997 issue of *Communications of the ACM*, the journal of the Association for Computing Machinery, guest editor Ramesh Jain noted the possibility of a major turning point: "Many disparate advances in technology are making visual information in computing as important as it is in ... biological human life. We humans are most adept and comfortable with visual information." With these advances, "we may again be at a turning point in the history of human civilization."[14]

We now know that the brain uses two contrasting strategies to handle information about the world. Each strategy is fundamentally different and therefore quite difficult to translate into the other—which is not at all surprising, given the brain's need to accommodate the requirements of such different modes of operation. It is apparent that both strategies are needed in the long run. For some time now, human culture has been almost entirely dominated by tools and technologies that support the sequential brain strategy—linked with words. However, quite suddenly, in historical terms, a new set of tools has been dumped into our laps. We should expect that moving from one strategy to the other will have powerful consequences.

Without being fully aware of the deep importance of what we are doing, we are now learning to use the tools and technologies that support the simultaneous strategy of the human brain—linked to images. Very possibly, this could be the most important change in the foundation of human culture for a very long time. And we are now only at the very beginning of the beginning. As we proceed along the way, however, we should expect the pace and direction to be set by strong visual thinkers, who will often ignore conventional verbal descriptions—instead putting themselves into their own mental models, talking with their hands, rolling on the floor, taking risks.

NOTES

1. Quoted in James Gleick, *Genius: The Life and Science of Richard Feynman* (New York: Pantheon Books, 1992), p. 321.

2. Gleick, *Genius*, p. 244.

3. Ibid., pp. 387–88.

4. Ibid., p. 398.

5. Ibid., p. 388.

6. Ibid., pp. 388–89.

7. Ibid., p. 389.

8. Sidney Coleman, quoted in ibid., p. 389.

9. Quoted in Jacques Hadamard, *The Psychology of Invention in the Mathematical Field* (New York: Dover, 1954), pp. 142–43.

10. Gleick, *Genius*, p. 244.

11. Quoted in ibid., p. 244.

12. Ibid., p. 245.

13. For more on the CAVE, see "CAVE Background," http://www.spcomm.uiuc.edu/classes/sp03/396-5/projects/ajgonzal/NCSA%20CAVE.htm (accessed August 9, 2004).

14. Ramesh Jain, "Visual Information Management," *Communications of the ACM* 40, no. 12 (December 1997): 31.

CHAPTER

17 MISSED OPPORTUNITIES AND CHEAP TOOLS

THE UNEXPECTED GIFT

Years ago, a young researcher was performing a laboratory procedure that had been devised to separate DNA into its component parts. She was annoyed, however, at not being able to make the procedure work as intended. Each time she measured the results of her work, she came up with more DNA than she started with; she should have gotten less. Something was wrong. Puzzled by her failure to make the procedure work, she consulted with her coworkers and repeated the procedure over and over again. But each time, she was disappointed to discover that she still obtained more DNA than she had originally introduced. Her coworkers were sympathetic and tried to help, but no solution to the problem could be found. Eventually, the effort was abandoned, and the researcher went on to other things.

For some reason, it did not occur to this researcher that to know how to create DNA is a great deal more useful than knowing how to destroy it— or, for that matter, being able to repeat someone else's laboratory procedure successfully. Some years later, another scientist in a different laboratory successfully developed a method to create DNA. Subsequently, he received a Nobel Prize for his discovery.[1] The first researcher and her former colleagues are still asking themselves how it is that they did not recognize what was really going on when her project repeatedly failed.

I was told this story by a scientist friend after dinner years ago. I asked if it had been published anywhere. He said that it had not been recorded anywhere to his knowledge and that I might use it. And what of the participants, his former colleagues? My friend observed that it had all just been too painful and that they wanted to forget all about it if they could. Such a narrow miss—why didn't they realize what was happening?

In the world of science and technology, sometimes a gift is seen only as a problem—a problem that would be quickly wished away if we could. However, sometimes the most important thing is to be able to recognize a gift for what it is, even though it was not asked for or wanted. It is helpful, sometimes, not to be wholly focused on the narrow interest of the moment—no matter how serious one's task, no matter how large the project, no matter how urgent the deadline. One has to be open to new possibilities, to looking at things in a different way, to being able to see what is available. Sometimes one can be too thorough in following projected lines of logic. We need to learn how to recognize and more fully appreciate the potential of the unexpected and the unwanted. We might ask ourselves whether the things we now see as problems are really opportunities in disguise—unwanted gifts.

SEEING THROUGH THE CLUTTER

The scientist friend who told me the story presented above, a cancer researcher, laments that the requirements of a scientific career seem to be at odds with seeing straight through the clutter—seeing gifts even when unwanted and unexpected. He said that he and his colleagues are so caught up in the grind of conventional scientific research that they do not have time to gain deeper understanding. While he is cautious of openly discussing this problem, deep down he suspects that many of the answers are just sitting out there waiting to be plucked from the existing experiments and stores of knowledge.

My friend acknowledges that he and his associates are compelled to churn out grant proposals, design more studies, and hire additional promising postdoctoral researchers. That is the system. Yet he suspects that no more studies are really needed, at least for a while. He suspects that there is enough information available now to fit the pieces of the puzzle together, if only there were time to sit in the library and quietly think it through. But there is no money for sitting in the library and thinking. So the grant applications are submitted, and more numbers are produced, to be reviewed by peers—leading to more studies and numbers once again. The machine grinds on with more new numbers but little new understanding.

If a person wishes to be really creative, it seems that it is sometimes essential to have time to be able to follow where one's thoughts lead rather than having to succeed in a series of tasks largely defined by one's career, one's competitors, or other outside forces. We can speculate about what might have happened to Einstein's early work without his period of independent study as a school dropout (following his own fancy), his lecture cutting and continued self-directed study during his university years, his two years of intermittent unemployment (with contrasting growth in intellectual excitement) after graduation, and then his relatively undemanding patent office job once he did enter the world of conventional work.

We might wonder what would have happened if Einstein had become immediately involved in the teaching, administrative, and social demands of a conventionally successful career. Early success might have resulted in a deeper failure. As he himself observed, in such a path there is a strong tendency to do research that is comparatively superficial and predictable—little steps that do not risk serious failure or threaten existing beliefs—modest research programs that can be relied upon to produce publishable results and supportive, unthreatened mentors. If one wants to be really creative, Einstein observed (as we saw in chapter 15), one needs to be able to look past the specialist knowledge to see the larger whole, avoiding getting tangled in "the more or less dispensable erudition."

Diverse Means Widely Available

These days, it is widely believed that most of science and technology development has to be backed by a lot of money. By contrast, we should keep in mind that the first personal computer was largely developed by hobbyists in their garage. But that was already a long time ago; now, many believe that nothing of importance can be done without a large research staff, expensive equipment, and a substantial budget. This may be true of much modern science and technology, but not, perhaps, in every case—and perhaps rarely where really significant changes are involved. A very old example may help to show what possibilities may still be open to us: the work of Wilbur and Orville Wright. Coming from the pantheon of American technological heroes, this example illustrates what cheap tools, common sense, basic capabilities, and determined effort may accomplish where experts with conventional research programs or gentlemen enthusiasts had failed repeatedly.

Periodically—as true then as it is now—there seems to come a time when all the tools and techniques become available cheaply enough for relatively ordinary people to draw together what they need in some novel way. Once these circumstances converge—once diverse means are widely available to the population at large—then the major additional needed ingredients are mainly vision and effort, along with a willingness to risk many small failures in order to inch forward into unknown territory. There is an aspect of evolutionary selection here as well. It matters most of all, perhaps, that at a particular time and place all the resources to get a job done are widely available. Many will fail, but a few will succeed. With cheap tools and widely distributed capabilities, the whole enterprise moves ahead at a much more rapid rate.

The Wright brothers had only their bicycle business and such tools, skills, and income as the business made available to them. Yet with these modest resources, they took what was essentially an off-season hobby and turned it into a dramatically successful achievement, one that had previously eluded all the efforts of professionals. Neither Wilbur nor Orville ever finished high school, although other members of the family were college educated. Their father was an educated religious leader and administrator, a traveling bishop of the United Brethren in Christ. Their sister eventually attended Oberlin College to earn her teaching credentials. The brothers initially went into business as job printers and publishers of several small local newspapers, but they eventually stumbled into the suddenly popular and modestly profitable bicycle business that started to flourish in the early 1890s. The business involved bicycle sales (with weekly installment payments), rental, and repair in the summer, with cottage industry manufacturing in the winter.

The two brothers, who were observed to "combine mechanical ability with intelligence in about equal amounts," ran the manufacturing operation easily. An old school friend who had previously been part of their printing operation performed the final bicycle assembly. Orville operated the enameling oven while Wilbur did the brazing, using a brazier that they had designed themselves. There seemed to be a relatively aimless quality about the young adult years of the two brothers in Dayton. Their printing business was in part a continuation of Orville's summer job in his high school years. Off and on Wilbur had considered going to college. But in high school a sporting injury and a "vaguely defined" heart ailment caused Wilbur to drop this plan, and he stayed at home for several years, partly taking care of his semi-invalid mother until her death in 1889—while his father's work continued to require extensive travel and long absences from home.

Wilbur's slow recovery and apparent lack of drive during these years exasperated his brother Reuchlin, who had married and moved to Kansas City. He could not understand how it was that Wilbur stayed at home for so long just reading and taking care of his ailing mother. Reuchlin wrote their sister Katherine, "What does Will do? . . . He ought to do something. Is he still cook and chambermaid?"[2] This is not exactly what one would expect of the senior member of the two pioneers of the dashing and daring field of early aviation. (It is not unusual, however, for highly creative people to have "fallow" periods for thought, research, and reflection—to allow their ideas to take shape. These periods, or alternating cycles of productivity and comparative inactivity, are often noted in biographies of creative people.)

CHEAP TOOLS READILY AT HAND

Without formal training or special resources, the self-taught Wrights seemed to have all they needed. Each necessary task was dealt with in a straightforward way with the resources commonly available and readily at hand. They had access to cheap tools and basic information. When they needed a windy site for their earliest glider experiments, they simply wrote to the US Weather Service. Their early trials were essentially large-scale kite experiments, but these yielded important information on lift, more efficient wing shapes, and novel devices for control in all three dimensions. Unlike many other early experimenters in aircraft design, they knew that they needed to teach themselves how to control the aircraft first. Consequently, well before employing an engine, they took many short, gliding practice flights down a large sand dune to develop their own reflexes—to give themselves some time to learn by trial and error the "feel" of the machine and the controls.

They found that the tables on wing shape and lift that had been published by a German professor were wrong, so they devised their own—partly from their own wind tunnel, itself made from simple parts, to their own design. Indeed, in time they came to distrust any data they had not tested themselves. They could find no automobile company willing to make the light and powerful engine they required, so they made their own engine to their own design, largely in their own shop, with the help of the machinist who worked in their bicycle business. At the time, it was falsely believed that air propellers were similar to water propellers. Consequently, the brothers found that they had to devise their own theory as well as develop their own design for the propellers needed to drive their machine. And throughout their flying experiments, they took photographs of everything they did so they could access their progress and make a permanent record of their achievements.

Those who are familiar with the way such a project would be staffed today—with teams of highly paid experts in dozens of fields—can easily see how rapidly budgets and development schedules for such an undertaking would balloon. Of course, a very great deal more is known now in many fields than was known then. But at the edge of the new, the situation—the same now as it was then—may not be as different as it might appear at first. Small, determined groups with fresh ideas (although less well educated and less experienced) may still move more rapidly and effectively. Sometimes it is good not to be an expert, not to know too much. Sometimes it is far more important to have a vision and to be willing to learn by taking risks and making mistakes that experts would not make. Sometimes it is good not to know beforehand all the reasons why it will never work and why it will never sell.

In the time of the Wrights, the head of the Smithsonian Institution, Samuel Pierpont Langley, a respected engineer and scientist, obtained a sizable grant of fifty thousand dollars from the War Department to develop a heavier-than-air aircraft, but his experiments sank in the Potomac, with "howls of derision from all quarters." Wilbur and Orville financed their experiments entirely out of their own modest personal resources, at a small fraction of the cost of the fully funded professional effort. According to one biographer, "For years the Wrights had been strict with their money. Their total out-of-pocket expenditures, right up to the point where they made their flights on December 17, 1903, had not quite reached one thousand dollars." Of course, the expenditures of Langley and the Wrights are not strictly comparable, since there is presumably no allowance for Wilbur's and Orville's own time, nor for that of their bicycle shop machinist, nor for the assistance they received from Kitty Hawk area locals. In any case, the difference is a dramatic indication of what can happen when fully qualified people embark on a project with ample resources. One Wright biographer pointed out, "As administrator of the country's most prestigious scientific institution, Langley was in an enviable position when it came to producing such an aircraft, but in some ways the wealth of manpower and resources at his disposal was a hindrance."[3]

THE LONE HACKERS OF 1903

We might ask, then, how the efforts of the Wrights, so long ago, could be relevant to the realities of our times. To answer the question, we need now to consider if—at this stage in the development of computer graphics and data visualization—we might not be at the beginning of a period in some important ways comparable to the time of the Wrights. In their own time, the Wrights had in their hands all the mechanical tools and skills needed for their novel task. Today, as more and more powerful electronic tools and skills have become increasingly available in the hands of ordinary people, one wonders what determined individuals and small groups may be able to accomplish where the great companies and laboratories have so far failed—or what discoveries they may make that would never occur to fully qualified employees in well-funded research laboratories. In the time of the Wrights, sophisticated mechanical capabilities had become widely available at modest cost to comparatively ordinary people—without special education or facilities. Today, extraordinarily sophisticated electronic capabilities have already become widely available (since many of us have computers with power similar to the early supercomputers) at modest cost to these same comparatively ordinary people.

On reflection, perhaps it is only a matter of time before we should expect modern-day electronic Wrights to devise some truly new things—perhaps things as yet unimagined by the professionals, or in areas where highly trained teams from "big science" and "big technology" have repeatedly failed before. They may not have the expensive equipment or the big budgets, but if they are really innovative, they may find a totally new way of doing the job. Sometimes, perhaps even now, what is needed is not so much big budgets but cheap tools and a big vision. Perhaps then we can be more open to new possibilities, to looking at things in a different way, and to being able to see what we have been given—and we can better appreciate the potential of the unexpected and the unwanted.[4]

Notes

1. In October 1993 the Nobel Prize in chemistry was awarded to Kary B. Mullis, of La Jolla, California, for "his invention of the polymerase chain reaction (PCR) method." With his method, it is "for example possible using simple equipment to multiply a given DNA segment from a complicated genetic material millions of times in a few hours, which is of very great significance for biochemical and genetic research"; see "Press Release: The 1993 Nobel Prize in Chemistry," Royal Swedish Academy of Sciences, October 13, 1993, p. 1.

2. Information on the Wright brothers in this section is taken from Fred Howard, *Wilbur and Orville: A Biography of the Wright Brothers* (New York: Ballantine, 1987); quoted material from pp. 7–9.

3. Harry Combs, with Martin Caidin, *Kill Devil Hill: Discovering the Secret of the Wright Brothers* (Englewood, CO: TernStyle, 1986), pp. 320–21; Howard, *Wilbur and Orville*, p. 125.

4. This chapter is adapted from a column that had incorporated material from the 1997 edition of my book *In the Mind's Eye* (Amherst, NY: Prometheus Books, 1997), pp. 199–202; and previously, pp. 185–86.

CHAPTER

18 JAMES CLERK MAXWELL, WORKING IN WET CLAY

If you can visualize the shape, you can understand the system.
—James Gleick, *Chaos: Making a New Science*

J ames Clerk Maxwell, acknowledged by many to be the most important physicist of the nineteenth century, knew how to be a supremely competent scientist and mathematician. Yet, when necessary, he could draw on the talents of the artist and sculptor—for he knew that if he could find a way to "visualize the shape," then he could begin to really understand the vast complexity of the system. Accordingly, when he wanted to understand some deep and complex pattern in nature, he often dismissed conventional analysis and notation. Instead, he used the visual and spatial tools of the craftsman, mechanic, and artist, modeling clay with wet hands to mold a tangible sculpture of the three-dimensional image in his mind's eye.

FIRST COLOR PHOTOGRAPH

The fame of "Maxwell's equations" has meant that the name of James Clerk Maxwell is familiar to most persons having any form of scientific training. However, the full extent of his work and accomplishment is relatively little known. Those interested in computer graphics may be especially interested to note that as early as 1860, Maxwell had begun the scientific study of color—and had developed the first color photograph. In addition to developing the electrodynamic theory of light, he also began the systematic application of statistical methods in physics—including original methods to explain the nature of Saturn's rings.

In 1868, Maxwell wrote the first important paper on cybernetic and control theory, so central to computer technology—through an analysis of the common spinning-ball governor. Along with important contributions to the geometry of optics, he also developed certain mathematical terms and coined terminology related to the study of vectors (familiar to many as the arrows used to represent the direction and magnitude of a force).[1]

Maxwell's accomplishments were indeed remarkable. But it is also apparent that he had a number of the distinctive mix of traits often seen in very strong visual thinkers. He seemed to have an unusual capacity to think in two ways: both visually and mathematically—and many of his considerable accomplishments may be traced to these dual abilities. However, like many strong visual thinkers, Maxwell also had language difficulties.

On the one hand, he had no difficulty with reading or writing—and was generally an excellent student for most of his life. However, on the other hand, he often had difficulty collecting his thoughts in order to answer on demand and under pressure an unexpected question. In addition, he stuttered severely, and this continuing difficulty adversely affected his career as lecturer and professor.

As a child, he had shown a great love of drawing and had near relatives who were artists. He had a hearty and whimsical sense of humor. And as an adult, he seemed to retain a childlike curiosity about everything, often seeing similarities and making connections among the most diverse and apparently unrelated things.

GIBBS'S "GRAPHICAL METHOD"

An important illustration of the operation of Maxwell's visual-spatial thinking is his early appreciation of the work of American physicist J. Willard Gibbs, one of the major figures in the development of the study of thermodynamics. In the 1870s, Gibbs published a series of papers addressing the complex thermodynamic behavior of water and other fluids—using an unusual and innovative "graphical method," as he called it.

This method involved a three-dimensional mental model comparable to what we would now call a "surface plot"—a kind of three-dimensional graph that shows numerous points covering an undulating surface with rises and depressions like small mountains, hills, and valleys. As any point (representing a particular temperature, volume, or pressure, etc.) moves over the surface plot, the conditions change in certain predictable ways, giving a deep understanding of the behavior of the complex system—based on being able to visualize the complex shape.

Gibbs wrote about his new method and described it mathematically, yet he made no effort to make a diagram of what was, apparently, clearly seen in his own mind's eye. The new method and the difficulty in having to visualize such complex material resulted in little attention from Gibbs's scientific colleagues, especially in the United States.

MAXWELL'S SCULPTURED "FANCY SURFACE"

Yet when Maxwell read Gibbs's papers in Britain, he immediately saw the power and the potential of the new graphical method. Indeed, so great was his interest that "he spent an entire winter" constructing a three-dimensional clay model of a surface using Gibbs's data.[2] As Maxwell explained in a letter to a scientist friend, "I have just finished a clay model of a fancy surface showing the solid, liquid, and gaseous states, and the continuity of the liquid and gaseous states."[3]

What Maxwell had made, then, was a kind of sculpture (looking like a mountain with two nearby hills)—patiently calculating the approximate position of each point in three-dimensional space and then adjusting the shape of the clay surface to correspond to the array of points in different positions (just as a sculptor or stonecutter would check his own work with a series of caliper measurements from an original model).

Maxwell sent a plaster of Paris cast of the clay model to Gibbs and kept two more in his own laboratory at Cambridge University. Gibbs's copy is still on display in a glass case outside the Yale University Physics Department—while Maxwell's own copy remains on display at the new Cavendish Laboratory just outside Cambridge in England. Sculpture is a reproducible and durable medium, even in plaster.

What is most important for our discussion, then, is the way the highly visually oriented Maxwell immediately seized upon Gibbs's unusual but strikingly apt visual-spatial approach. Because Maxwell by this time was famous among scientists while Gibbs was entirely unknown, Maxwell was eventually able to move a whole generation of American and European scientists to appreciate the true value of Gibbs's novel approach.

However, whereas Gibbs's method and approach in mathematical form came to be fully appreciated over time, the visual and spatial model on which the method was based has been almost completely ignored for more than a century—until very recent times. That is, for more than a century, students of nearly every technical occupation have memorized Gibbs's equations, yet the visualizations on which these equations are based received virtually no attention at all during this period.

REDISCOVERING THE GEOMETRY OF THERMODYNAMICS

As explained by University of Iowa chemistry professor Kenneth R. Jolls, "For those who could not follow the elaborate verbal manipulation of lines and planes in space that permeates [Gibbs's] writings, the physical meaning and the artistic beauty of these brilliant analogies were lost. Indeed, the interesting connections between thermodynamics and geometry, which were the essence of Gibbs's theoretical development, have all but vanished from the literature."

Recently, however, with the development of computer-generated 3-D graphics, all this has begun to change. Professor Jolls and his graduate student Daniel Coy developed a means of doing what Maxwell had done—but this time rapidly on a powerful graphics computer rather than over several months in modeling clay and plaster. According to Jolls, "there can be no doubt in the mind of any serious thermodynamicist" that images like those being produced on their computer screen "were vividly in Gibbs's mind as he wrote his famous trilogy [of papers] in the mid-1870s."[4]

So it is that the visually thinking Maxwell immediately perceived the value of a visual-spatial approach, which he could model in clay—but which we can now see modeled on a computer screen or in a virtual reality display. The technology and the speed are enormously different, but the concept and the visual image in the mind's eye are exactly the same.

ANTICIPATING PIXAR AND THE NSF

The reference to the art of sculpture is especially apt in the case of Maxwell. As I have noted in previous columns, strong family connections can often be observed between those with some form of dyslexia or learning disability and strong talents in the visual or performing arts. Also, it is commonly observed that many inventors have been artists or closely related to artists.

This connection is of particular interest to C. W. F. Everitt, one of Maxwell's biographers, as he attempts to gain a better understanding of Maxwell's extraordinary abilities: "The persistence of the artistic gift in a family so practical in outlook is a striking fact, one that must be born in mind in analyzing Maxwell's genius. Each generation threw up clever artists, among whom not the least able was Maxwell's cousin Jemima . . . whose brilliant watercolor paintings of Maxwell's childhood are a perpetual delight to Maxwell scholars."[5]

It is of perhaps no small import that the display case at the new Cavendish Laboratory outside Cambridge, which holds Maxwell's plaster model, also holds two rotating drums with slits designed by Maxwell with images painted in watercolor with his own hand. One animation portrays a man and woman dancing; the other animation visualizes two smoke rings interacting. Accordingly, we can easily say that in one glass case we have concrete evidence that Maxwell anticipated, with all else, the basics of the animated cartoon—brought to full, computerized, 3-D feature length a short time ago by Pixar and Disney—as well as the first scientific visualization, long promoted at the supercomputer centers and elsewhere by the National Science Foundation.

MAXWELL "IN A PROP"

Maxwell's early biographers, Lewis Campbell and William Garnett (1882), describe the period from 1847 to 1850, when Maxwell was between the ages of sixteen and nineteen:

> When he entered the University of Edinburgh, James Clerk Maxwell still occasioned some concern to the more conventional amongst his friends by the originality and simplicity of his ways. His replies in ordinary conversation were indirect and enigmatical, often uttered with hesitation and in a monotonous key. . . .
>
> When at table he often seemed abstracted from what was going on, being absorbed in observing the effects of refracted light in the finger-glasses, or in trying some experiment with his eyes—seeing round a corner, making invisible stereoscopes, and the like. Miss Cay [his aunt, the sister of his late mother] used to call attention by crying, "Jamsie, you're in a prop" [i.e., a mathematical proposition]. He never tasted wine; and he spoke to gentle and simple in exactly the same tone. On the other hand, his teachers . . . had formed the highest opinion of his intellectual originality and force.[6]

The brief description of Maxwell at the dinner table is particularly telling in establishing his relative disinterest in conventional table conversation and his persistent preoccupation with observing the operation of light and other natural phenomena, whatever the situation.

It is also notable that all these examples are of a visual nature ("trying some experiment with his eyes—seeing round a corner, making invisible stereoscopes"). These examples lend themselves to building mental models of optical interaction and spatial relationships, which are, in turn, closely related to the mathematics of area, field, line, and force.

Maxwell relied heavily upon visual, mechanical, and geometric approaches in his mathematical and scientific work. As Everitt observes, "Maxwell's starting point in mathematics was Euclidean geometry. Euclid is now so out of fashion that few people know the excitement of his intellectual rigor. . . . With Maxwell the love of geometry stayed. . . . The love of geometry also helped interest Maxwell in Faraday's ideas about lines of force."[7]

The common thread throughout the great variety of Maxwell's accomplishments is the interplay of force and substance in a largely visual-spatial arena. The visual-spatial dominated his work. However, from the stories of his daily life we might also infer that he was thinking in geometric terms much of the time, wherever he was and whatever he was doing.

SHIFTING PERSPECTIVES

Maxwell's writing and research show an unusual flexibility of mind, which seems to be characteristic of some strong visual thinkers. Maxwell could move from one structure to another quite different structure with relative ease, retaining underlying similarities of approach. Everitt states, "Maxwell . . . was continually changing his outlook. His five leading papers on electromagnetic theory written between 1855 and 1868 each presented a complete view of the subject, and each viewed it from a different angle. It is this variety that makes Maxwell's writings, in [physicist James] Jeans's words, a kind of enchanted fairyland: one never knows what to expect next."[8]

Maxwell was a professional scientist, but he was able to see well beyond the conventional science of his day. He was as fully at home in the intuitive and visual world as he was with the world of the "professed mathematicians." He knew mathematics but did not think in the same way as the conventional mathematicians of his time. He knew their ways but was not restricted by them.

He approached physical phenomena with complex mechanical models, yet when he was finished, all such analogies were made impossible (at least for a time). The consequences of his work were so extensive and profound that they set the research agenda for the next half-century; yet during his lifetime, he never received the recognition given his contemporaries of lesser stature.

Maxwell was well educated, but his career was only modestly successful. His speech difficulties limited his professional advancement throughout his life. Although he was eventually appointed head of the new Cavendish Laboratory at Cambridge University, it was only after two other preferred candidates had declined the position.

Unfortunately, he died too young to elaborate his work fully or to gain full recognition for his accomplishments. Yet in the physical sciences his work came to be acknowledged as the most important product of the entire nineteenth century. Maxwell was never able to lecture well, but he taught generations—sometimes because he was willing both to renounce troublesome words and notation and to attempt to visualize complex patterns in nature by molding wet clay with bare hands.[9]

NOTES

    1.   C. W. F. Everitt, "Maxwell's Scientific Creativity," in *Springs of Scientific Creativity*, ed. Rutherford Aris et al. (Minneapolis: University of Minnesota Press, 1983), p. 74.

2.   Kenneth R. Jolls and Daniel C. Coy, "Art of the Thermodynamics," in *IRIS Universe*, no. 12 (1990): 35.

3.   Maxwell, letter to Thomas Andrews, November 1874, quoted in ibid., p. 35.

4.   Jolls and Coy, "Art of the Thermodynamics," pp. 31–35.

5.   Everitt, "Maxwell's Scientific Creativity," p. 79.

6.   Lewis Campbell and William Garnett, *The Life of James Clerk Maxwell* (London: Macmillan, 1882; reprint, New York: Johnson Reprint, 1969), pp. 105–106.

7.   Everitt, "Maxwell's Scientific Creativity," p. 121.

8.   Ibid., p. 120.

9.   Parts of this chapter have appeared previously in different form in my book *In the Mind's Eye* (Amherst, NY: Prometheus Books, 1991 and 1997).

CHAPTER

19   DIGITAL ARTIST AS HERO

Artists Rescue National Economy!

With . . . petroleum-rich . . . countries now bankrupt and unable to purchase more US weaponry, our leading export has evaporated. The number two export, media, has stepped in to save the day with new developments in interactive television, networked games, educational media, and home shopping services. Budding artists in elementary school are being aggressively recruited by industry-funded media arts colleges and universities who hope to mold them into the media design geniuses of tomorrow. For the first time since the Renaissance, parents are happy to hear their children announce, "I want to be an artist when I grow up."

—From an imaginary newspaper story by Jane Veeder

J ane Veeder, of San Francisco State University, has underscored the radical changes the worlds of art and computer graphics have gone through over the years with her imaginary newspaper article "Artists Rescue National Economy!"[1] Indeed, this fabricated story seems especially prophetic, as it was first used in a talk she gave in 1991. As she observed during a SIGGRAPH conference panel in 1997, "We are almost there."[2] With a sudden explosion in market demand and some remarkably high salaries at the time of her comment, digital artists and animators became a markedly valued resource—virtually overnight, it seemed. Yet this trend, even though relatively short-lived, may have had wider implications than was first apparent. Indeed, it is possible that this renewed interest in the artist may be the initial phase in a longer-term, genuine growth in appreciation by the wider society of the power of the image.

BACK TO MORE BASIC BASICS

Just as our media are full of stories of redoubled efforts in verbal literacy and basic academic skills, we may be seeing the slim beginnings of the first broad reconsideration of the significance of visual literacy and the reassessment of a set of nonverbal skills that are far more basic than the academic and clerical skills that normally receive the focus of attention. If, as I have argued previously, we are really beginning to move slowly from a world of words to a world of images, then it is indeed useful to briefly catch the public attention with the specter of shortage and the gloss of high demand. However, it is especially useful that this flash of brief public attention may also be of help in allowing us to circle back as a culture—to reassess the value of core fundamental skills such as seeing and observing—and to reconsider the emerging and important role of the arts in all education, and at all levels.

Well-intended but misguided efforts toward educational reform place too much emphasis on, as I have mentioned in previous chapters, what are really the skills of a medieval clerk: reading, writing, counting, and memorizing texts. In contrast, it seems that what we should now be focusing on are the skills that will be important in the lives of the children of today—not the skills that were important for our grandparents. And these are likely to be the skills of a Renaissance visual thinker like Leonardo da Vinci, using new visualization technologies to understand patterns in the world largely using the rapid and integrative visual-spatial intelligence—perhaps learning in the near future, as a culture, to employ the other side of our brain, after centuries of relative disuse.

LEARNING HOW TO SEE

Speaking on the same panel as Jane Veeder, Ed Catmull, one of the two founders of Pixar, noted that there are several widely held misconceptions about the education of digital artists. At Pixar, they receive thousands of reels showing student work, yet most of these reels are rejected after ten seconds. Catmull observed that the first misconception is that "computers offer a shortcut to becoming an artist." Many believe that if you learn to use an animation program, "you are, voila, an animator with exciting job prospects in a rapidly growing industry." This is simply "wrong!" As an old song goes, cowboy clothes do not make a cowboy—similarly, animation software cannot make an animator. Rather, in Catmull's view, the aspiring digital artist needs the solid traditional curriculum of the artist. "In fact, what is needed is to take a lot of drawing classes, figure drawing classes, composition classes—in fact, the basic classes that are offered in art school—and not skip past them."

Catmull notes that "most people think that they can't draw—and they are probably right." However, he notes that it is also true that "most people think that they can't learn to draw—and in that they are profoundly wrong." There is a great misconception, Catmull observes, about the ability to draw, indeed, about the larger nature of art. It is not generally understood, but "learning to draw is important because it develops observational skills," and these kinds of skills are "extremely important in computer graphics." "It is ironical that we call ourselves a visual culture," he notes, because when "funding is cut in schools, art is the first thing to go." There is an important distinction that needs to be more widely understood: "Art isn't just about becoming an artist. Art is about learning how to see."

There are no real shortcuts. The basic skills of art must be mastered first before someone can become truly creative. "In fact," says Catmull, "all the creative people I know have spent years developing their craft and their skills. And it is upon their craft and skills that they apply their creativity." Accordingly, he declares, "This is true whether they are animators or programmers. If students do not understand this, they will not become good. It is imperative that teachers teach them that this is important to do." He believes that the "same things apply to technical people" as well. They need to "take classes in color and color theory because they will see things that they would not see otherwise." Catmull also noted another misconception apparent in the student reels submitted to Pixar. Students seem to believe, in spite of teacher warnings, that the reel they are putting together is "their magnum opus—so it must be long." His response, once again: "Wrong!" Indeed, what students need to understand is that really good artists learn to work within constraints. Time is a major constraint. Accordingly, Catmull observes that if students "cannot learn to work within constraints, they will not become good artists."

AN EARLY VISION: CREATIVITY

The need for constant attention to learning one's craft was echoed by fellow panelist Robin King, from Sheridan College, in Toronto. He told the story of speaking to Loren Carpenter just after he won the Academy Award for *Tin Toy*. Asking him what he was going to do next, Carpenter replied, "I am going back to school to learn to write a story—because I want to make a motion picture." For King, that reply was instructive. "The lesson being that learning to be an animator is a lifetime occupation. No matter how good you are, it is a craft to be perfected." And for King, the problem for educators is to learn to work with business and industry to design educational systems that will effectively "put people on that road."

But for King, putting students on that road has been the result of many years of work—based on an early vision of how emerging graphic technologies might relate to creativity in many fields. In the 1970s, with training in physics and chemistry and working as head of the applied photography program at Sheridan, King wanted to employ scientific techniques to a study of creativity in the arts. "Science does not recognize creative activity. . . . Yet many great discoveries were made by people in a different state of consciousness: dreams, sudden inspiration—what we call the Aha! experience, nothing to do with intellectual thought. In the arts everyone is supposed to be a little strange, relying on drugs or the muse in order to perform. I wanted to marry the two worlds. If we understand artistic creativity, we can improve on it."[3] It is clear that King and his associates have learned something about how to improve it. With demand for Sheridan's students legendary in the field, it is all the more impressive that the whole process started so early, from what would appear to be a more theoretical than applied perspective. King believes that schools of art and photography need to embrace the new technologies rather than resist them, as teachers and professors were doing in the early days of computer graphics. He felt that "a teaching institution must, by definition, be cutting-edge."

However, like Catmull and others, when it comes to the basics of art, King is a traditionalist: "At Sheridan, the computer animation students are artists first and foremost." One graduate, currently at Industrial Light and Magic, reported, "At Sheridan, there were regular classes in storyboarding and storytelling. The emphasis was not on knowing the software; it was on knowing how to give things life. I constantly watched footage of animals moving and interacting; we spent hours at the zoo. That's why life drawing is a must; you have to understand anatomy and the whole makeup of the body." King is reported to have told one young computer whiz to put away his computer for six months—so he could have time "to read, to watch, to do carving and sketching." King asked the student to "Try to understand the real world. . . . Tell people stories. Learn to think and to observe."

Thus it appears that several of those working at the forefront of the field, even at the new (if short-lived) boom time for the digital artist, still underscore for us the need for thorough training in the traditional basic skills of the artist, especially those of seeing and observing. Perhaps, then, educating the other side of our brain will allow us to see new solutions to new problems—perhaps, in time, even leading the larger society to understand how one-sided our modern culture has become. There is, then, a striking possibility that new digital artists—using new tools to imitate nature once again, with great precision, on many levels, after long avoidance—may find themselves back in the mainstream of a culture that has found good reason to follow their lead once again. Those at the forefront also indicate the new recognition of the importance of creativity in all aspects of life and work. As Robin King has observed, "Creativity, not science, lies at the leading edge of the evolution of the human species; that is the delightful and beautiful paradox."

NOTES

1. Jane Veeder, "Artists Rescue National Economy!" unpublished imaginary newspaper article made available to the author on request.

2. Charles S. Swartz et al., eds., "Educating the Digital Artist for the Entertainment Industry: The Collision of Academia and Business," panel summary, *Computer Graphics*, Proceedings of ACM SIGGRAPH 97, Annual Conference Series 1997, pp. 456–58. Panelists: Edwin E. Catmull (Pixar), Robin King (Sheridan College), Richard Weinberg (University of Southern California), Jane Veeder (San Francisco State University), Charles S. Swartz (UCLA Extension). All panelists' quotations in this chapter are from this source. The SIGGRAPH conference of 1997 represented a high point in the boom in computer graphics, with increased salaries, raids on digital artists from other companies, and concerns about hiring computer graphics professors who were then not available to teach a new supply of students. But, of course, the boom did not last. In time, the story became more complex. Some companies, like Pixar, did very well indeed, while other companies did not so well. Eventually, the computer graphics business began to contract with the rest of the general economy—and by 2003, even the often dazzling SIGGRAPH conference became more modest in scope and size. The August 2004 SIGGRAPH conference reflected a substantial recovery, however.

3. Quoted in Veronica Cusack, "A Mickey Mouse Operation: Now That Animation Studios . . . from Disney to Dream Works, Are Recruiting Sheridan Students by the Dozen, Robin King's Job Is Done. Next Stop, Singapore," *Toronto Life*, August 1996, education section. All King quotes in this chapter are taken from this article.

CHAPTER

20 IS A VISUALIZATION LANGUAGE POSSIBLE?

*Just after the invention of the Phoenician alphabet, words and images . . .
began to take separate routes. It is true that . . . in ancient Egypt, the two
forms were combined. . . . But, by and large, the visual and the verbal
went their separate ways. . . . Each had its own vocabulary . . . , each its
own department in the university. . . . Everybody knew that you were
either a word person (which was most of us) or a picture person (i.e., the
artists). It was all part of a great either/or division that we have relied
upon for millennia.*

—Robert E. Horn, *Visual Language:
Global Communication for the 21st Century*

In his book *Visual Language: Global Communication for the 21st Century,*[1]
Robert E. Horn argues that whether we know it or not, we are all now
involved in building a truly new language, a visual language—one that is
bringing together the pieces that have been mostly separate for so long.
Horn explains that with the tight integration of words and visual elements
we are now building a new global means of communication. And he claims
that this new entity will be a true language with its own special syntax,
semantics, and the other formal structures expected of a true language.

INTO PRACTICE

Horn's book is interesting on several levels—not the least of which is that
he puts into practice what he preaches. For the first four pages, his book is
mostly text, with just three unpretentious illustrations. However, with
pages 5 and 6, the format changes dramatically and becomes the thing he
is talking about. The story of visual language is told with visual language.
From that point on, nearly everything is explained, argued, and illustrated

with images and arrows and webs—with labels, brief explanations, and short paragraphs. In some cases he even reduces his two-page spread in size and adds labels to his labels—to explain what he has done on his pages and why.

In addition, nearly everything is rendered in plain clip art style. He says that he recognizes "that using clip art gives this book a particular look that may be dismissed by some critics, which is often the fate of clip art." However, he wants to show how much can be done by anyone (artistic or not) with simple and easily available images—believing that in time "different styles will soon become available that will make it an increasingly graceful and aesthetically pleasing communications tool."

The approach does promote a tendency to feel we are not getting the full measure of certain ideas and concepts, since many topics are dealt with extreme brevity in one- or two-page segments. Clearly, the approach is highly suitable for some topics and less suitable for others. However, on the whole, the approach does seem to work quite well.

Given the acknowledged limitations of his format, Horn is able to easily carry his subject as he adds a bit of unexpected charm and levity. He puts himself in the picture (literally) every few pages. Mostly, he draws himself into the margin, helping us to understand some point, gesturing with his hands or holding a coffee cup, in his suit and tie, or with his jacket off and sleeves rolled up. Thus Horn succeeds in projecting a persuasive and personable presence—in spite of the comparatively crude form of drawing he employs.

Indeed, Horn uses his visual-language method so successfully throughout his book that it seems a bit obtuse to try to write a review of the book and the method without also resorting to using the method as well. Suffice it to say that seeing his method in use suggests the benefit of future experimentation.

BRIDGES AND SIMULTANEOUS REVOLUTIONS

Although there can be no doubt about the essential usefulness of visual knowledge and visual literacy within the computer graphics community, this awareness is still hardly known in the world at large—especially among educational institutions where the word is still undisputed king. (Indeed, as we can see from ill-fated attempts at reform, most educators, at most levels, are so deeply rooted in this perspective that they can hardly view education in any other way.) Accordingly, it is therefore all the more important that a book like Horn's is available to organize and synthesize a vast amount of material—building bridges in a way that can be understood even by a largely word-oriented culture.

Whether it is recognized or not, Horn argues that the momentum of visual language is now growing widely and rapidly. "Currently, visual language is in a period of tremendous growth all over the world and in all areas of human communication. Such global developments make it difficult to get an accurate perspective on very recent developments. . . . One thing is certain: When a complete history of the language is written, our times are sure to be remembered as a flourishing of creativity in the use of visual language."

Horn also reminds us that "visual language is one of many simultaneous communications revolutions." He explains that the World Wide Web promotes the use of hypertext, which permits many connections and therefore gives writers greater flexibility while also "fragmenting the document from the reader's point of view." With rapid transit between many "context-less destinations," the Web also promotes being "lost in cyberspace." With multimedia we are now able to communicate with almost all the senses "after a long period during which the print-oriented media restricted the focus" of human senses. The use of virtual reality will "add a third dimension of space, further complicating and enriching communication." The fragmentation of specialist information "into smaller, more flexible—but less coherent—chunks creates challenges for coherence and context in new media environments."

WORDS WITH IMAGES

Horn's approach invites us to consider that we are not exactly moving from a world of words to a world of images. Rather, as we really knew, we should more properly see that we are moving to a world of words with images—but this time both will be used in an unfamiliar tight and mutually reinforcing integration.

We may think immediately of the rare individuals who are both artists and writers—such as Leonardo da Vinci or William Blake—where scholarly editors and cost-conscious publishers have produced expensive editions of either the words or the images alone, rarely displaying both together. It has been a marketing problem, a departmental problem, even a technological problem. But all this may change.

EMERGING VISUAL CULTURE

An example of Horn's method is his two-page spread on "What Is Driving the Emergence of Visual Culture?" Here he shows a mountain-rimmed horizon with a rising sun of "visual culture" and many broad arrows in the foreground. Each arrow shows the direction of movement and linkage of a score of driving forces—ranging from the "increasing importance of presentations" and the "rapid globalization of work & organizations" to the "large increase in capacity for scientific visualization" and the "worldwide spread of comic books."

Using his illustration as case in point, Horn describes how each image and set of words works in the overall design. He describes much that is almost painfully obvious. But in so doing he also shows how much we already know about the shared rules of visual language that have gradually and informally built up over time. He also systematizes a wealth of information and artistic convention from many different sources.

In another example, quoting one of Marshall McLuhan's major interpreters, Horn observes that "'the alphabet is a funnel' but visual language unleashes the full power of communication." These words themselves are not as suggestive as seeing the funnels themselves illustrated, one compressing all information into a thin line of words surrounded by empty white space. The other expands and amplifies information in a spreading richness of possibility.

SPEED AND BEST PRACTICE

Throughout, Horn guides us in what we need to know and what we should do. He indicates widely understood conventions and visual metaphors—such as time as an arrow. Citing well-known graphic designer and author Edward R. Tufte and others, he also indicates what we have learned about the best ways to show information: Graphs should not have "clashing optical effects." Charts should be simplified, maximizing data and minimizing unnecessary lines and other elements with a desirable "data to ink ratio." We need to organize information so that we do not try to hold more than "4 to 7 chunks in short-term memory simultaneously."

Horn claims the superiority of integrated visual language and cites a number of studies to support this view. He claims that "basic scientific research is beginning to bear out the thesis of this book—that people find it easier and more effective to communicate by using combinations of words and images."

He cites one study comparing integrated text and diagrams with separated text and diagrams. The results indicated that with the integrated information students got more answers correct. Another study indicated visual-language approaches produced higher scores in less time. In business environments, studies indicate that the use of visual language is more persuasive, promotes faster decision making and broader group consensus, makes a better impression, and shortens meetings.

PATHS TO THE COMPLEX

Those of us who have been enthusiastic about information visualization have anticipated that one of the most important long-term effects would be the ability to really see the big picture. Often it is important to see all parts of a problem together in a simultaneous fashion—rather than just advocating a particular point of view among many, as is often the case. Horn and others dealing with sophisticated graphical and text displays of information see opportunities for resolving truly complex issues.

With global politics or the role of carbon dioxide in global climate change, Robert Holmes reports in *The New Scientist* that some see this approach as a major innovation. Using these techniques they hope "that by developing an argumentation analysis we can help people stop hyperventilating and get clearer on what things they disagree on, and which of those are factual and which are emotional issues." As a discussion evolves, others want to "use the computer to put a map on the wall. Then people would really see and understand the causes and effects and what to do about it."[2]

OPPORTUNITIES MISSED OR GAINED

In the end, it seems clear that Bob Horn has provided us with a major milestone on the road to a sophisticated understanding and use of images and words in tight association. His concept of visual language may help all of us to see that rapid change may be leading us back to a more natural reintegration of our senses and thought processes. His extensive use of clip art makes his book at once unpretentious and accessible. The book does go a long way to help us understand the extent of what we already know—and the large potential and possibilities that are still almost invisible to many.

However, we may wonder whether there may be a deep cultural and economic resistance to the full adoption and recognition of visual language—so that vast potential might remain unrealized, as with television. Some clearly had a vision for educational TV, but it never really happened. Mostly, the medium's potential has been diverted to selling products and, from time to time, political images—although we must acknowledge that TV had much to do with bringing down a hastily constructed wall or two in Eastern Europe. But perhaps the history of television is not so much a failure as it is just one further step to a larger vision of possibility.

As one earlier visionary, quoted by Horn, puts it, "Sight, even though used by all of us so naturally, has not yet produced its civilization. Sight is swift, comprehensive, simultaneously analytic and synthetic. It requires so little energy to function, as it does, at the speed of light, that it permits our minds to receive and hold an infinite number of items of information in a fraction of a second. With sight, infinities are given at once; wealth is its description."[3]

NOTES

1.   Robert E. Horn, *Visual Language: Global Communication for the 21st* Century (Bainbridge Island, WA: MacroVU, 1998).

2.   Robert Holmes, "Beyond Words: Bogged Down by Complex Arguments?" *New Scientist,* July 10, 1999, pp. 32–37.

3.   Caleb Gattegno, *Towards a Visual Culture: Educating through Television* (New York: Onterbridge and Dienstfrey, 1969); quoted in Horn, *Visual Language.*

CHAPTER

21   FOLLOWING THE GIFTS
ART, VISUAL TALENT, AND TROUBLES WITH WORDS

Previous chapters have dealt mostly with visualization and the large and small consequences that we might expect as these technologies and techniques are more widely used by the world at large. To a much lesser extent, these chapters have dealt with my other main interest: the fact that, in many cases, the early development of the human brain seems to gain a range of high visual-spatial talents at the expense of a variety of verbal proficiencies. In this chapter, I will focus mainly on the latter interest.

With the development of the brain, there seems to be a kind of trade-off. As noted previously, researchers have found that if a person demonstrates above-average talent on the visual-spatial side, he often (but not always) experiences some inefficiency with language processing in the left hemisphere of the brain. This inefficiency can take many forms. Sometimes there are persistent problems with spelling, hesitant speech, or unusual difficulty with recalling names or with learning foreign languages. Sometimes the complex of verbal problems will fit the definition of dyslexia or other learning difficulties.[1]

The specifics are of less interest here than the general observation that individuals who are especially talented in visual-spatial modes (e.g., sculptors, painters, architects, engineers, designers, some mathematicians, creative scientists, craftsmen, athletes, photographers, surgeons, and computer-graphic artists) should not be surprised when they (and their close family members) have difficulties with some aspect of a mostly word-dominated educational system—especially in their early years.

I expect this pattern is of special interest to readers involved with computer graphics in some way—because so many are so visually oriented. If one brings up this kind of topic in a group that is visually oriented, one should expect to find many individuals who will recognize something of this pattern in themselves, their coworkers, or family members. Indeed, when I mentioned this pattern very briefly in a panel I had organized on visualization at the SIGGRAPH conference in the summer of 1993, several members of the audience came up afterward and told me of their dyslexia, their great difficulty in early education, or the way their dyslexia seemed to help them with their visual work.

It is also noteworthy that certain occupational groups seem to understand and acknowledge the visual-verbal trade-off, whereas other occupational groups tend to be in a state of massive denial. Many surgeons and engineers seem to understand this pattern. Some neuroscientists familiar with dyslexia lore joke that you should never trust a surgeon who can spell (see chap. 6).

The field of architecture serves as a counterexample. I have been told that the field of architecture is "awash with dyslexics." However, I have also been told by those familiar with the profession that in general this pattern is never discussed, either informally or officially, in schools of architecture. We might wonder how many superior architects are turned away from architectural schools because official thinking does not expect highly talented students to have unusual difficulties with reading, writing, and other verbal and academic tasks. On a visit to give a talk at the Glasgow School of Art in Scotland years ago, I was told by the local dyslexia support person that she hoped that my talks and seminar there would help the architecture lecturers to see their own dyslexic traits in a more positive light—hoping to help them better understand themselves and their students.

A STUDY OF LONDON ART STUDENTS

About the same time as my visit to Glasgow, I was invited to give several talks in England where there is a growing awareness in this pattern, in some ways far more sophisticated than that in the United States. That year a study was done of first-year students in a major art college in London, Central St. Martin's College of Art and Design.

College authorities were concerned with the high levels of dyslexia among incoming students, and they employed a psychologist, Dr. Beverly Steffart, to perform some assessments. According to an early report, "her remarkable findings are that up to three-quarters of the 360 foundation-year students assessed have a form of dyslexia." Steffart's assessments found that "the typical students were intellectually gifted—most of them doing well enough to put them in the top 10 percent of the population. Their visual spatial skills were also at a superior level—but they had many problems with reading, writing and spelling." She observed, "my research so far seems to show that there does seem to be a 'trade-off' between being able to see the world in this wonderfully vivid and three-dimensional way, and an inability to cope with the written word either through reading or writing."[2]

TURNING TOWARD VISUAL GIFTS

Around the world, teachers, psychologists, and neuroscientists studying dyslexia and similar conditions have generally focused on the problems and have sought ways to try to fix these problems. A great deal has been learned in the last couple of decades about the ways that dyslexia is linked to different brain structures and different patterns of "wiring" in the brain. Accordingly, it seems time now to begin focusing on the other half of the condition—on the gifts and talents that are often, but not always, associated with dyslexia and other language difficulties. We should learn to turn toward and embrace the gifts—by beginning to focus on talents as well as difficulties.

In a world of fundamental technological and economic change, we can no longer afford to focus mainly on traditional academic skills that are themselves rapidly becoming less and less important. In an increasingly competitive global economy, compounded with increased machine power and global outsourcing in recent years, it has become clear that we are all less protected by traditional technological and geographic barriers. As barriers decline, opportunities increase—but only for those who see and develop their own special capabilities, their own distinctive advantage. Consequently, it seems that we all will have to seek to work in our areas of greatest strength, whatever those strengths may be. Teachers and professors need to focus on the realities of life for our children and grandchildren, however different these may be from long-standing tradition.

As computer visualization of information gradually but powerfully comes into use in field after field, I believe visual-spatial talents will become more and more highly valued—shifting the perception of high value from words and numbers to the sophisticated understanding of complex images. Time would appear to be on the side of dyslexics and other strong visual thinkers. If these expectations are correct, it is clearly important that proper regard be given to developing areas of visual strength throughout the population (as well as remediating areas of language weakness). Some professionals and teachers argue, however, that such concerns can be a distraction from a proper focus on building up literacy and other basic skills. Indeed, we are in the middle of yet another cycle of national emphasis on verbal literacy and other standard academic basic skills—completely ignoring the future need for sophisticated "visual literacy."

In reply, it can be argued that the varied and distinctive mix of talents often found among visually talented people with language difficulties has long been important to human culture and economy—although they are difficult to assess using traditional, word-dominated, academic methods. Current trends can be expected to restore full value to the natural abilities of many visual thinkers and dyslexics, while semi-intelligent machines take over and devalue many of the clerical skills to which traditional educational systems devote so much time and effort.

DIFFERENT MEASURES OF TALENT

Talent does not develop in linear fashion—nor is major talent always recognized by traditional educational institutions. It should be remembered that Winston Churchill, for example, was never permitted to attend university in Great Britain because he could not learn Latin and Greek. Yet, of course, as is often observed, he was probably one of the most important leaders of the twentieth century, helping to save Western civilization and much of the world from a new Dark Age. Today, with extensive academic preparation required in almost every field (using traditional verbal modes of instruction and testing), it seems quite clear that many highly talented dyslexics and strong visual thinkers with language problems are being excluded by groups and disciplines that would otherwise greatly profit from their vision, energy, enthusiasm, perceptiveness, and originality.

BABY DINOSAURS

An example of what might have easily been lost in one discipline is provided by highly innovative paleontologist John R. (Jack) Horner. Eventually, he came to revolutionize his field, although in the beginning he flunked out of his university six times because of his dyslexia. A report on the impact of Horner's work noted that "his brilliant synthesis of evidence . . . forced paleontologists to revise their ideas about dinosaur behavior, physiology, and evolution."

However, in the beginning, Horner reports he was clearly expected to fail. "Back in the days when I was growing up, nobody knew what dyslexia was. . . . So everybody thought you were lazy or stupid or both. And I didn't think I was, but I wasn't sure. I had a lot of drive, and if somebody told me I was stupid, that usually helped—it really helped me take a lot more risks. For someone that everybody thinks is going to grow up to pump gas, you can take all the risks you want. Because if you fail, it doesn't matter."

Horner's story forces us to reconsider in a deep fashion what is really important in one's work and what is not. Horner proved to have extraordinary difficulties with things that are largely peripheral to the discipline (reading, composition, test taking) but also proved to be unusually gifted in those things that lie at the heart of the discipline (being unusually observant while looking for fossils, being able to interpret the surprising patterns that emerge from fossil evidence, thinking his way beyond his associates, and developing original and persuasive arguments based on the evidence).

Horner never earned an undergraduate degree. "He flunked out of the University of Montana six times, failing just about all his science courses, and never completing his undergraduate work." Although he had difficulty passing his courses, all the time he was really learning, gaining the knowledge and experience needed to revolutionize a field. According to the curator of the museum of vertebrate paleontology at the University of California at Berkeley, "A lot of people have tended to underestimate Jack because he hasn't come through the traditional academic route. But he is, without question, one of the two or three most important people in the world today studying dinosaurs." Horner sees things differently, and he sees things others do not see. For example, he feels that it is of little interest to find the fossil bones of a big adult dinosaur. What he wants to find is many dinosaurs of many sizes, in context, to try to understand the growth and development of the animals and the ways they interacted with each other. Horner is known not only for his different perspectives but also his remarkable ability to see in the field the tiny fossils of baby dinosaurs that other experts cannot find. He has been known to find in fifteen or twenty minutes fossils that other researchers in the field have sought for weeks. Apparently, Horner can build models in his mind of the long-term changes in the landscape, with upthrusts and erosion, so he can guess where the sought-after fossil bones would end up. According to one colleague, "He has a gift. . . . He can see things the rest of us don't see."[3]

Envisioning Solutions

The world of entrepreneurship and business innovation often seems more accommodating to the dyslexic and visual-thinker talent mix than the academic world. Here, the ability to anticipate trends is paramount. Charles Schwab, who started the highly successful discount stock brokerage company of the same name, explained that his struggle with his own dyslexia helped him to develop other abilities: "I've always felt that I have more of an ability to envision, to be able to anticipate where things are going, to conceive a solution to a business problem than people who are more sequential thinkers."

Schwab often refers to his own dyslexia in press interviews. He and his wife have established a foundation concerned with dyslexia and other learning difficulties. They have worked for years to help parents, teachers, children, and others understand and deal with these problems successfully. His coworkers and associates describe him as a big-picture thinker who sees what is needed and leaves the details to others—a combination that seems to be working quite well to keep his company a leader in the industry.[4]

DYSLEXIC VISIONARY

Another visual-thinking dyslexic who has become a major success in business is Craig McCaw, who developed the wireless mobile cellular telephone industry in the earliest days and eventually sold his company to AT&T. It is notable that in a cover article for the business magazine *Fortune*, the cover text refers to McCaw's dyslexia as well as his new business interests: "Craig McCaw's Cosmic Ambition: The Dyslexic Visionary Who Fathered Cellular Looks to Launch an Even Bigger Industry." The article notes that Bill Gates was persuaded to invest over $10 million of his own money in McCaw's new venture because Gates said that "Craig . . . thinks ahead of the pack and understands the communications business and where it's going better than anyone I know."

It is notable that the article explicitly associates McCaw's entrepreneurial talents to his dyslexia: "His thoughts often seem to progress in a nonlinear fashion, which McCaw says stems from [his] dyslexia. . . . He has difficulty absorbing lengthy written documents and usually avoids them. That leaves time for him to do what he prefers anyway, which is to think and to stand back and take in the big picture. . . . McCaw [says] that he is good at seeing circumstances from the other person's point of view, or at least in a different way from most. That helps him do what great entrepreneurs do, which is not to invent but to see the hidden value of an idea already in plain sight, a value that seems obvious as soon as it is given voice. McCaw didn't discover wireless communications—he was merely the first to truly understand what it was worth." Clearly, in his own way, Craig McCaw also sees things in ways that other people do not see.[5]

BEING DIGITAL

The varied talent mix of dyslexics and strong visual thinkers seems to be especially well recognized in the world of computers—where performance is measured by demonstrating systems and where anticipating technological trends is more highly valued than paper credentials and traditional academic skills. Years ago, Nicholas Negroponte, the dyslexic founder of the Media Lab at MIT, was featured on the cover of *Wired* magazine. Playing on the title of Negroponte's book *Being Digital*, the *Wired* article is titled, "Being Nicholas: The Media Lab's Visionary Founder . . . Is the Most Wired Man We Know (and That Is Saying Something)."

In the interview, Negroponte is asked whether he would rather read text on a computer screen or on paper. His answer reveals the matter-of-fact, by-the-way manner many successful dyslexics have come to speak of their learning difficulties. "I don't read long articles period. I don't like to read. I am dyslexic and I find it hard. When people send me long [e-mail] messages, I ignore them. The only print medium I read every day is the front page of the *Wall Street Journal*, which I scan for news of the companies I am interested in. All the rest of my reading is on screens, and often not very good screens, because I travel so much."

Early in 1995, Negroponte was touring the United States promoting *Being Digital*—a compilation of articles he had originally written for *Wired*. Despite the title of his book, remarkably, the first sentence on the first page of the introduction is not about computers at all: "Being dyslexic, I don't like to read." It is important that Negroponte started his book with this oblique but telling observation because it encapsulates for us the paradox that we frequently observe: contrary to what we have been taught to believe, some of the most brilliant and forward-thinking individuals in our culture have had trouble with words—sometimes, a great deal of trouble.[6] It is also worth noting that Negroponte observed on radio talk shows during his book tour that dyslexia is so common at MIT that it is known locally as the "MIT disease."

Unconventional Gifts for Work and Life

As the usefulness of computer data visualization continues to develop, the same visual-thinking abilities that have long served the most brilliant mathematicians and scientists, as well as artists, craftsmen, and mechanics, may increasingly come to serve the most creative and highest-level thinkers in business and other fields. We should expect that these visual thinkers will often see the emerging trends and new developments that their conventionally trained competitors will not see. For some, this extra edge may make all the difference.

When we survey examples of highly successful visual thinkers and dyslexics, we can see that they have many strengths that are often not properly recognized in school or university—but are recognized in work and in life. We need to find ways of seeing and developing the gifts and talents hidden under the difficulties. Successful visual thinkers and dyslexics succeed by following their substantial gifts, not by focusing on their difficulties. We need to find ways to bring traditional education more in line with the changing requirements of work and life. The more we are able to do this, the more likely we will, in the long run, really help dyslexics and strong visual thinkers—as well as the larger society.

NOTES

1. For a more complete discussion, see "Constellations of Traits: Some Neurological Perspectives," chap. 3 in *In the Mind's Eye: Visual Thinkers, Gifted People with Learning Difficulties, Computer Images, and the Ironies of Creativity* (Amherst, NY: Prometheus Books, 1997), pp. 73–100. See also Ellen Winner, *Gifted Children: Myths and Realities* (New York: Basic Books, 1996), pp. 7ff., for discussion of "The Myth of Global Giftedness."

2. "The Art of Being Dyslexic," *Independent*, February 27, 1997, education supplement, p. 1.

3. All quotes on Horner from K. A. MacDonald, "The Iconoclastic Fossil Hunter," *Chronicle of Higher Education*, November 16, 1994; see also West, *In the Mind's Eye*, pp. 265–66.

4. R. Mitchell et al., "The Schwab Revolution," *Business Week*, December 19, 1994; see also West, *In the Mind's Eye*, p. 265; and Betsy Morris, "The Dyslexic CEO," *Fortune*, May 13, 2002, pp. 54–70.

5. *Fortune*, May 26, 1996; see also West, *In the Mind's Eye*, pp. 264–65.

6. T. A. Bass, "Being Nicholas: The Media Lab's Visionary Founder Nicholas Negroponte Is the Most Wired Man We Know (and That Is Saying Something)," *Wired* 3.11, November 1995, pp. 146 ff., 204; see also West, *In the Mind's Eye*, pp. 267–68.

CHAPTER

22   NIKOLA TESLA AND THINKING IN PICTURES

When I get an idea I start at once building it up in my imagination. I change the construction, make improvements and operate the device in my mind. It is absolutely immaterial to me whether I run my turbine in thought or test it in my shop. I even note if it is out of balance. There is no difference whatever; the results were the same. In this way I am able to rapidly develop and perfect a conception without touching anything. When I have gone so far to embody in the invention every possible improvement I can think of and see no fault anywhere, I put into concrete form this final product of my brain. Invariably my device works as I conceived that it should, and the experiment comes out exactly as I planned it. In twenty years there has not been a single exception.

—Nikola Tesla, *My Inventions*

Nikola Tesla is of special interest for this book because of his extraordinarily powerful visual imagination. As he says, his imagination appears to have been so highly developed that he could create complete models of devices in his mind, building them and running them as if they were real. But it is probably of no small consequence that he seems to have experienced, initially, this powerful ability to visualize things not as a useful talent or a wonderful gift but instead as a problem.

"A PECULIAR AFFLICTION"

In his autobiography, Tesla explains, "In my boyhood I suffered from a peculiar affliction due to the appearance of images, often accompanied by strong flashes of light, which marred the sight of real objects and interfered with my thought and action." He makes clear that although these images were powerful in their projection, they were not hallucinations. "They were pictures of things and scenes which I had really seen, never of those I had imagined. When a word was spoken to me the image of the object it designated would present itself vividly to my vision, and sometimes I was quite unable to distinguish whether what I saw was tangible or not. This caused me great discomfort and anxiety. . . . These certainly were not hallucinations . . . for in other respects I was normal and composed."[1]

The son of a Serbian Orthodox priest, Tesla was relatively well educated in literature, science, and mathematics and had a strong inclination toward practical inventiveness. He was a lonely man with many odd habits and strong compulsions. For example, at each meal he would have to calculate the cubic area of each bite of food before eating it. Similarly, he had to finish reading whatever he started, even when it ran into many volumes, whether or not he had lost interest or had decided that he was getting little return for his effort.

In 1884, he immigrated to the United States during a time of great excitement over technical innovations—the telephone, electric lights, and other new inventions. He even worked for Thomas Edison for a while (with extraordinary energy and dedication) when he first arrived in the United States but finally had to leave Edison's company to pursue his own highly innovative but incompatible ideas—inventing, eventually, the alternating-current electric power system, used around the world today.

In order to control his strong visual imagination in his youth, Tesla experimented with various mental exercises and flights of the imagination. In time, it became clear that the "affliction" was the negative side of what turned out to be a special and unusual talent. He continued these exercises "until I was about seventeen, when my thoughts turned seriously to invention. Then I observed to my delight that I could visualize with the greatest facility. I needed no models, drawings, or experiments. I could picture them all as real in my mind. Thus I have been led unconsciously to evolve what I consider a new method of materializing inventive concepts and ideas, which is radically opposite to the purely experimental and is in my opinion ever so much more expeditious and efficient."[2]

Tesla explains that if something is constructed before it is fully developed and worked out in the mind, then the experimenter is often distracted by comparatively unimportant details of apparatus construction. In Tesla's words, "The moment one constructs a device to carry into practice a crude idea, he finds himself unavoidably engrossed with the details and defects of the apparatus. As he goes on improving and reconstructing, his force of concentration diminishes and he loses sight of the great underlying principle. . . ."[3]

POWERS BEYOND BELIEF

Some might question Tesla's claims. He was known to have a tendency to make extravagant statements, especially to eager young reporters. We know also that Tesla was a great showman when demonstrating his new electrical devices to the public—more like a magician than an engineer or scientist. Yet his tricks were based on scientific and engineering knowledge that was not known by others in his field until decades later. In addition, many of his extravagant tales of the technological advances he proposed, such as laser beams, long-distance microwave power transmission, and ocean thermal-electricity generation, are only comparatively recently coming into serious consideration and use.

For many, Tesla's claims were hard to believe (although those who did believe in him, in contrast, accorded him a status almost like that of a cult figure). However, we now have reason for taking Tesla at his word. He does provide some justification for why this should be so: "Why should it be otherwise? Engineering, electrical and mechanical, is positive in results. There is scarcely a subject that cannot be mathematically treated and the effects calculated or the results determined beforehand from the available theoretical and practical data. The carrying out into practice of a crude idea as is being generally done is, I hold, nothing but a waste of energy, money and time."[4]

MODELS IN MIND AND MACHINE

We are now learning that Tesla was, in most respects, to be believed. It is perhaps a sign of our times that what might be seen as a bizarre tale spun by Tesla in a magazine article published in 1919 is now, over eighty years later, exploding into prominence at the center of industry and commerce. Tesla argued that it is a waste of time and money to build a model or prototype of anything until a number of variations have been tested in a powerful visual imagination such as his own. Virtually the same point is being made in recent years by designers, engineers, and managers, but this time they are talking about the machine equivalent of Tesla's remarkable and unusual imagination—that is, what is now known as three-dimensional (3-D) computing.

With 3-D computing, working models of aircraft, automobiles, golf clubs, or nuclear power plants can be (and have been) constructed inside a powerful graphics computer and displayed on a screen. These models can be operated and tested and modified much as Tesla was apparently able to do with his imagination alone. Proponents claim many advantages for the widespread use of 3-D computing: for example, in one early study of the use of 3-D computing in five US and Japanese companies, "The speed and

power of 3-D computing has all but eliminated the requirements to produce physical prototypes and models. This allows management and engineers to economically pursue more creative and sometimes high-risk
design options. NASA/Ames uses [3-D] workstations to simulate a wide
number of options for a Mach 25 aircraft that would have been cost pro-
hibitive using the traditional wind tunnel practices."[5]

Tesla noted the speed and ease with which his mental modeling pro-
ceeded, free of the distractions of building an actual physical prototype.
This is not an unusual observation. Creative designers often lament the
time required to build a physical product of what could be built so quickly
in their mind. Thus it may not be surprising that, in practice, another
important consequence of 3-D computing is a marked decrease in frustra-
tion along with a marked increase in productivity:

> Users of 3-D computing reported increases in individuals' productivity of
> 20 percent to 50 percent. This higher productivity was used to expand the
> scope of individual job functions and to reduce the actual time to com-
> plete a project. The ability to 'handle' the realistic electronic model led to
> improved interaction between the designer and the model, resulting in a
> more intimate and accurate understanding of the model. This also
> resulted in more creativity, less frustration. We consistently observed that
> users had a positive work attitude and they preferred working in a 3-D
> environment as compared to the manual or 2-D environment in which
> they had previously worked.[6]

Such reports make one wonder whether this is just one more step in an
old progression or whether these developments, by now well established in
some areas, can be seen as the beginning of something that is really quite
new. Such changes may make it possible for comparatively ordinary people
to do with ease and speed what before only extraordinary people like Tesla
could do inside their heads. And, as we have noted before, this new direction in development might very well favor those who are much better with
the manipulation of images than the manipulation of codes, words, and
even mathematical symbols.

With Tesla, the power of the visual imagination takes on a whole new
dimension. He was clearly an intensely creative visual thinker. He had
some related problems, such as a curious inability to make drawings, but
these did not appear to affect him adversely. Perhaps his greatest liability
was the fierce independence and lack of social skill that repeatedly caused
him to fall out with his coworkers and benefactors, eventually preventing
him from continuing his work.

Tesla, however, provides us with an example of visual thinking that
illustrates, in a most concrete way, the power and potential of this ability.
What Faraday, Maxwell, and Einstein may have been able to do with

abstract images, imaginary mechanical analogies, or related mathematical formulas, Tesla seems to have been able to do in his mind with almost real mechanical devices and working machinery. Tesla provides us not only with important new insights but also with a standard against which other visual thinkers may be assessed. He also provides us with an example of what, in time, more ordinary people may be able to do with the new tools that are becoming cheaper, more powerful, and easier to use as they become more and more widely available.

THINKING IN PICTURES IN ANOTHER DIMENSION

When I did my research for my book *In the Mind's Eye*, I decided to include Nikola Tesla because of his wonderful descriptions of his own powerful visualization abilities—in spite of the fact that he had no indication of the language-related learning problems I was also interested in. He had many unusual characteristics, but he seemed in most respects entirely unlike most of the other individuals I had included in that book. I suspected there was a significant pattern to Tesla's unusual mixture of traits, but I had no idea what it was.

Then I read Temple Grandin's book *Thinking in Pictures: And Other Reports from My Life with Autism.*[7] Grandin, who is autistic herself, describes the traits typically seen in a form of high-functioning autism known as Asperger syndrome. In one chapter she deals with the possible relationship of giftedness or even genius in relation to the syndrome, describing several important historical figures who would appear to have shared many of the appropriate traits. Although she does not explicitly name Tesla, Grandin had clearly supplied the pattern I had been looking for.[8] Common characteristics of Asperger syndrome include excellent rote memory, a notable lack of social skills and lack of sensitivity to various social cues, strong focus and single-mindedness of thought and action, and eccentric, sometimes compulsive behavior.

In recent years, there has been an explosion of interest in autism and Asperger syndrome. This increase in interest is mainly due to very large increases in the numbers of children (and their parents) being diagnosed. By now it is well known that these increases are often associated with areas of the country where many high-technology industries are located. An article by Steve Silberman for *Wired* magazine, titled "The Geek Syndrome," summarized the situation in 2001:

> At clinics and schools in [Silicon] Valley, the observation that most parents of autistic kids are engineers and programmers who themselves display autistic behavior is not news. And it may not be news to other communi-

ties either. Last January, Microsoft became the first major US corporation to offer its employees insurance benefits to cover the cost of behavioral training for their autistic children. One Bay Area mother [reported] that when she was planning a move to Minnesota with her son, who has Asperger syndrome, she asked the school district there if they could meet her son's needs. "They told me that the northwest quadrant of Rochester, where the IBMers congregate, has a large number of Asperger kids," she recalls. "It was recommended I move to that part of town."[9]

Links with a range of technical occupations have been widely observed. Some call Asperger syndrome "the engineers' disorder." Certain high-tech entrepreneurs and company heads are sometimes linked to the condition as well. Silberman's article in *Wired* notes that "Bill Gates is regularly diagnosed in the press: His single-minded focus on technical minutiae, rocking motions, and flat tone of voice are all suggestive of an adult with some trace of the disorder." A strong visual orientation is not necessarily a major component of autism or Asperger syndrome; however, for both Nikola Tesla and Temple Grandin (and others), visualization and visual thinking are central components of their thought processes.

An April 2004 article in the *New York Times* by Amy Harmon focuses on the rapidly spreading awareness of Asperger syndrome among adults with the condition. Most have long been puzzled by the traits in themselves but did not know until recently that there was a diagnosis and a name. They thought they were alone; but now many are gathering together in support groups. "They all share a defining trait: They are what autism researchers call 'mind blind.' Lacking the ability to read cues like body language to intuit what other people are thinking, they have profound difficulty navigating basic social interactions. The diagnosis is reordering their lives. Some have become newly determined to learn how to compensate. They are filling up scarce classes that teach skills like how close to stand next to someone at a party, or how to tell when people are angry even when they are smiling."

The new and rapidly spreading awareness has many effects in many directions, especially within families, observes Harmon. "This new wave of discovery . . . is also sending ripples through the lives of their families, soothing tension among some married couples, prompting others to call it quits. Parents who saw their adult children as lost causes or black sheep are fumbling for ways to help them, suddenly realizing that they are disabled, not stubborn or lazy."

In addition, Harmon points out that the support groups are having important effects on those affected: "Some are finding solace in support groups where they are meeting others like themselves for the first time. And a growing number are beginning to celebrate their own unique way of seeing the world. They question the superiority of people they call 'neu-rotypicals' . . . and challenge them to adopt a more enlightened, gentle outlook toward social eccentricities."[10]

It is a remarkable fact that Mark Haddon's mystery novel *The Curious Incident of the Dog in the Night-time,*[11] a much-acclaimed bestseller (as evidenced by its demand in bookshops in both the United States and Great Britain in spring 2004), has as narrator a fifteen-year-old boy with Asperger syndrome. Haddon, who had some early work experience with autism and similar conditions, explains that he really chanced upon the flat "voice" of the narrator—who loves mathematics and patterns and describes exactly what he is seeing but never fully understands its social significance. Haddon said that when he chanced upon this voice and realized how useful it would be to himself as writer he thought he had something very special. "When you're writing in that voice, you never try and persuade the reader to feel this or that about something. And once I realized that, I knew that the voice was gold dust."[12]

With Tesla, from Visualization to Asperger

We started out with the story of Nikola Tesla helping us to understand the great power of certain forms of visual imagination and visualization. Then his story served as a bridge to help us understand the possibilities as new computer visualization systems extend some of this visualization power to individuals having conventional brains but unconventionally powerful machines. But beyond this, never in the original plan, we are then led to see that many aspects of Tesla's strange behavior and his remarkable talents can be better understood in the context of the newly identified patterns in autism and Asperger syndrome—both relatively recently recognized conditions. The former was first described and named in the 1940s (by two separate individuals), while the latter did not appear in US diagnostic manuals until the 1990s. Both were thought to be extremely rare, until, just in the last few years, large increases in incidence became evident and demanded attention. Tesla's example has helped us understand a new way of seeing the world—one that would appear to be closely linked to the use of the newest visual technologies. Yet, remarkably, it would appear that there is a new recognition of whole groups of children and adults who would seem to be more or less like Tesla, especially in those parts of the country where the newest technologies, of all kinds, are being created and developed.

Some argue that the numbers of children with "autism spectrum" disorders is increased because these new computer technology centers tend to draw together (and reward highly) large numbers of those having a few or moderate autistic traits. As a consequence, it is said, some of the affected adults then marry each other (in larger numbers than would have happened otherwise), and they have children who may have autistic traits that are much more pronounced than either parent alone (a pattern known as assortative mating).

According to Silberman's article, Dan Geschwind, director of the neurogenetics lab at UCLA, sees some similarities between dyslexia and autism, since both challenge conventional ideas about human intelligence: "Certain kinds of excellence might require not just various modes of thinking, but different kinds of brains. 'Autism gets to fundamental issues of how we view talents and disabilities,' [Geschwind] says. 'The flip side of dyslexia is [having, with reading problems] enhanced abilities in math and architecture. There may be an aspect of this going on with autism and assortative mating in places like Silicon Valley. In the parents, who carry a few of the genes, they're a good thing. In the kids, who carry too many, it's very bad.'"[13]

In a similar vein, Grandin quotes researcher Robin Clark, who observes that a "disorder may occur if a person receives too big a dose of genetic traits which are only beneficial in smaller amounts. For example, a slight tendency to fixate on a single subject can enable a person to focus and accomplish a great deal, whereas a stronger tendency to fixate prevents normal social interaction."[14]

A NEW UNDERSTANDING

As a new awareness comes into public consciousness through various sources such as Grandin's book, Silberman's *Wired* article, or Haddon's novel, it is hoped that all of us will develop a better understanding about why some people behave the way that they do—as well as gain some insight into how they are able to do things the rest of us cannot do. We may become more tolerant or we may come to be more aware of the power of real diversity (and its price). Or, we may be more willing to have certain services available for affected children and adults. Or, some of us may see some of these traits in ourselves or our friends or our family members.

Whatever our reaction, it gradually becomes apparent that we may be on the edge of not one but two major changes. The new visual and other technologies may allow us to use our brains in far more powerful ways than the conventional technologies of words and numbers and books alone. But at the same time, without being fully aware of what we are doing and how we are doing it, we may be helping to create more individuals who are unusually well suited to work within these new worlds. It may be far too early to understand what is going on here or what it signifies. However, there do seem to be some parallels with dyslexia research that might be helpful.

PARADOX AND SOCIAL BENEFIT

Dyslexia was first recognized and described more than a century ago, in the 1890s, some fifty years before autism was described. Like autism, it was initially thought to be extremely rare. Now it is seen as affecting up to 15 to 20 percent of the population, depending on the definitions used, and as having profound effects on education, employment, and life success. There was little scientific or government attention paid to dyslexia until the last decade or two, when both increased greatly, with substantial funding for research. Throughout there has always been a tendency to look at the problems associated with dyslexia, and the focus has been on ways to fix the problems. However, there has always been a very small group of individuals who believed that with dyslexia come certain advantages (sometimes, or even often, but not always).

Among these was the late Harvard neurologist Norman Geschwind (a distant relative of Dan Geschwind). He believed that the same unusual neurological formations that lead to dyslexia could also promote a range of superior abilities. Accordingly, he has provided a discussion that may also may have some relevance to autism spectrum disorders: if the problem condition also has advantages (in some cases), he wondered, then how can we learn to control the condition and not give up the (sometimes considerable) advantages? Geschwind's comments on the possible prevention of dyslexia take on an extra dimension of significance when we consider autism as well: "The dilemma . . . becomes obvious. Not only do many dyslexics carry remarkable talents that benefit their society enormously, but the same talents exist in unusually high frequency among their unaffected relatives. If we could somehow prevent these brain changes, and thus prevent the appearance of dyslexia, might we not find that we have deprived the society of an important and irreplaceable group of individuals endowed with remarkable talents?"

In spite of this, Geschwind was hopeful that the advantages and disadvantages are not necessarily connected. This hope was based on evidence that there are many nondyslexic "individuals among the relatives of dyslexics who are . . . possessed of remarkable spatial talents. . . . We know that especially frequently the sisters of dyslexics are likely to share the talents without the disadvantages of dyslexia. Once we gain intimate information as to the mechanisms of formation of the anomalies that lead to the superior talents, we should be able to retain the advantages while avoiding the disadvantages."[15]

Thus Geschwind hoped to eventually have one without the other. We too may well hope for this (with dyslexia and with autism), but we also need to consider the possibility that it may not always be possible. It may be an essential part of the nature of things that, in a significant number of cases, one cannot have one without the other.[16] Is it possible that our brains have such design constraints? Is it possible that unusually high proficiency in one area will often mean a significant lack of proficiency in another? Or, conversely, is it possible that a deficiency in one area may indicate the likelihood of special abilities in other areas? Or, given a third case, if one has fairly balanced capabilities, is it probable that, in many instances, extraordinary abilities (in either of two incompatible modes) may be precluded? Most recent neurological evidence suggests that this may in fact be so.

Albert Galaburda, an associate of Norman Geschwind, carried out microanatomical studies of the brains of dyslexics. After detailed examination of several cases, Galaburda and his associates described the role of microscopic lesions (areas of damage or diminished growth) and the unusual symmetry of certain formations that had been observed in all the dyslexic brains that they had examined. Galaburda observed that the microscopic lesions may be capable of suppressing the development of some areas, but he suggested a role for them in actually increasing the development of other areas. This research suggests a biological basis for the frequent, paradoxical coexistence of special abilities and disabilities in the same individual: "We all know that these lesions may in fact be capable of reorganizing the brain. But they don't always reorganize the brain to produce dyslexics. I am sure that similar mechanisms are used to reorganize the brain to produce geniuses too, and sometimes both of them occur in the same person."[17]

Norman Geschwind pointed out that the study of dyslexia is filled with paradoxes. If the observations of Geschwind and Galaburda are borne out by further research, then perhaps one of the most striking such paradoxes is that many of those with the greatest abilities can also be expected to have unusual difficulty in areas that are easy for those with average abilities. Similarly, we could find that the study of Asperger syndrome and other autism spectrum disorders may also be filled with paradoxes, the greatest of which may be that when we come to learn more about autism (as with dyslexia), is it possible that we may find that we cannot live entirely without it, at least in some moderate measure? As Dan Geschwind noted above, these studies tend to take us to deeper levels, forcing us (as did Tesla's story) to think in fresh ways about human intelligence and ability.

NOTES

1. Nikola Tesla, *My Inventions: The Autobiography of Nikola Tesla*, ed. Ben Johnston (Williston, VT: Hart Brothers, 1982), pp. 31–32.

2. Ibid., p. 33.

3. Ibid.

4. Ibid.

5. KPMG Peat Marwick, "Competitive Benefits from 3D Computing," 1989, p. 10.

6. Ibid., p. 12.

7. Temple Grandin, *Thinking in Pictures: And Other Reports from My Life with Autism* (New York: Doubleday, 1995). When Grandin was on her book tour promoting the paperback edition of *Thinking in Pictures*, she came to Washington, DC, for a book signing and a lecture to an autism parent group. At the book signing, I asked her to sign the copy of her book that I had just purchased (although I had already read an earlier version). At the same time I presented her with a copy of my book, *In the Mind's Eye*. She took one look at my book and said that she had always wanted to read it. I asked how she knew of it. She said she had seen a review of my book when she was correcting the proofs for *Thinking in Pictures* and found it quite interesting. It was too late to put anything more into her text, but she could add a book to her list of readings—where to my surprise she pointed it out. The next day we had a long telephone conversation about the similarities and differences between her treatment of visual thinking in relation to autism and my treatment of visual thinking in relation to dyslexia. I had always hoped to look more into these connections, but whenever I brought it up to researchers in the field, I was told that the two conditions were too dissimilar. Nothing could be learned, they explained, from looking at them together. For some time I have suspected that they could be wrong. I thought that the high visual aspect in two rather different but overlapping conditions might lead to some insight both unexpected and valuable (perhaps more valuable because unexpected). Perhaps we will see, one way or the other, in the not too distant future whether my hunch is correct.

8. Grandin, *Thinking in Pictures*, pp. 177–88. According to the National Institute of Neurological Disorders and Stroke, "Asperger syndrome (AS), one of the autistic spectrum disorders, is a pervasive developmental disorder characterized by an inability to understand how to interact socially. AS is commonly recognized after the age of 3. People with high-functioning autism are generally distinguished from those with AS because autism is associated with marked early language delay. Other characteristics of AS include clumsy and uncoordinated motor movements, limited interests or unusual preoccupations, repetitive routines or rituals, speech and language peculiarities, and nonverbal communication problems. Generally, children with AS have few facial expressions. Many have excellent rote memory and become intensely interested in one or two subjects (sometimes to the exclusion of other topics). They may talk at length about a favorite subject or repeat a word or phrase many times. Children with AS tend to be self-absorbed, have difficulty making friends, and are preoccupied with their own interests. There is no specific course of treatment or cure for AS. Treatment may include psychotherapy, parent education and training, behavioral modification, social skills training, educational interventions, and medications for specific behavioral symptoms"; see "NINDS Asperger Syndrome Information Page," http://www.ninds.nih.gov/health_and_medical/disorders/asperger_doc.htm (accessed July 8, 2004). Organizations that deal with

Asperger syndrome and other autism-related disorders include the Asperger Syndrome Coalition of the United States, http://www.asc-us.org; the Autism Network International, http://ani.autistics.org; the Autism Society of America, http://www.autism-society.org; Cure Autism Now, http://www.canfoundation.org; and the Learning Disabilities Association of America, www.ldaamerica.org (all accessed July 8, 2004).

9. Steve Silberman, "The Geek Syndrome," *Wired*, December 2001.

10. Amy Harmon, "Answer, but No Cure, for a Social Disorder That Isolates Many," *New York Times*, April 29, 2004.

11. Mark Haddon, *The Curious Incident of the Dog in the Night-time* (London: Vintage, 2003).

12. Mark Haddon, transcript of interview with Martha Woodroof, *Weekend Edition Sunday*, National Public Radio, October 12, 2003, p. 2.

13. Silberman, "The Geek Syndrome."

14. Quoted in Grandin, *Thinking in Pictures*, p. 177. Interest in links between high intelligence and Asperger syndrome (AS) have been popping up in various scientific journals for some time. For example, a brief article in *Science* magazine (vol. 287, February 25, 2000, p. 1395) referred initially to an article in the December 1999 issue of *Neurocase*: "Psychologist Simon Baron-Cohen and colleagues at the University of Cambridge report on a study of three men with AS: a 38-year-old mathematician and two students, a physicist, and a computer scientist. The mathematician, anonymous in the paper but who acknowledged his identity to *Science*, is Richard Borcherds, a recipient of the Fields Medal, math's equivalent of the Nobel Prize (*Science*, 18 August 1998, p. 1265)." Along with a control group, the subjects took tests measuring how well they could read emotions in photographs. They also took tests to measure their understanding of "folk physics." As it turned out, "The subjects did far better than the controls on the physics test, but they were far worse at reading moods. The results 'strongly suggest that social intelligence is independent of other kinds of intelligence, and may therefore have its own unique evolutionary history,' the psychologists write. Other recent research has indicated that autism is more common in families of physicists, engineers, and mathematicians." The article goes on to explain that "Borcherds, now at the University of California at Berkeley, is frank about his condition, although he describes himself as being 'at the fuzzy borderline' of Asperger syndrome. He's not sure the research says anything new. Mathematicians' social ineptness has long been part of the profession's self-deprecating folklore, he observes: 'I seem to have a hell of a lot of colleagues who are not too much unlike me.'"

15. Quotations from Norman Geschwind from Thomas G. West, *In the Mind's Eye* (Amherst, NY: Prometheus Books, 1997), pp. 22–23.

16. In dyslexia, like autism and Asperger syndrome, there may be special talents and abilities, but by no means always. In a personal communication of March 25, 1986, Howard Gardner pointed out, "Dyslexics can be totally ungifted, and nondyslexics may have all the gifts which some dyslexics exhibit."

17. Albert Galaburda, Orton Dyslexia Society tape no. 30, 1984. The Orton Dyslexia Society is now the International Dyslexia Association; see http://www.interdys.org for more.

CHAPTER

23 SEEING THE UNSEEN
CONCLUDING REMARKS

In writing these essays, I had originally meant only to find topics of interest to myself and my readers, following the likely implications of these new technologies, as their growing power and broad use made their imagined potential ever more manifest. I had no idea that this variety of heterogeneous topics would tend to converge on a set of themes and issues that would seemingly continue to grow more and more significant and relevant with each passing year.

For example, with the work of Jerry Uhl and others (see chap. 1), we have seen very briefly how the sophisticated use of graphical computers can effectively teach calculus to a wide range of university students while at the same time completely transforming basic conventions in teaching and learning. I had originally seen Uhl speaking on a short film made for the early Apple Macintosh computer, the only personal computer at the time capable of running the graphics-intensive CALCULUS & *Mathematica* program. I later introduced myself to Uhl after his presentation at a SIG-GRAPH education panel session, and we discussed the role of visualization in teaching and learning mathematics. Subsequently, I learned that the CALCULUS & *Mathematica* program was widely seen as the most radical departure from conventional teaching methods—as well as being the most dependent on computer graphics and interactive visualization techniques. Much later, I learned that the approach of Uhl and his associates had finally come to be seen by many to be the most effective teaching approach—they learned that you should teach visually first, then have the students describe the visual steps and consequences in their own words, then, finally, teach the basic theoretical concepts and the conventional mathematical symbols.

In a way, it seems obvious, really. Take a new powerful tool like the graphical computer and drop it in the middle of a place where it fits; make use of it in a highly intelligent way. It should not be surprising that the effects will reverberate in every direction, transforming a great many of the conventional ways of doing things. And, of course, most important, these students are not just memorizing formulas as before; rather, they actually understand what they are doing and can apply their knowledge many years afterward, something that very rarely happened in the old days, using the old teaching methods. We may wonder how long it will be before other academic disciplines modify old methods to take advantage of these new tools, now available almost everywhere.

Such brief encounters have provided small insights of growing significance—brief observations suitable for brief description in brief columns. In similar fashion, with the work of John Allman (chap. 13), we have seen how a careful investigation of the earliest primates may underscore the essential interdependence of hand, eye, and brain—suggesting that whenever we think of visual design we must also think of hands-on interaction as well. With Chuck Close (chap. 10), we have seen how an artist can work systematically to illuminate the fundamentals of human perception—and, what is more surprising, receive front-page recognition and credit from specialist scientists. With Ed Catmull from Pixar Animation Studios and Robin King from Sheridan College (chap. 19), we have seen how artists, animators, and designers (long disparaged in conventional "basic" education) may sometimes have a far greater worldwide economic impact than those who have followed higher-prestige, conventional educational paths.

With our brief profile of Nikola Tesla (chap. 22), we have seen the use of extremely strong visual abilities that foreshadow our use of the newest and most powerful graphical computers—but we also see evidence of a kind of mind that seems to be growing more and more common in certain areas in recent years. With Leonard Shlain and others (chap. 6), we have seen how an investigation of eighth-century iconoclasts may help us to gain insight into the wars and threats that fill our headlines today. Linking a *Science* essay on infectious disease with a science fiction story (chap. 5), we may gain some understanding of the unexpected power of graphic technologies and those who use them. With "Thinking Like Einstein on the *Hokule'a*" (chap. 2), we have seen that the considerable accomplishments of a traditional culture may not be so different from some of the greatest accomplishments of modern science. Sometimes, if we take the long view, we can see patterns that hold true over long stretches of time. Trends and fashions in technology and thought may come and go, but there are a few overarching trends that seem to endure. Among these, I would submit, are the long-term trends first described in some detail by Norbert Wiener.

CYCLES OF COMPETITION

In his book *Cybernetics*, published over fifty years ago, mathematician Norbert Wiener predicted a sequence of events that we see unfolding today. He also set forth the context in which we might usefully think about technology in education and work in a rapidly changing world economy. According to Wiener, we are seeing a repeating cycle. As briefly mentioned in chapter 1, in the last century, muscle power was taken over by machines, and no one could make a living wage in competition with the new machines. Similarly, in the near future, those with old-fashioned clerical skills or even those with pedestrian academic, managerial, or professional skills may find it increasingly difficult to find buyers for their services in the marketplace. (More recently, of course, this situation is exacerbated, as Internet technologies open the global marketplace to new forms of direct global competition. But the main engine of change moves on relentlessly.)

As noted previously, we know that machines have replaced assembly line workers and bank tellers, and we may not be surprised to see an erosion of opportunities for those with certain manual or clerical skills. However, many of us still may not be ready to adjust our fundamental thinking based on unprecedented changes in many managerial and professional roles. Wiener, one of the fathers of computing and control systems, saw it all coming long ago. Writing from the National Institute of Cardiology in Mexico City in 1947, he explained, "Perhaps I may clarify the historical background of the present situation if I say that the first industrial revolution, the revolution of the 'dark satanic mills,' was the devaluation of the human arm by the competition of machinery." Once this form of competition was in place, there would be "no rate of pay at which a . . . pick-and-shovel laborer can live which [would be] low enough to compete with the work of a steam shovel."

In the next phase, which is currently unfolding all around us, "the modern industrial revolution is similarly bound to devalue the human brain, at least in its simpler and more routine decisions." There are likely to be some exceptions: "Of course, just as the skilled carpenter, the skilled mechanic, the skilled dressmaker have in some degree survived the first industrial revolution, so the skilled scientist and the skilled administrator may survive the second." However, the overall trend is clear: "Taking the second revolution as accomplished, the average human being of mediocre attainments or less has nothing to sell that is worth anyone's money to buy."[1]

We can easily see the prescience of Wiener's somber observations, as machines have increased in power by many orders of magnitude since his day—and as his second revolution moves closer to fulfillment with increasing rapidity. We now know that many of the most basic and routine functions of the copyeditor, bank clerk, and bookkeeper, for example, are being done more rapidly and more cheaply by machines. In similar fashion, we are seeing the beginnings of a less expected trend: computer systems learning to reliably replicate the more routine professional judgments of attorneys, engineers, accountants, architects, physicians, and investment bankers. Referring to the work of economist Paul Krugman, *The Economist* magazine observed some time ago, "Lawyers and accountants . . . could be today's counterparts of early-19th-century weavers, whose incomes soared after the mechanisation of spinning only to crash when the technological revolution [finally] reached their own craft."[2]

In the half-century since Wiener's appraisal, much has come about that was unexpected, but the basic form and direction of this relentless and accelerating trend has remained unchanged. It has become increasingly clear that not only clerical and other "low-level" functions are subject to threat but also, in time, many functions and jobs that formerly were thought to require a high level of intelligence and advanced degrees.

These changes should force us to rethink the fundamentals of education and work. The rules of the game are changing in dramatic and unexpected ways. We will all need to adjust our ideas of talent and intelligence. And, in this world turned upside down, we may expect that many of the students who are at the bottom of the class in the old, word-dominated system will rise (or have already risen) to the top of the class in a new world, where high-value work will involve the insightful observation and manipulation of visual-spatial patterns.

GROUPTHINK WITHOUT IMAGINATION

While I was revising this final chapter in late July 2004, the report of the 9/11 Commission was released. It instantly caught my attention that the commissioners said that among many failures, the lack of imagination was perhaps the most important failure of all. Other broadcast commentators spoke about the problem of "groupthink" in the Central Intelligence Agency (CIA) and elsewhere. Although I had no desire to introduce new material to this book at the last moment, I felt compelled to address this matter, even if in the briefest possible manner.

In the report section titled "Institutionalizing Imagination: The Case of Aircraft as Weapons," the commissioners state: "Imagination is not a gift usually associated with bureaucracies. For example, before Pearl Harbor the U.S. government had excellent intelligence that a Japanese attack was coming. . . . In retrospect, available intercepts pointed to Japanese examination of Hawaii as a possible target. But, another historian observes, 'in the face of a clear warning, alert measures bowed to routine.' It is therefore crucial to find a way of routinizing, even bureaucratizing, the exercise of imagination."[3]

I felt compelled to deal with this matter, however briefly, since I had dealt with very similar themes only three months earlier. I had been asked to give talks at conferences of the British Dyslexia Association at the University of Warwick early in March and the Irish Dyslexia Association in Dublin in April. As always, I had been searching for a new way to catch the attention of conference attendees—boldly making my case that dyslexics, especially dyslexics who were strong visual thinkers, frequently have talents and capabilities that are hidden or misunderstood. After much consideration, I settled upon linking an e-mail I had recently received from a dyslexic, visual-thinking cryptographer, Roy Follendore, with a recent cover article in *Fortune* magazine on the long-term failure of cancer research.

Follendore had told me that he believed that one of the major roles of dyslexics in the workplace was to keep "groupthink" from happening. He said he thought that every research and investigation team should have at least one dyslexic on it. This bold (and improbable) measure could ensure that the group would not get stuck in some eddy of thought and not be able to move forward—or alternatively, would avoid the group moving forward in the wrong direction. Of course, many people, including myself, had long argued along similar lines that visual-thinking dyslexics seem to be remarkably creative and original in their thinking. Indeed, being too original was often part of their problem. However, Follendore's observations stuck in my mind. I found his observations especially interesting because he had already worked on many government-related teams in this way—and because he is notably creative in his own right, having invented and coined the name for the most widely used data encryption system for networking companies and government agencies on the Internet, known as the Virtual Private Network (VPN).[4]

It would appear that the *Fortune* cancer story would have no relevance to our discussion. However, strangely, it is right on target. The article claimed that the striking lack of real progress in cancer research over many years was significantly linked to the "groupthink" of the dominant cancer research culture: "Virtually all [the] experts offered testimony that, when taken together, describes a dysfunctional 'cancer culture'—a groupthink that pushes tens of thousands of physicians and scientists toward the goal of finding the tiniest improvements in treatment rather than genuine breakthroughs; that fosters isolated (and redundant) problem solving instead of cooperation; and rewards academic achievement and publication over all else."

How can so much effort be expended by so many brilliant people and yet so have little real accomplishment? The article quotes an outside observer who seems to have caught the essential nature of the effort: "'It's like a Greek tragedy,' observes Andy Grove, the chairman of Intel and a prostate cancer survivor, who for years has tried to shake this cultural mindset as a member of several cancer advisory groups. 'Everybody plays his individual part to perfection, everybody does what's right by his own life; and the total just doesn't work.'"[5]

It is, of course, extraordinarily bold to suggest that including dyslexic visual thinkers on research teams and investigative bodies might contribute to real solutions for systemic problems and failures within the cancer research establishment as well as the systemic problems and the failures within the US security and intelligence establishment. However, it seems that we have arrived at a time when we clearly need to deeply rethink where we stand in a number of areas. In such times, perhaps we should give some thought to such a bold and improbable approach. The adoption of a surprising approach might help avoid surprises in the future. Could it be that institutionalizing the role of dyslexic visual thinkers in investigative bodies might help to institutionalize the use of imagination? Perhaps institutions with enough imagination to see the potential value of innovative, visual-thinking dyslexics may have enough imagination to anticipate and outwit future threats. If some neurologists are correct, this is the role that strong visual thinkers and dyslexics have played for many thousands of years: having different brains and different perspectives—to allow individuals and groups to see unexpected patterns, to see what is coming over the horizon, to see what others do not see. It is a bold and unconventional suggestion, but in a time of unconventional threat, it may be exactly what is wanted. Time will tell.

REVERSALS IN THINKING AND SEEING

After centuries of comparative continuity, we may be seeing the beginnings of a need for fundamental change. Over time, the prestige of the verbal, academic approach largely overwhelmed the long tradition of multisensory, hands-on learning. Perhaps we will now see a movement back the other way. We might move forward by seeming to move backward. For today's students and workers, many of the basic verbal and clerical skills that have long dominated education at all levels will cease to be as important and valued as they once were. In the new economy, these tasks will be increasingly taken over by semi-intelligent machines, as predicted by Norbert Wiener long ago.

In the new economy and global marketplace, visual-spatial talents, big-picture thinking, pattern recognition, and creative problem solving are expected to become increasingly important. The recognition of this trend will accelerate as greater use is made of data visualization, computer graphics, and interactive, multisensory technologies to understand complex systems and predict formerly unexpected trends.

Many companies and employers will find that in order to survive they will need to adjust to new categories of thought and new rules of practice. In a similar fashion, educators will need to adapt to new realities, as they try to free themselves from an almost universal preoccupation with the instruments of the old technology. Accordingly, as we all struggle to adapt ourselves to deep changes in thinking and working, some strong visual thinkers will doubtless play once again their oft-repeated role. We should expect to find them working creatively at the edge of the new frontier, reading little but learning much, experimenting, innovating, using their imagination, finding ways around groupthink, establishing a new path forward—learning from direct experience, anticipating where things are going, seeing what others do not see—seeing the unseen.

NOTES

1. Norbert Wiener, *Cybernetics*, 2nd ed. (New York: MIT Press, 1961), pp. 27–28.

2. "Seeing Is Believing," *Economist*, August 19, 1995, p. 71.

3. Thomas H. Kean, Lee H. Hamilton, et al., *The 9/11 Commission Report: Final Report of the National Commission on Terrorist Attacks upon the United States*, authorized ed. (New York: W. W. Norton, 2004), p. 344.

4. Follendore had explained in the e-mail and later conversations that conventional encryption systems usually employ complex mathematics. Often these could be cracked, he explained, in time, using mathematical techniques and superfast computers. Prior to VPN, the model of networked cryptography revolved around protecting files as continuous streams of content passed though expensive dedicated telephone links. In contrast, Follendore visualized VPN encryption at the "primitive level" of packets in order to produce simultaneous "virtual networks" within the Internet. Encrypted packets can be made more difficult to crack and are more difficult to track, capture, and assemble for analysis.

After conceiving VPN, Follendore moved on to design cryptographic systems using a chain of visual analogies that control mathematics in ways that could not be understood by means of conventional computer programs. The side effect was that extremely complex relationships of encrypted content can be understood, managed, and presented without needing to decrypt that content. Essentially, instead of a packet-level VPN, Follendore had visualized the potential of a multilevel, content-based VPN.

Trained originally in the visual arts and with a later degree in communications, Follendore backed into the encryption business and claims that he could not have come up with the VPN encryption concept without his dyslexia. His dyslexia allowed him to see the encryption problem in a different way—and come up with a very unusual solution.

5. Clifton Leaf, "Why We Are Losing the War on Cancer [and How to Win It]," *Fortune*, March 22, 2004, p. 80.

ACKNOWLEDGMENTS

I t is customary to acknowledge the assistance of those who have helped with research and have read drafts of a book. However, as it happens, this book has been written bit by bit over a number of years—and is not so much a conventional book project as the tangible result of an education. Accordingly, I think it is appropriate to acknowledge those who have been my guides and teachers (in many large and small ways) over these years. Some may be surprised that they are remembered here for some small piece of information or clarification they have forgotten but I have not.

Of course, I want to thank especially those who have read and commented on the articles, columns, and early drafts of this book. But I want also to thank those who have been kind enough to introduce me to this complex, exciting, and ever-changing world—where visual technologies interact with visual brains—and have been patient enough to help me see what it all might mean and to consider where it all might be taking us.

Initially, I specifically want to express my appreciation to Steven L. Mitchell at Prometheus Books, who, aware of the enduring reader interest in *In the Mind's Eye*, asked me to write another book for them—giving me the opportunity to say, "Well, I've got this series of articles and columns. . . ." I also want to thank Benjamin Keller, who has been persistent and patient in his efforts to impose some order and discipline on a set of informal and heterogeneous short pieces.

I am grateful to Karen Sullivan, who, as guest editor of *Computer Graphics*, first asked for the article that is now chapter 1. And, of course, I want to express my gratitude to Gordon Cameron for persuading me to start the series of columns, for his editing over the years, and for his foreword, written while on vacation. I also want to thank my wife, Margaret, for her suggestions and many shared enthusiasms.

I thank those who invited me to a workshop in the summer of 1990 and an education conference in Spain in April 1991, where I first began to become familiar with the deeper issues and the remarkable openness of the SIGGRAPH community. I am also grateful to those who participated in two small visualization conferences: at the Aspen Institute in Aspen, Colorado (October 1995), and at the National Library of Medicine in Bethesda, Maryland (February 2000). I want to the express my appreciation to colleagues, associates, and friends at the National Library of Medicine and the Krasnow Institute for Advanced Study, especially to Dr. Donald A. B. Lindberg and Dr. James L. Olds for their continued interest and encouragement.

Individuals from many institutions and groups have been helpful over the years. Chief among these are individuals from the National Center for Supercomputing Applications; the Johns Hopkins University Center for Talented Youth; the Electronic Visualization Laboratory of the University of Illinois, Chicago; the Media Center of the University of Oregon at Eugene; the Arts Dyslexia Trust; Green College, Oxford University; the Royal College of Art and the Central St. Martins School of Art and Design—together with many other computer centers and art schools in the United States and Great Britain. I am similarly grateful to many artists and technologists, animators and musicians, scientists and technologists, writers and researchers—their visualizations and animations, exhibitions and demonstrations, lectures and informal comments have helped me over time to see the development of these new technologies in a larger context. Many have helped me directly and indirectly—but, of course, the observations as well as any errors and omissions are my responsibility alone.

Finally, I want to thank especially those members of the SIGGRAPH community who from the very beginning welcomed me as a newcomer, knowing almost nothing. They generously shared their enthusiasm, experience, and knowledge about this varied and ever-changing field. Our informal discussions, e-mail correspondence (some long ago but well remembered), and my early inclusion in seminars and workshops contributed greatly to my deeper appreciation of the broad implications of these new technologies. As I look back over the years, I am amazed at the openness that I feel privileged to have shared, as Gordon Cameron noted, the "wonderfully creative and inclusive synergy . . . that remains a typical and unique characteristic of the SIGGRAPH organization."

Accordingly, I want to express my great appreciation and gratitude to the following individuals: Vincent Argiro, John Andrew Berton, Jim Blinn, Judy Brown, Huguette Chesnais, Donna Cox, Dan Coy, Steve Cunningham, Valerie Delahaye, Janet Dreyer, William Dreyer, Jim Foley, Roy Follendore, Walter Frey, Mark Friedhoff, Patricia Galvis-Assmus, Nahum Gershon, Dan Geschwind, Jeff Gilger, Temple Grandin, Elizabeth Gruben, Fabian Hercules, Laurin Herr, Craig Hickman, Mary Higgins, Ken Jolls, Brandon King, Janet Laylor, Wayne Lytle, Jock MacKinlay, Ted Malloch, Carol Marshall, Bruce McCormick, Mike McGrath, Carol Mills, Barbara Mones-Hattal,

Harold Morowitz, Philip Morris, Ken O'Connell, Scott Owen, Ian Padgett, Sue Parkinson, Tom Pauls, Duane Preble, John Remmer, Harry Renwick, Terence Ryan, Dan Sandin, Gordon Sherman, Ben Shneiderman, Karl Sims, Larry Smarr, Alvy Ray Smith, Ken Smith, Vic Spitzer, Vijay Srinivasan, Beverly Steffert, Karen Sullivan, Clive Summerville, Judy Thomas, Patience Thomson, Jerry Uhl, Andries Van Dam, Willem Velthoven, Catya Von Karolyi, Kim Wallace, Dave Warner, Oliver West, and Mark Whitney.

The quotes about and from Einstein that introduce the book, on page 9, are from the following sources: C. P. Snow, "Albert Einstein, 1879–1955," in *Einstein: A Centenary Volume*, ed. A. P. French (Cambridge, MA: Harvard University Press, 1979), p. 3; Albert Einstein, letter to James Frank, quoted in Ronald W. Clark, *Einstein: The Life and Times* (New York: World, 1971), p. 10; and Albert Einstein, quoted in Jacques Hadamard, *The Psychology of Invention in the Mathematical Field* (1945; reprint, New York: Dover, 1954), pp. 142–43.

COPYRIGHT ACKNOWLEDGMENTS

I am particularly grateful to the Association for Computing Machinery (ACM) and to ACM SIGGRAPH for originally providing a venue in *Computer Graphics* for publication of much of this material and for their copyright policy: "As a contributing author, you retain copyright to your article and ACM will make every effort to refer requests for commercial use directly to you." The following is a listing of chapter numbers and the *Computer Graphics* articles or columns (in the series "Images and Reversals") with which they are partly or wholly associated.

Part 1. Visual Thinking

1. "Forward into the Past: A Revival of Old Visual Talents with Computer Visualization," vol. 29, no. 4 (November 1995): pp. 14–19.
2. "Thinking Like Einstein on the *Hokule'a*—Visual Thinking through Time," vol. 35, no. 3 (August 2001): pp. 15–16.
3. "Visual Thinkers and Nobel Prizes," vol. 35, no. 1 (February 2001): pp. 16–17.
4. "Word Bound: The Power of Seeing," vol. 31, no. 1 (February 1997): pp. 5–6.
5. "When the World Plague Was Stopped by a Digital Artist," vol. 34, no. 4 (November 2000): pp. 11–12.
6. "Smashing Images," vol. 33, no. 3 (August 1999): pp. 16–17.

Part 2. Visual Technologies

7. "Is Visualization No Longer a 'New New Thing'?" vol. 34, no.1 (February 2000): pp. 15–16.

8. "Talking Less, Drawing More," vol. 30, no. 3 (August 1996): pp. 81–82.

9. "Unintended, Unexpected Consequences: SIGGRAPH 96," vol. 30, no. 4 (November 1996): pp. 3–5.

10. "Artist Discoveries and Graphical Histories," vol. 33, no. 4 (November 1999): pp. 12–13.

11. "Transforming Spheres—in Three Parts," vol. 32, no. 4 (November 1998): pp. 14–15.

Part 3. Visual Brains

12. "Make All Things Make Themselves," vol. 33, no. 2 (May 1999): pp. 15–16.

13. "Enormous Eyes and Tiny Grasping Hands," vol. 34, no. 3 (August 2000): pp. 14–15.

14. "Brain Drain: Reconsidering Spatial Ability," vol. 32, no. 3 (August 1998): pp. 13–14.

15. "Knowing What You Don't Need to Know," vol. 32, no. 1 (February 1998): pp. 14–16.

Part 4. Visual People

16. "Feynman Diagrams and Spreading Illusions," vol. 32, no. 2 (May 1998): pp. 12–14.

17. "Missed Opportunities and 'Dispensable Erudition,'" vol. 31, no. 3 (August 1997): pp. 11–13.

18. "James Clerk Maxwell, Working in Wet Clay," vol. 33, no. 1 (February 1999): pp. 15–17.

19. "Digital Artist as Hero," vol. 31, no. 4 (November 1997): pp. 13–14.

20. "Is a Visualization Language Possible?" vol. 34, no. 2 (May 2000): pp. 15–16.

21. "Following the Gifts: Visual Talents and Troubles with Words," vol. 31, no. 2 (May 1997): pp. 8–9.

APPENDIX

For many readers, this book deals with familiar technologies and familiar products of these technologies. For these readers, I hope it will provide useful perspectives and insights. However, for many others I hope that this book will serve as a brief introduction to a family of new technologies that may come, in time, to reshape our world.

It is of the essence of these new technologies that their products cannot be displayed adequately in a book. In a book, we can talk about these new technologies, but we cannot show them in action. Some time ago, I had thought of providing some sort of CD-ROM or DVD. However, soon I saw clearly that the richest source of information and best examples are mainly sitting out there waiting for us on the World Wide Web itself. In addition, there is a large archive of materials on VHS and DVD available from ACM SIGGRAPH.

A short sampling of information on varied topics referred to in these chapters is provided below. In the age of the World Wide Web and especially the search engine Google, it seems quite superfluous to give lengthy descriptions and extensive contact information. Details have been provided for sections of ACM SIGGRAPH, but other organizations will be allowed to speak for themselves through their own Web sites. Sometimes I have provided an address for a specific text article of interest; however, of course, the more general publication root Web address is also contained in the longer specific address. All Web addresses given below assume the prefix http://. Many Web addresses have dropped the secondary prefix www.

ACM SIGGRAPH PUBLICATIONS

To order proceedings, slides, and other materials:

ACM Order Department
P.O. Box 12114
Church Street Station
New York, NY 10257
Tel: + 1-800-342-6626 (credit card orders)
E-mail: acmhelp@acm.org

To order SIGGRAPH video reviews:

SIGGRAPH Video Review
(Same address and telephone as above)
E-mail: svorders@siggraph.org
www.siggraph.org/library/SVR/SVR/html

ACM SIGGRAPH Home Page
www.siggraph.org

For general questions on ACM and/or SIGGRAPH membership:

Member Services
Tel: + 1-212-626-0500
E-mail: acmhelp@acm.org

For information on some eighty professional and student chapters around
the world, see the following Web site:

chapters.siggraph.org

SIGGRAPH Conference for 2005

Los Angeles, CA
July 31–August 4, 2005
Chair, James L. Mohler
E-mail: chair-s2005@siggraph.org

SIGGRAPH Conference History, 1974–2005

www.siggraph.org/conferences/

Sample Web Sites of Interest

ACM Symposium on Virtual Reality Software and Technology (VRST)
www.cs.cityu.edu.hk/~vrst2004/

Animusic: Computer Animated Music
www.animusic.com

Caltech Computer Graphics Group
www.gg.caltech.edu

Computer Graphics World
www.cgw.com

Cornell Theory Center
www.tc.cornell.edu

Electronic Visualization Laboratory
www.evl.uic.edu

Geometry Center, University of Minnesota
www.geom.uiuc.edu

IEEE Symposium on Visual Languages and Human-Centric Computing
vlhcc04.dsi.uniromaI.it/index.php

IEEE Visualization Conference
vis.computer/vis2004/cfp/

International Dyslexia Association
www.interdys.org

Johns Hopkins University Center for Talented Youth
www.cty.jhu.edu

Kid Pix
www.kidpix.com

Krasnow Institute for Advanced Study
krasnow.gmu.edu

Massive Computer Animation Software
www.massivesoftware.com

MIT Media Lab
www.media.mit.edu

MIT Media Lab Europe
www.medialabeurope.org

NASA Scientific Visualization Sites Listing
www.nas.nasa.gov/Groups/VisTech/visWeblets.html

National Center for Supercomputing Applications (NCSA)
www.ncsa.uiuc.edu/~cox/
www.ncsa.uiuc.edu/AboutUs/People/Divisions/divisions4.html
nirl.ncsa.uiuc.edu/virdir/

Pixar Animation Studios
www.pixar.com

San Diego Chapter, SIGGRAPH, Historical Influences, SIG KIDS
san-diego.siggraph.org/sigkids/Influences.html

Silicon Graphics
www.sgi.com

Sims, Karl, artificial life creatures, movies
alife.ccp14.ac.uk/ftp-mirror/alife/zooland/pub/research/ci/Alife/karl-sims/

Softimage
www.softimage.com

VFXWorld: An Animation World Network Publication
"3D Animation Takes Off in Education: Mary Ann Skweres Uncovers the
    Rapid Rise of 3D Animation as a Valuable Teaching Tool in Education"
vfxworld.com/?sa=adv&code=57c5ed8a&atype=articles&id=2165

Wired Magazine
"The Geek Syndrome"
www.wired.com/wired/archive/9.12/aspergers_pr.html

REFERENCES AND READINGS

Agassi, Joseph. *Faraday as a Natural Philosopher*. Chicago: University of Chicago Press, 1971.

Allen, William. "Scientific Visualization: Where Science and Art Merge." *Supercomputing Review* 2, no. 8 (August 1989): 28–30, 32–33.

Allman, John Morgan. *Evolving Brains*. New York: Scientific American Library, 1999.

Apostol, Tom M., Basil Gordon, James F. Blinn, et al. *Project Mathematics! Program Guide and Workbook to Accompany the Videotape on the Theorem of Pythagoras*. Animated computer graphics by James F. Blinn et al. Pasadena: California Institute of Technology, 1988.

Apple Computer. "Macintosh + Mathematica = Infinity." In *The Apple User Group Connection Videotape* Series (13 minutes, 7th item). VHS. Cupertino, CA: Apple Computer, 1989.

Argiro, Vincent. "Seeing in Volume." *Pixel: The Magazine of Scientific Visualization*, July–August 1990, pp. 35–39.

Arieti, Silvano. *Creativity: The Magic Synthesis*. New York: Basic Books, 1976.

Arnheim, Rudolf. *New Essays on the Psychology of Art*. Berkeley and Los Angeles: University of California Press, 1986.

———. *Visual Thinking*. Berkeley and Los Angeles: University of California Press, 1969.

Auletta, Ken. *World War 3.0: Microsoft and Its Enemies*. New York: Random House, 2001.

Baker, Peter. "Defector Says Bin Laden Had Cash, Taliban in His Pocket." *Washington Post*, November 30, 2001, pp. A1–A25.

Bass, T. A. "Being Nicholas: The Media Lab's Visionary Founder Nicholas Negroponte Is the Most Wired Man We Know (and That Is Saying Something)." *Wired* 3.11, November 1995, pp. 146 ff., 204.

Beeson, Curtis, and Kevin Bjorke. "Skin in the 'Dawn' Demo." *Computer Graphics* 38, no. 2 (May 2004): 14–19.

Benbow, Camilla Perrson. "Physiological Correlates of Extreme Intellectual Precocity." *Neuropsychologia* 24, no. 2 (1986): 719–25.

———. "Sex Differences in Mathematical Reading Ability in Intellectually Talented

Preadolescents: Their Nature, Effects, and Possible Causes." *Behavioral and Brain Sciences* 11 (1988): 169–232.

Benbow, C. P., and R. M. Benbow. "Extreme Mathematical Talent: Hormonal Induced Ability?" In *Duality and Unity of the Brain*, edited by D. Ottoson, pp. 147–57. New York: Macmillan, 1987.

Benbow, C. P., and J. C. Stanley. "Sex Differences in Mathematical Ability: Fact or Artifact?" *Science* 210 (1980): 1262–64.

Bogen, J. E., and G. M. Bogen. "The Other Side of the Brain III: The Corpus Callosum and Creativity." *Bulletin of the Los Angeles Neurological Societies* 34 (1969): 191–220.

Bronowski, Jacob. *The Visionary Eye: Essays in the Arts, Literature, and Science.* Selected and edited by Piero E. Ariotti in collaboration with Rita Bronowski. Cambridge, MA: MIT Press, 1978.

Brooks, Frederick P., Jr. *The Mythical Man-Month: Essays on Software Engineering.* Reading, MA: Addison-Wesley, 1995. Twentieth anniversary edition, with four new chapters.

Brown, D., H. Porta, and J. J. Uhl. "CALCULUS & *Mathematica*: A Laboratory Course for Learning by Doing." In *The Laboratory Approach to Teaching Calculus*, edited by L. C. Leinbach, J. R. Hundhausen, A. M. Ostebee, L. J. Senechal, D. B. Small, pp. 99–110. Rev. ed. MAA Notes, vol. 20. Washington, DC: Mathematical Association of America, 1991.

Brown, Judith R., Rae Earnshaw, Mikael Jern, and John Vince. *Visualization: Using Computer Graphics to Explore Data and Present Information.* New York: John Wiley & Sons, 1995.

Bunn, Austin. "Welcome to Planet Pixar." *Wired* 12.06, June 2004, pp. 126–68.

Calder, Nigel. *Timescale: An Atlas of the Fourth Dimension.* New York: Viking, 1983.

Campbell, Lewis, and William Garnett. *The Life of James Clerk Maxwell, with a Selection from His Correspondence and Occasional Writings and a Sketch of His Contributions to Science.* London: Macmillan, 1882; reprint, New York: Johnson Reprint, 1969.

Card, Stuart, Jock MacKinley, and Ben Shneiderman, eds. *Readings in Information Visualization: Using Vision to Think.* San Francisco: Morgan Kaufman, 1999.

Caroe, G. M. *William Henry Bragg, 1892–1942: Man and Scientist.* Cambridge: Cambridge University Press, 1978.

Clark, Kenneth. *Civilisation: A Personal View.* New York: Harper and Row, 1969.

Clark, Ronald W. *Einstein: The Life and Times.* New York: World, 1971.

Combs, Harry, with Martin Caidin. *Kill Devil Hill: Discovering the Secret of the Wright Brothers.* Englewood, CO: TernStyle, 1979, reprint 1986.

Cotswold Wardens and the Ramblers Association. *Country Walks around Blockley.* Gloucester, UK: Gloucestershire County Council, Shire Hall, 1991.

Davis, W., H. Porta, and J. Uhl. *CALCULUS & Mathematica.* Courseware, including software and four texts. Reading, MA: Addison-Wesley, 1994.

"Documents Detail Al Qaeda Training of Foreign Fighters." *Washington Post*, November 22, 2001, p. A35.

Dukes, Helen, and Banesh Hoffmann. *Albert Einstein: The Human Side.* Princeton, NJ: Princeton University Press, 1979.

Einstein, Albert. *Albert Einstein, The Human Side: New Glimpses from His Archives.* Selected and edited by Helen Dukas and Banesh Hoffmann. Princeton, NJ: Princeton University Press, 1979.

——. *Autobiographical Notes.* Translated and edited by Paul Arthur Schilpp (German and English on opposing pages). La Salle and Chicago, IL: Open Court, 1979. Originally published as vol. 7 of *The Library of Living Philosophers* (Evanston, IL), 1949.

——. *The Collected Papers of Albert Einstein.* Vol. 1, *The Early Years: 1879–1902.* Edited by John Stachel. (Documents in German and other original languages, with introduction, commentary, and notes in English.) Princeton, NJ: Princeton University Press, 1987.

——. *The Collected Papers of Albert Einstein.* Vol. 1, *The Early Years: 1879–1902.* English translation by Anna Beck. (Companion volume with English translation of documents only.) Princeton, NJ: Princeton University Press, 1987.

——. *The Collected Papers of Albert Einstein.* Vol. 2, *The Swiss Years: Writings, 1900–1909.* Edited by John Stachel. (Documents in German and other original languages, with introduction, commentary, and notes in English.) Princeton, NJ: Princeton University Press, 1989.

——. *The Collected Papers of Albert Einstein.* Vol. 2, *The Swiss Years: Writings, 1900–1909.* English translation by Anna Beck. (Companion volume with English translation of documents only.) Princeton, NJ: Princeton University Press, 1989.

——. *Einstein: A Centenary Volume.* Edited by A. P. French. Cambridge, MA: Harvard University Press, 1979.

——. "On the Electrodynamics of Moving Bodies." In *Einstein: A Centenary Volume,* edited by A. P. French. Cambridge, MA: Harvard University Press, 1979. Originally published in German in 1905.

——. *Relativity: The Special and the General Theory.* Authorized translation by Robert W. Lawson. New York: Crown, 1961. Originally published in German in 1916.

Everitt, C. W. F. "Maxwell's Scientific Creativity." In *Springs of Scientific Creativity: Essays on Founders of Modern Science,* edited by Rutherford Aris, H. Ted Davis, and Roger H. Stuewer. Minneapolis: University of Minnesota Press, 1983.

Faraday, Michael. *The Chemical History of a Candle.* New York: Harper & Brothers, 1903.

——. *Experimental Researches in Electricity.* Vols. 1–3. London: Taylor and Francis, 1839 and 1855; reprint, New York: Dover, 1965.

Feldman, David Henry, with Lynn T. Goldsmith. *Nature's Gambit: Child Prodigies and the Development of Human Potential.* New York: Basic Books, 1986.

Ferguson, Eugene S. *Engineering and the Mind's Eye.* Cambridge, MA: MIT Press, 1992.

Foley, James, Andries van Dam, Steven K. Feiner, and John F. Hughes. *Computer Graphics: Principles and Practice.* 2nd ed. Reading, MA: Addison-Wesley, 1987.

Freedberg, David. "The Power of Wood and Stone: The Taliban Is Not the First to Fear the Mysterious Lure of Art." *Washington Post,* March 25, 2001, p. B2.

Frey, Walter. "Schools Miss Out on Dyslexic Engineers." *IEEE Spectrum,* December 1990, p. 6.

Friedhoff, Richard Mark, and William Benzon. *Visualization: The Second Computer Revolution.* New York: Harry N. Abrams, 1989.

Galaburda, Albert M., ed. *Dyslexia and Development: Neurobiological Aspects of Extra-Ordinary Brains.* Cambridge, MA: Harvard University Press, 1993.

Gannon, Kathy. "Afghan Soldiers Give Clinic on Blowing Up Buddhas." *Wisconsin State Journal,* March 27, 2001, p. A5.

Gardner, Howard. *Frames of Mind: The Theory of Multiple Intelligences.* New York: Basic Books, 1983.

———. *Intelligence Reframed: Multiple Intelligences for the 21st Century.* New York: Basic Books, Perseus Books, 1999.

Garrett, Laurie. *The Coming World Plague: Newly Emerging Diseases in a World out of Balance.* New York: Penguin Books, 1994.

Geschwind, Norman. "Biological Associations of Left-Handedness." *Annals of Dyslexia* 33 (1983): 29–40.

———. "The Brain of a Learning-Disabled Individual." *Annals of Dyslexia* 34 (1984): 319–27.

———. "Why Orton Was Right." *Annals of Dyslexia* 32 (1982). Orton Dyslexia Society Reprint no. 98.

Geschwind, Norman, and P. Behan. "Left-Handedness: Association with Immune Disease, Migraine, and Developmental Learning Disorder." *Proceedings of the National Academy of Sciences* 79 (1982): 5097–5100.

Geschwind, Norman, and Albert M. Galaburda, eds. *Cerebral Dominance: The Biological Foundations.* Cambridge, MA: Harvard University Press, 1984.

———. *Cerebral Lateralization: Biological Mechanisms, Associations and Pathology.* Cambridge, MA: MIT Press, 1987.

Geschwind, Norman, and W. Levitsky. "Human Brain: Left-Right Brain Asymmetries in Temporal Speech Region." *Science* 161 (1968): pp. 186–87.

Gibbs, Josiah Willard. *The Scientific Papers of J. Willard Gibbs.* Vol. 1, *Thermodynamics.* London, New York, and Bombay: Longmans, Green, 1906; reprint, New York: Dover, 1961.

Gleick, James. *Chaos: Making a New Science.* New York: Viking Press, 1987.

———. *Genius: The Life and Science of Richard Feynman.* New York: Pantheon Books, 1992.

Gollifer, Sue, et al., eds. *Art and Animation Catalog, SIGGRAPH 2004.* A *Computer Graphics* Annual Conference Series, 2004. A publication of ACM SIGGRAPH.

Gould, S. J. *Eight Little Piggies: Reflections in Natural History.* New York: W. W. Norton, 1993.

Grandin, Temple. *Thinking in Pictures: And Other Reports from My Life with Autism.* New York: Doubleday, 1995.

Guyer, Barbara. "Dyslexic Doctors: A Resource in Need of Discovery." *Southern Medical Journal* 81 (1988): 1151–54.

Hadamard, Jacques. *The Psychology of Invention in the Mathematical Field.* 1945; reprint, New York: Dover, 1954.

Haddon, Mark. *The Curious Incident of the Dog in the Night-time.* London: Vintage, 2003.

Haddon, Mark. Interview by Martha Woodroof. *Weekend Edition Sunday,* National Public Radio, October 12, 2003. Transcript p. 2.

Hampshire, Susan. *Susan's Story: An Autobiographical Account of My Struggle with Words*. London: Sphere Books, 1983. (Includes on pp. 157–58 the quotation used at the beginning of the introduction to Leonardo da Vinci's *Anatomical Notebooks*.)

Harmon, Amy. "Answer, But No Cure, for a Social Disorder that Isolates Many." *New York Times*, April 29, 2004.

Hart, John C. "ACM Transaction on Graphics." *Proceedings of ACM SIGGRAPH* 23, no. 3 (August 2004): 222–24.

Herr, Laurin, et al. *Volume Visualization: State of the Art*. VHS. A special issue of the ACM SIGGRAPH Video Review, issue 44. 1989. (With transcript.)

Hillard, Bill. "Building 3D User Interface Components Using a Visualization Library." ACM-SIGGRAPH *Computer Graphics* 1, no. 1 (February 2002): 4–7.

Hiltzik, Michael. *Dealers of Lightning: Xerox PARC and the Dawn of the Computer Age*. New York: HarperBusiness Book, 2000.

Holton, Gerald. "On Trying to Understand Scientific Genius." *American Scholar* 41 (1972): 95–110.

Howard, Fred. 1987. *Wilbur and Orville: A Biography of the Wright Brothers*. New York: Ballantine, 1987.

Icely, H. E. M. *Blockley through Twelve Centuries*. Alburgh, Harleston, and Norfolk, UK: Published for the Blockley Antiquarian Society by Erskine Press, 1974, reprint 1996.

Jain, Ramesh. "Visual Information Management," *Communications of the ACM* 40, no. 12 (December 1997): 31.

Johnson, George. "The Jaguar and the Fox: Hard as He Tried, Murray Gell-Mann Could Never Make Himself into a Legend Like His Rakish Colleague and Collaborator Richard Feynman—Even If He Was Probably the Greater Physicist." *Atlantic Monthly*, July 2000, pp. 82–85.

Jolls, Kenneth R. "Drawings and Conclusions: The Art of Doing Science." Paper presented at IFIP conference on Computer Graphics and Education, Barcelona, Spain, April 4–6, 1991. Preprint 91106, October 1990, College of Engineering, Iowa State University.

Jolls, Kenneth R., and D. C. Coy. "The Art of Thermodynamics." *IRIS Universe: The Magazine of Visual Processing* 12 (1990): 31–36.

Kaku, Michio. *Einstein's Cosmos: How Albert Einstein's Vision Transformed Our Understanding of Space and Time*. New York: W. W. Norton, 2004.

Kaufmann, William J., and Larry L. Smarr. *Supercomputing and the Transformation of Science*. New York: Scientific American Library, 1993.

Kawaharada, Dennis. "Wayfinding (Non-Instrument Navigation)." Polynesian Voyaging Society Web site. http://leahi.kcc.hawaii.edu/org/pvs/L2wayfind.html (accessed June 23, 2004). (See also Nainoa Thompson, "Voyage Into the New Millennium," *Hana Hou!* magazine, February/March 2000, pp. 41 ff.)

Kean, Thomas H., Lee H. Hamilton, et al. *The 9/11 Commission Report: Final Report of the National Commission on Terrorist Attacks upon the United States*. Authorized ed. New York: W. W. Norton, 2004.

Keim, Daniel A. "Visual Exploration of Large Data Sets." *Communications of the ACM*, August 2001, pp. 39–44.

Kolata, Gina. "Computer Graphics Comes to Statistics." *Science*, September 3, 1982, pp. 919–20.

KPMG Peat Marwick. *Report Summary. The Competitive Benefits from 3D Computing: A Study of Silicon Graphics' Customers.* Mountain View, CA: Silicon Graphics, 1989.

Kress, Gunther, and Theo van Leeuwen. *Reading Images: The Grammar of Visual Design.* London: Routledge, 1996.

Krim, Jonathan. "EU Likely to Order Microsoft to Unbundle: Putting Media Player in Operating System Said to Stifle Competition." *Washington Post*, March 16, 2004, pp. E1–E5.

Leaf, Clifton. "Why We're Losing the War on Cancer (and How to Win It)." *Fortune*, March 22, 2004, pp. 76–97.

Lederberg, Joshua. "Infectious History." *Science*, April 14, 2000, pp. 287–93. Part of series, "Pathways of Discovery." (Dr. Lederberg is a Sackler Foundation Scholar heading the Laboratory of Molecular Genetics and Informatics at Rockefeller University, New York. He is a Nobel laureate [1958] for his research on genetic mechanisms in bacteria.)

Ma, Kwan-Lui. "Visualization: A Quickly Emerging Field." *Computer Graphics* 38, no. 1 (February 2004): 4–7.

Mandelbrot, Benoit B. "Fractals and an Art for the Sake of Science." In *Computer Art in Context: SIGGRAPH '89 Art Show Catalog*, pp. 21–24. New York: Pergamon Press, 1989. (Supplemental Issue 1989 of *Leonardo*, the journal of the International Society for the Arts, Sciences and Technology, Berkeley, CA, and Boulogne-sur-Seine, France. Published in conjuction with the SIGGRAPH '89 Art Show, July 31–August 4, 1989, Boston, MA.)

———. *The Fractal Geometry of Nature.* Updated and augmented edition. New York: W. H. Freeman, 1983.

McCormick, Bruce, Thomas A. DeFanti, and Maxine Brown. "Visualization in Scientific Computing," special issue, *Computer Graphics* 21, no. 6 (November 1987).

McDonald, Kim A. "The Iconoclastic Fossil Hunter." *Chronicle of Higher Education*, November 16, 1994, pp. A9–A17.

Miles, T. R. 1993. *Dyslexia: The Pattern of Difficulties.* 2nd ed. London: Whurr, 1993.

Miller, Arthur I. *Imagery in Scientific Thought: Creating 20th-Century Physics.* Cambridge, MA: MIT Press, 1986.

Mitchell, Russell, et al. "The Schwab Revolution." *Business Week*, December 19, 1995.

Morris, Betsy. "The Dyslexic CEO: Charles Schwab, Richard Branson, Craig McCaw & John Chambers Triumphed over America's No. 1 Learning Disorder. Your Kid Can Too." *Fortune*, May 20, 2002, pp. 54–70.

Negroponte, Nicholas. *Being Digital.* New York: Knopf, 1995.

———. "000 000 111: Double Agents." *Wired* magazine 3.03, March 1995, p. 172.

Norman, Donald A. *Things that Make Us Smart: Defending Human Attributes in an Age of the Machine.* Reading, MA: Addison-Wesley, 1993.

O'Brien, Jeffrey. "The Next Intel: Meet Nvidia CEO Jen-Hsun Huang, The Man Who Plans to Make the CPU Obsolete." *Wired* magazine 10.07, July 2002, pp. 100–103.

O'Connell, Kenneth R., Vincent Argiro, John Andrew Berton Jr., Craig Hickman, and Thomas G. West. "Visual Thinkers in an Age of Computer Visualization." In *Computer Graphics*, the Proceedings of the Annual Conference of ACM SIG-GRAPH, August 1993, pp. 379–80.

Padgett, Ian, and Beverly Steffert, eds. *Visual Spatial Ability and Dyslexia: A Research Project*. London: Central Saint Martins College of Art and Design, in association with the Arts Dyslexia Trust, 1999.

Pais, Abraham. *"Subtle is the Lord . . .": The Science and the Life of Albert Einstein*. Oxford: Oxford University Press, 1982.

Park, Kyungmee. "A Comparative Study of the Traditional Calculus Course vs. the CALCULUS & *Mathematica* Course." PhD diss., Graduate School of Education, University of Illinois at Urbana-Champaign, 1993.

Pearson, E[gon] S[harpe]. *Karl Pearson: An Appreciation of Some Aspects of His Life and Work*. Cambridge: Cambridge University Press, 1938.

———. "Some Aspects of the Geometry of Statistics: The Use of Visual Presentation in Understanding the Theory and Application of Mathematical Statistics." In *The Selected Papers of E. S. Pearson*. Berkeley and Los Angeles: University of California Press, 1966. Presented as the inaugural address of the president to the Royal Statistical Society in 1956.

Pearson, Karl. *The Life, Letters and Labours of Francis Galton*. Vol. 1, *Birth 1822 to Marriage 1853*. Cambridge: Cambridge University Press, 1914.

Petroski, Henry. *To Engineer is Human: The Role of Failure in Successful Design*. New York: St. Martin's Press, 1985.

Richard, Paul. "So Much Irony in This Passion." *Washington Post*, February 29, 2004, pp. B1–B5.

Ritchie-Calder, Peter. *Leonardo & the Age of the Eye*. New York: Simon and Schuster, 1970.

Robertson, Barbara. "Hot Bots: The Three Laws of Robotics—Digital Domain and Weta Digital create animated CG robots for the film *I, Robot*." *Computer Graphics World* 27, no. 8 (August 2004): 24–30.

Robins, Cynthia. "One Man's Battle against Dyslexia: How Financier Charles Schwab Is Helping Others Whose Kids Have Learning Disabilities." *San Francisco Examiner*, March 8, 1992, pp. D-3, D-10.

Satori, Giuseppe. "Leonardo Da Vinci, Omo Sanza Lettere: A Case of Surface Dysgraphia?" *Cognitive Neuropsychology* 4, no. 1 (1987): 1–10.

Scott, Remington. "Sparking Life: Notes on the Performance Capture Sessions for the *Lord of the Rings: The Two Towers*." *Computer Graphics* 37, no. 4 (November 2003): 17–21.

"Seeing Is Believing." *Economist*, August 19, 1995, p. 71.

Shlain, Leonard. *The Alphabet versus the Goddess: The Conflict between Word and Image*. New York: Viking, 1998.

Shneiderman, Ben. *Leonardo's Laptop: Human Needs and the New Computing Technologies*. Cambridge, MA: MIT Press, 2002.

Silberman, Steve. "The Geek Syndrome: Autism—and Its Milder Cousin Asperger's Syndrome—Is Surging among the Children of Silicon Valley. Are Math-and-tech Genes to Blame?" *Wired* magazine 9.12, December 2001.

Snow, C. P. "Albert Einstein, 1879–1955." In *Einstein: A Centenary Volume*, edited by A. P. French, pp. 3ff. Cambridge, MA: Harvard University Press, 1979.

Spalter, Anne Morgon. *The Computer in the Visual Arts*. Reading, MA: Addison-Wesley Longman, 1999.

Steen, Lynn Arthur, ed. *Heading the Call for Change: Suggestions for Curricular Action*. Washington, DC: Mathematical Association of America, 1992.

———. "Mathematics Education: A Predictor of Scientific Competitiveness." *Science*, July 17, 1987, pp. 251–52, 302.

———. "The Science of Patterns." *Science*, April 29, 1988, pp. 611–16.

Stross, Randall E. "Microsoft's Big Advantage: Hiring Only the Supersmart." *Fortune*, November 25, 1996, pp. 159–62. (Excerpt from *The Microsoft Way*.)

———. *The Microsoft Way*. New York: Addison-Wesley, 1996.

Suplee, Curt. "Six Awarded Nobel Prizes in Chemistry, Physics: 'Information Age' Contributions Honored." *Washington Post*, October 11, 2000, p. A2.

Tauber, Alfred I., and Scott H. Podolsky. *The Generation of Diversity: Clonal Selection Theory and the Rise of Molecular Immunology*. Cambridge, MA: Harvard University Press, 1997.

Tenner, Edward. *Why Things Bite Back: Technology and the Revenge of Unintended Consequences*. New York: Vintage Books, 1997.

Tesla, Nikola. *Experiments with Alternate Currents of High Potential and High Frequency: A Lecture Delivered Before the Institution of Electrical Engineers, London; With an Appendix by the Same Author on the Transmission of Electric Energy Without Wires . . . [and] with a New Portrait and a Biographical Sketch of the Author*. New York: McGraw, 1904.

———. *My Inventions: The Autobiography of Nikola Tesla*. Edited and introduced by Ben Johnson. Williston, Vermont: Hart Brothers, 1982. Republication of a series of six articles that originally appeared in the *Electrical Experimenter*, February–June and October 1919.

Thomas, Lewis. *Late Night Thoughts on Listening to Mahler's Ninth Symphony*. New York: Bantam Books, 1984.

———. *The Medusa and the Snail*. New York: Viking Press, 1979.

———. *The Youngest Science: Notes of a Medicine-Watcher*. New York: Bantam Books, 1983.

Thompson, D'Arcy Wentworth. *On Growth and Form*. Vols. 1 and 2. 2nd ed. Cambridge: Cambridge University Press, 1942; reprint, Deventer, The Netherlands: Ysel Press, 1972.

Thompson, Nainoa. "Voyage into the New Millennium." *Hana Hou!* February–March 2000, pp. 41 ff.

Thompson, Pamela Kleibrink. "Oppor-toon-ities in Animation and Computer Graphics." *Computer Graphics* 38, no. 3 (August 2004): 25–27.

Tolstoy, Ivan. *James Clerk Maxwell: A Biography*. Chicago: University of Chicago Press, 1981.

Tufte, Edward R. *Envisioning Information*. Cheshire, CT: Graphics Press, 1990.

———. *The Visual Display of Quantitative Information*. Cheshire, CT: Graphics Press, 1983.

———. *Visual Explanations: Images and Quantities, Evidence and Narrative*. Cheshire, CT: Graphics Press, 1997.

Upson, Craig, ed. *Chapel Hill Workshop on Volume Visualization: Conference Proceed-*

ings, May 18–19, 1989. Chapel Hill: University of North Carolina at Chapel Hill, 1989. ACM SIGGRAPH Special Publication 429892.

Uth, Robert. *Tesla: Master of Lightning.* VHS. Produced and directed by Robert Uth. Written by Robert Uth and Phyllis Geller. PBS Home Video. Distributed by Warner Home Video. New Voyage Communications, 2001.

Waldrop, M. Mitchell. *Complexity: The Emerging Science at the Edge of Order and Chaos.* New York: Simon & Schuster, 1992.

Walker, D. R., A. Thompson, L. Zwaigenbaum, et al. "Specifying PDD-NOS: a Comparison of PDD-NOS, Asperger syndrome, and Autism." *Journal of the American Academy of Child Adolescent Psychiatry* 43, no. 2 (2004): 181–82.

Watson, James D. *The Double Helix: A Personal Account of the Discovery of DNA.* With a foreword by Sir Lawrence Bragg. New York: Atheneum, 1968.

Wiener, Norbert. *Cybernetics: Or, Control and Communication in the Animal and the Machine.* Cambridge, MA: MIT Press, 1961.

West, Thomas G. "The Abilities of Those with Reading Disabilities: Focusing on the Talents of People with Dyslexia." Chap. 11 in *Reading and Attention Disorders: Neurobiological Correlates,* edited by Drake D. Duane. Baltimore: York Press, 1999.

———. "Advanced Interaction: A Return to Mental Models and Learning by Doing." *Computers & Graphics* 18, no. 5, special issue on advanced interaction (September–October 1994): 685–89.

———. "Awakening to Dyslexic Talents in the 'New Economy.'" In "Innovations and Insights," *Dyslexia: An International Journal of Research and Practice* 1, no. 1 (1995).

———. "Following the Gifts: Visual Talents and Trouble with Words." *Computer Graphics* 31, no. 2 (May 1997): 8–9.

———. "Forward into the Past: A Revival of Old Visual Talents with Computer Visualization." *Computer Graphics* 29, no. 4 (November 1995): 14–19.

———. "A Future of Reversals: Dyslexic Talents in a World of Computer Visualization." *Annals of Dyslexia* 42 (1992): 124–39.

———. *Geniuses Who Hated School.* Translated by Katsumi Kushimoto. Tokyo: Kodansha Scientific, 1994. Japanese translation of *In the Mind's Eye.*

———. *In the Mind's Eye: Visual Thinkers, Gifted People with Learning Difficulties, Computer Images, and the Ironies of Creativity.* Amherst, NY: Prometheus Books, 1991.

———. *In the Mind's Eye: Visual Thinkers, Gifted People with Dyslexia and Other Learning Difficulties, Computer Graphics, and the Ironies of Creativity.* Updated ed. Amherst, NY: Prometheus Books, 1997.

———. "Medieval Clerk to Renaissance Thinker: Design, Visualization and Technological Change." Presentation published on CD-ROM documenting the proceedings of the first "Doors of Perception" conference, Stedelijk Museum, Amsterdam, Holland, October 30–31, 1993. Also published in September 1994 as part of *Mediamatic* magazine (Amsterdam) 8, no. 1.

———. "Playing with Images: A Return to Thinking in Pictures." *Computers in Physics* (American Institute of Physics) 10, no. 5 (September–October 1996): 413.

———. "A Return to Visual Thinking." *Computer Graphics World,* November 1992.

———. "A Return to Visual Thinking." In *Proceedings, Science and Scientific Computing: Visions of a Creative Symbiosis. Symposium of Computer Users in the Max*

Planck Gesellschaft, Göttingen, Germany, November 1993, edited by P. Wittenberg and T. Plesser. Göttingen: MPG, 1994. (Paper published in German translation: "Rückkehr zum visuellen Denken, Forschung und wissenschftliches Rechnen: Beiträge anläßlich des 10. EDV-Benutzertreffens der Max-Planck-Gesellschaft in Göttingen, November 1993.")

————. "Slow Words, Quick Images: Dyslexia as an Advantage in Tomorrow's Workplace." In *Learning Disabilities and Employment,* edited by Paul J. Gerber and Dale Brown. Austin, TX: ProEd, 1997.

————. "Special Talents in a Not-So-New Population." In *Hidden Abilities in Higher Education: New College Students with Disabilities,* edited by Linda Lucas Walling, pp. 7–12. Monograph Series 21. Columbia: University of South Carolina, 1996. (National Resource Center for the Freshman Year Experience & Students in Transition, University of South Carolina. Based on a keynote address given February 18, 1994.)

————. "'Strephs,' Tumbling Symbols and Technological Change: The Implications of Dyslexia Research in a World Turned Upside Down." Paper presented at "On the Leading Edge of Dyslexia Research: Neuroscience, Genetics and Implications for the Future," preconference symposium before the Annual Conference of the Orton Dyslexia Society, Boston, November 7–9, 1996. Audio tape. St. Petersburg, FL: Convention Recordings International, 1996.

————. "Unintended, Unexpected Consequences: SIGGRAPH '96." *Computer Graphics* 30, no. 4 (November 1996): 3–5.

————. "Upside Down: Visual-spatial Talents and Technological Change." *Understanding Our Gifted* 8, no. 3 (January–February 1996): 1–11.

————. "Visualization in the Mind's Eye." *IRIS Universe: The Magazine of Visual Processing,* no. 14 (November 1990).

————. "Visual Thinkers, Mental Models and Computer Visualization." In *Interactive Learning Through Visualization: The Impact of Computer Graphics in Education,* edited by S. Cunningham and R. Hubbold. Heidelberg: Springer-Verlag, 1992.

————. "Word Bound: The Power of Seeing." *Computer Graphics* 31, no. 1 (February 1997): 5–6.

Whitmore, J. R., and C. J. Maker. "Intellectually Gifted Persons with Specific Learning Disabilities—a Case Study: Marcia." In *Intellectual Giftedness in Disabled Persons.* Rockville, MD: Aspen Systems, 1985.

Whitney, Mark, and Carlo Pedretti. *Leonardo's Deluge.* VHS. Art on Film Series, A Joint Venture of the Metropolitan Museum of Art and the J. Paul Getty Trust, 1990.

Winner, Ellen. *Gifted Children: Myths and Realities.* New York: Basic Books, 1996.

Wired magazine staff. "Savior of the Plague Years 1996–2020." In "Wired Scenarios," special supplement to *Wired,* Fall 1995, pp. 84–148. Image manipulation by Eric Rodenbeck.

Witt-Miller, Harriet. "The Soft, Warm, Wet Technology of Native Oceania." *Whole Earth Review,* Fall 1991, pp. 64–69.

Yoo, Terry S. "Taking Stock of Visualization in Scientific Computing." *Computer Graphics* 38, no. 3 (August 2004): 4–6.

————. "Visfiles: Taking Stock of Visualization in Scientific Computing." *Computer Graphics* 38, no. 3 (August 2004): 4–6.

Zakaria, Fareed. *The Future of Freedom: Illiberal Democracy at Home and Abroad.* New York: W. W. Norton, 2003.

Zeki, Semir. *Inner Vision: An Exploration of Art and the Brain.* Oxford: Oxford University Press, 1999.

Zimmermann, Walter, and Steve Cunningham, eds. *Visualization in Teaching and Learning Mathematics.* Washington, DC: Mathematical Association of America, 1991.

INDEX